NO TIME FOR TEARS

LORA WOOD HUGHES

NO TIME FOR TEARS

Illustrations by Edwin Earle

University of Nebraska Press
Lincoln and London

Copyright 1946 by Lora Wood Hughes
All rights reserved
Manufactured in the United States of America

First Bison Book printing: 1985
Most recent printing indicated by the first digit below:
1   2   3   4   5   6   7   8   9   10

Library of Congress Cataloging in Publication Data
Hughes, Lora Wood.
  No time for tears.
  "Bison book"—Verso t.p.
  1. Hughes, Lora Wood.   2. Nurses—United States—
Biography.   I. Title.
RT37.H78A36   1985   610.73'092'4 [B]   85-8644
ISBN 0-8032-2336-6
ISBN 0-8032-7229-4 (pbk.)

DEDICATION

To my friend and collaborator, Nell Lewis Macgregor, I here give grateful acknowledgment for her long toil in editing and revising the manuscript for this book. She supplied the technical skill which I lacked, as well as an unswerving confidence that we could produce the book I had so long dreamed about. Without her encouragement and able help I should not have had the hardihood to make my dream a reality.

CONTENTS

PART I.   Kansas Homestead 1

PART II.   California 35

PART III.   Honolulu 65

PART IV.   Montana 87

PART V.   Alberta 203

PART VI.   Puget Sound Country 255

KANSAS HOMESTEAD

KANSAS HOMESTEAD

I WAS SIX YEARS OLD when I made a discovery one day.

It was a matter of tremendous importance to me. I twisted my head around to look up at Mama, who at the moment was soothingly attending a carbuncle on my back. Papa had just lanced it with his jackknife. There wasn't a doctor within fifty miles of our Kansas homestead that winter of 1879.

'Mama,' I announced proudly, 'I've learned to think!'

'That's nice, Lora.'

Mama didn't sound a bit excited. She kept on dressing my carbuncle. I must make her understand. I was certain I'd figured out why I had carbuncles every fall and late on into the winter. They were awful torture, and the thought of Papa's lancing each one as it came to a head made me writhe.

'And so you can think?' Mama patted me comfortingly. 'You know, I wouldn't be surprised if that's what caused your carbuncles!'

She was trying to make me laugh, but I was only hurt and embarrassed. I couldn't tell her now about my Great Discovery, though I wanted desperately to know if I were right. When my condition became so much worse that it was necessary to get a doctor to come the long distance to see me, I determined to find out. The big, bearded doctor with his saddle-bags full of boxes and bottles of medicine fascinated me. When the chance came, I opened the subject.

'Doctor Stone, I wondered —— Every summer I get poison ivy and things. And then I get sugar of lead put on me. Rex — he was our dog — he ate up a dish of it one day and it made him sick. And then he got a lot of boils on him. And pretty soon he died. I wondered — could that sugar of lead I get rubbed on me make these carbuncles come?'

I can still remember Mama's mildly disapproving 'Oh, Lora!' and the quizzical look in the doctor's eyes as he smiled at me.

'Sugar of lead all summer, eh? Hm-m-m-m. Of course it could be.'

My little ego fairly swelled with pride. I'd thought that all out by myself. The aching sorrow when I hadn't known how to help poor old Rex, the memory of hellish moments when Papa plunged his jackknife into my tortured flesh, that wonderful loss of pain which came after Mama gave me some of the little pills the doctor left in case I hurt too much — all these stirred in my childish mind a steadily increasing mania to relieve suffering.

I would be like Mama. No distance was ever too great over those prairies and no night too dark when neighboring homesteaders came for her. And she nearly always made sick people well. Once I went with her to the Gavins', a hill-billy family down the creek from us. Their littlest baby was in convulsions, all black in the face and frightening to see. Mama put it in a warm bath and in a short time it was all right.

'When I grow up,' I said to my brother Ted, telling him about it later, 'I'm going to tie salve on people too, and make them well.'

I'd never heard of a nurse. I doubt if there was one within two hundred miles of us.

My family had gone from Missouri to homestead on the Kansas prairies when I was only two months old. I've always regretted I was too young to enjoy that early spring trek. From much telling, Mama's stories made it so vivid that I was sure I remembered the covered wagons crawling along, the herders driving the cattle in advance. Surely I had seen Grandma in her black-and-white calico dress and buffalo-hide jacket, a fascinator over her scant gray hair, perched on the high seat of the front wagon, driving the black team. And Papa, in fur coat and cap, driving the four matched bays to the next wagon. There was a stove in that one to warm Mama and Ted and me. It always shamed me to be told that I cried night and day the whole trip. It's a good thing I got done with crying early. There has been no time for tears since.

When Mama used to send me to the dugout, which in my memory served only as a root-house, I'd often forget to go back, so interested I'd become in reconstructing it as our first Kansas home, before the stone house was built. It was a twelve by fourteen excavation in the cutbank. A level horseshoe flat stretched before it to the clear, sparkling creek and high limestone bluffs from which had been quarried the stone for our permanent house. The sides and back wall of the dugout were dirt, and the front was of logs, sod-filled, with a crude door flanked on either side by tiny windows. Poles laid together and covered with sod and dirt made the roof.

We hadn't moved into it at first. Papa had insisted that the covered wagon boxes, taken off their trucks and put on the ground, would serve until the stone house could be built. They were comfortable enough, with their heavy canvas, a stove, and only bare necessities in the line of furnishings. Most of our furniture was stored in the sod house for safety.

Mama had three mortal terrors: Indians, lice, and high winds. She never looked up at the top of the stone quarry across the creek without expecting to see the hideously painted face of an Indian peering at her. And of course many of the cowhands had lice. And her fear of wind was certainly not without cause, since terrific ones often roared through the cottonwoods and box elders along the creek. And cyclones were not uncommon. But Papa thought it all foolishness to worry about such things.

Once, when he had gone to the Missouri River trading post and we were alone with the men, ominous green clouds, zigzagged by lightning, rolled up late in the afternoon. Mama called the cowhands and had them move all our bedding and goods into the dugout as fast as they could. The stuff was no sooner in — and we with it — before clouds of dust blotted out all daylight. It was terrifying, with the roaring and crashing about us. Then rain came, and it was as though we were under a waterfall. The lightning was continuous and the thunder loud as cannon fire. When the storm was over, the creek was within a few inches of the dugout with its flood waters. The wagons, torn and smashed, lay bottom up in the stream. The cowhands' large tent had blown away entirely, and their stoves and bedrolls lay forlornly on the ground. After this we lived in the dugout until our house was finished. Mama lined the walls and ceiling with sheets, and it wasn't really too bad, she said, though with all the extra furniture, there wasn't much room for the necessary cookstove, table, bed, and the one little rocker and the small chest of drawers which had held the baby clothes of two generations. — I still have it.

We weren't poor as poverty was rated in those days. There were quilts and feather beds and ticks for hay or straw, pillows, comforters, and blankets. There were rag carpets, soap and linens, drugs and toilet articles. Our foodstuffs were ample and varied, with dried corn and beans, apple butter and pumpkin jerk, besides staples. Game was plentiful. And Mama had eleven precious hens in weasel-tight coops. Our cows furnished us dairy products.

One of my favorite stories was that of our first Thanksgiving in the sod house. The garden had been good, the grass excellent, and the stock increase above the average. And everyone was well. As a special celebration, one of the hens, a vicious old dominecker that picked her eggs and ate her chicks before they were hatched, was sacrificed for the occasion and made into a luscious pie. The cowhands were crowded in with the family around the table. Even I was to have a bone to suck. While every mouth watered from the aroma, Mama bowed her head in silent thanksgiving for such a feast. But just as she lifted her eyes, there was a muffled sound overhead, and before anyone could move, the sheets above parted and in a rain of black dirt, a great fat toad dropped sprawling right in the middle of the chicken pie!

Many an incident such as this Mama turned from tragedy to comedy by her philosophical humor. As she often said to me, 'Don't eat a sour plum raw. Make it into jam!'

The site chosen for the stone house was a level plot in a grove of cottonwoods, between the creek and the abruptly lifting hill. A square of ground was cleared and the work began almost as soon as we arrived on our homestead, but so many other things claimed the menfolk's attention that it progressed slowly. Papa, with the aid of some of the neighbors, sawed and chiseled sandstone blocks and laid them in trim, beautiful walls. Among the low sod prairie houses our two-story stone dwelling was most impressive. There were three large rooms on the first floor and a huge unfinished one above. We moved in just before Christmas.

My brother Willie was born there the next year. When I was five, Mama decided Ted and I were old enough to graduate from the trundle bed and have quarters of our own, so we moved upstairs to sleep. One of our chief pleasures in winter was to remove the packing Mama had painstakingly stuffed around the windows to keep out snow in blizzards, and make tracks with our bare feet in the little drifts that formed on the floor.

Ted was twenty-two months older than I, and with his fair skin and thick yellow curls was a beautiful child. And knew it. Because of the airs he gave himself and his pitying attitude toward me, he quite convinced me I was ugly. Later in life my mother was shocked to learn I'd believed such a thing, which she insisted was not true. Never above normal weight in maturity, it's hard to believe I was so fat a little girl as my pictures show me. My hair was thin and fine and straight, about the color of raveled rope. It refused to grow to any length, and in those days a girl without long hair wasn't anything much. My cheekbones were high and my eyes deep-set, and with skin which tanned and weathered easily, I looked just like an Indian, according to Ted.

We had a well on the place. It was not very deep. Ted and I often amused ourselves by leaning over the curb and looking down into it. We'd lower the bucket into the water, then, when the surface was mirror-smooth, touch the rope ever so lightly. In the little petals of waves forming from the center, we'd gaze, fascinated, at our distorted faces.

One day as we watched our images smooth into familiar outline, Ted said to me, 'Don't you wish you had nice curls like I have?'

I wished for a moment I hadn't given him this chance to compare ourselves, for my full-moon face and straight hair looked homelier than ever, but after all it was a sort of game. 'Yes, I do,' I replied. 'But don't you wish they didn't make you look like a girl? And don't you wish you could read as well as I could? And don't you wish Ike Bush would ever take you up on his horse to ride with him, like he does me?' (Ike Bush was our favorite cowhand and to ride with him was a thrilling treat.)

Fate was eventually kind to me, for when Ted and I had diphtheria after I was in school, our hair fell out and Ted's came in brown and streaked, though it was still wavy, but mine came in thick and dark and curly. It seemed nothing short of miraculous that I might at last achieve long, spiraling curls to swing down on my shoulders.

Papa traded two steers for an organ one year, and hauled it all the way from the Missouri River trading post. Mama had a lovely voice and now we could have music. She also had a sewing machine, and with these two outstanding pieces of furniture, a big Boston rocker and a smaller one, gay rag carpet, a long shelf of books, a chest of drawers, chintz-covered stools, and white ruffled curtains at the windows, the memory of our living-room in the stone house still brings me a sense of luxurious well-being.

Because we children had shoes — and sometimes wore them — and because Mama usually had some neighbor's daughter hired to help her with the housework, some of the near-by homesteaders at first declared we were 'stuck-up.' But with all Mama's unselfish giving of herself they soon learned otherwise. With her experience, abetted by Doctor Jackson's *Home Treatment of the Sick* — the huge, thumb-worn book from which I learned to read — she nursed people through many sicknesses. She taught the hill-billies down the creek to read and write and to use scissors instead of butcher knives in cutting out garments. Papa also was always ready with a helping hand, and these people soon became staunch, self-sacrificing friends through drought, grasshoppers, cyclones, sickness, and death.

The life and heart of the stone house was the living-room fireplace, with its huge stone mantel-shelf, where, as I remember, there always stood a lovely orange-and-black glazed pot containing honey and sage for sore throats. In the center of the shelf a big pendulum clock ticked away the years and struck the hour and half-hour with a business-like chime loud enough to be heard almost down to the cowsheds. One day I discovered the clock had stopped.

'Quick, Mama!' I ran to her in panic. 'The clock is sick!'

She smiled at me reassuringly. 'Let's doctor it.' She poured kerosene into a cup and found a strong chicken feather, then mounted a bench before the mantel. I can still see her vividly in her blue-and-white calico dress, with her hair hanging in two heavy braids below her knees. The hair was unusually beautiful, and a jeweler who made gold- and silver-mounted hair chains once offered her twenty-five dollars for it.

'I'll hold on to your hair, Mama,' I told her. 'Then you can't fall.'

'That will help a lot,' she assured me. So I held tightly to the ends of her braids, proud to be holding her up.

With a twist of the knob, Mama removed the face of the

clock and applied the dripping feather to the great and thrilling mystery of little notched wheels and clicking things. Kerosene was a popular remedy for many ills. A few drops on a lump of sugar for a cough, a hot kerosene rub for a chest cold, could work wonders. And sure enough, in a few minutes the ticking began, steady and loud.

'Now the clock is well,' I declared. I helped Mama down by still grasping her braids.

Grandma and Papa's sister, Mary (the latter came to Kansas from Chicago after the stone house was built), took up claims adjoining ours. They built a nice log-and-frame house directly across the creek from us. Aunt Mary opened the first school in our district, using what few schoolbooks and reading charts were available. Up to this time our books had been limited, but we subscribed to the *Toledo Blade* and the *Ladies' Home Journal*. When Aunt Mary began making yearly trips to Chicago, bringing back books each time, Papa had to keep adding shelves to hold them.

We always had a hired man to help with the farming, herders out on the range miles away, and a cowhand to attend to the stock close to home in the huge fenced-in pasture. Our cowhand, Ike Bush, was the hero of my childhood.

He was not more than twenty when he came to the prairie with our outfit, but he was our most valued and dependable man. He was a long-legged, loose-jointed Texan, with black hair which fell in wisps over his eyes when the wind blew. Unlike most of his kind, who lived in their big hats, Ike often fastened his to a fencepost to await his return. Or if he took it he'd probably carry it under his arm or crush it down on the saddle-horn. I've seen him come riding into the yard with his sombrero on his horse's head, with the buckskin's ears sticking through holes he'd cut. His vividly blue eyes were the merriest I have ever seen.

Before I could walk, Ike began taking me up on the saddle in front of him when he rode pasture fences to locate holes or weak spots. He was my companion, guard, and playfellow.

I'll never forget how he comforted me on one occasion when I felt as though my life was utterly ruined. There was to be a celebration of some sort at our house, which Mama had invested with great mystery. Everyone in the country around had been invited and they were all to be surprised, the grown-ups said, smiling among themselves. For a week there was house-cleaning, carpet-beating, and cooking of all sorts. It was most exciting. After what seemed ages of suspense, the great day at last arrived.

'Wonder how the Logans will feel about this,' I heard Papa say to Mama as she was helping dish up breakfast.

Mama shook her head. 'I sort of hated to invite them, Jasper. They'll probably think we're silly — with all our children. But we'll set them a good example.'

That mystified me more than ever. The Logans always seemed like awfully nice people, *but they weren't married to each other!* That was a terrible sin, worse even than horse-stealing. It made their children something that was a bad word. The Gavin children sometimes made faces at them, and even Aunt Mary argued with Mama about the wisdom of our playing with them.

About one o'clock in the afternoon, people began to arrive. Some had started at six that morning to get there. Both rooms downstairs were crowded. I stood by Ike, gripping his hand in excitement. He was wearing store pants and a boiled shirt, with a big bow tie streaming out under his square chin. All morning, as he did last-minute chores for Mama, I had been admiring him.

And now I realized I hadn't seen Mama around for some time. Papa either. Aunt Mary and Grandma were getting everyone in place and asking them to be quiet, as there was to be a surprise in a few minutes. I wondered what in the world it was going to be. Ted looked at me questioningly from across the room. We had speculated endlessly on the mystery. I saw one of the neighbor women try to make Willie quit squirming. I felt squirmy myself in my stiffly starched dress and pantalets.

And then Matt Hermas, who'd been a music teacher over in the Old Country where he used to live, began playing the organ. 'My land! Who's getting married?' one of the women near me whispered to another. 'That's the wedding march!' Ike lifted me in his arms so I could see what was going on. The preacher stepped into the doorway between the two rooms. Everyone grew so quiet I was scared. The stairs creaked and my heart almost jumped out of my chest. There was the sound of footsteps coming down. And then Papa and Mama appeared, arm in arm. Breathless, I stared at them as they moved in slowly and sort of sad-looking, to stand before the preacher.

Mama had on a dress of white dotted Swiss with a full skirt so long it trailed behind her. On her hands were white lace mitts and she carried a white satin-and-ivory fan and a lace handkerchief. With her heavy braids wound around her head like a crown and a glistening ornament over her forehead, she looked more beautiful than Grandma's picture of Queen Victoria when she was young.

Papa, who usually wore his trousers tucked into his boots, looked a foot taller in his black broadcloth suit and white collar and tie. He was always close-shaven. His thin, dark hair grew far back on his forehead and he held his head high. His nose was slightly Roman and his deep-set blue eyes, rather close together, were piercing and proud. I had always wished he looked more like joyous Ike Bush, instead of being so stern and dignified, but today I was proud of him. I looked around at the other men and was glad he was different.

The preacher opened a little book and began reading in a very solemn voice. 'Dearly beloved, we are gathered together ——' Several women wiped their eyes. I looked around in alarm. They were sorry for Papa and Mama. The slow words of the preacher terrified me. 'Jasper, do you take this woman — ?' 'Mary, do you take this man — ?' As I listened to each saying 'I do,' a sudden appalling conviction smote me. I wiggled down out of Ike's arms, unable to bear the thought of anyone seeing me in this moment of sickening shame. I ran out-of-doors sobbing. My parents were like the Logans! After all these years together, they were just now getting married. And I — !

It was Ike who dragged me out of the smokehouse where I'd hid. He slapped his legs and roared with laughter when I gulped out my misery, then sobered quickly and explained how mistaken I was. 'You see, honey' — he stood me up and tried to straighten my crumpled dress — 'when a man and woman is willin' to stand up and promise them things all over again after they've tried each other out as right smart a time as your pa and ma has, it shows they've got the real thing. Now let's get back and see if the eatin's begun. My mouth has sho' been waterin' for them fixin's ever sence I got up this mornin'.'

Ike had reclaimed me from dishonor, and with inarticulate gratitude I built up his pedestal higher still. But never since have I liked anniversary ceremonies.

When the guests had gone home late that afternoon, I went into the bedroom with Mama while she took off her wedding dress. 'Where'd you hide it all this time?' I asked her.

'It was in the trunk with the fan and mitts and handkerchief. You've seen them all many times.'

'Not the dress,' I insisted. 'Just the other things.'

Mama smiled. 'No, you've never really seen it. You probably thought it was a bundle of rags tied up with a string. It would have rotted long ago if I'd put it away with all the starch in it, so I'd rinsed it out and just tied it up. But all it needed to make it look like new again was to be starched and ironed. I'd never shown it to you because I meant to surprise you some day.'

'You looked beautiful, Mama. But don't ever get married again, will you? I don't like getting married.'

With my developing ability to think for myself, a problem all out of proportion to my childish reason began to worry me. It had to do with God and sickness.

Papa was something of a skeptic in matters of religion. Mama had been raised in the faith of her Lutheran forebears, but they had not made much of an issue of their beliefs. She had taken what she had been taught with little question. On the prairie there was not much occasion for creed or ritual.

We said our prayers at night, bowed our heads at table — with a swift glance at Papa, who was always impatient — learned poems and songs about Jesus, and took Mama's word for everything about being kind and unselfish to people and animals.

The 'saddle-bagger,' fat Elder Lockard — God help him out of the hell he created for himself and little children! — came to our place every few weeks, held several meetings and came in for a vast amount of fried chicken and, from most people, awed respect. To him was left the task of instructing us children in religion. I think I disliked the man from the first time I ever looked at him. When Mama would tell him of some misfortune or illness among the neighbors, he would sigh, put his palms a little apart in front of him, fingertips touching, and say, in a resigned, subdued sort of voice, 'Whom the Lord loveth, He chasteneth.' When it was at last made clear to me that the Lord didn't actually chase anyone, but that he supposedly sent sickness and suffering to make people better, I was frightened.

We were told to love God, but I didn't. I couldn't forget the night Mama came home with Mrs. Gavin's baby in her arms and said Mrs. Gavin was dead. There were six little children in that family. What if God took Mama to make me better? I was more than ever afraid when Brother Lockard folded his hairy hands across his fat stomach, nodded his head and said, 'The Lord giveth, and the Lord taketh away. Blessed be the name of the Lord.' Bewilderment filled me. If God really wanted people to get sick so they could die, then wasn't it wrong to try to make them well, as Mama did?

I'll always remember a bout I had with the circuit rider one day. He had arrived in the early afternoon, and Hannah Peters, our hired girl, spent hours preparing a worthy supper. As she dished up at mealtime, I eyed the great platter of fried chicken hungrily. The livers had been piled together on one side for the preacher. Brother Lockard was fond of livers. So was I. And when he came he got all of them. Temptation overcame me and when I thought myself unseen, I snatched a couple of the coveted giblets and popped them into my mouth.

But as I turned, I faced Hannah's wrath. I shouldn't have attempted to deny her accusation. I couldn't swallow the dry livers fast enough to make my denial convincing as I hurried out. She was cross with me anyway. I had ripped off all the *Toledo Blades* which she'd used to paper the inside of the backhouse a few days before. I thought the grained wood too nice to hide. Mama hadn't punished me very severely, since she felt as I did. Lumber was scarce in Kansas. This was a good opportunity for Hannah to get even with me, and she announced my sin to the whole table when Papa began forking the livers onto the Elder's plate. With all eyes on me, I rashly denied it again.

'She's lyin'!' declared Hannah flatly.

'Maybe I had better have a little talk with Lora after supper,' suggested the Elder grimly, before Mama could smooth things over.

I pushed back my chair and left the table, hating those two who'd ruined my appetite for that wonderful food. Mama didn't call me back. I think the preacher's too-ready interference irked her. It seemed to me I'd scarcely settled down to play with my lap full of the snakes' eggs I'd been collecting before I was summoned into The Presence. The Elder sat before the blazing fireplace. He pulled me between his knees and held me tightly as I squirmed under the cold gaze of his pale little eyes.

His voice was so solemn it frightened me. 'My child, God has prepared a deep hole as big as this earth and filled it with fire a million times hotter than the one in this fireplace, and He has called it hell. Unless little girls who steal and tell lies confess their sins and pray to be forgiven, He will throw them into that fire that knows no quenching and they will burn forever in hell!'

I tried to jerk away. 'Then I hate God!' I shrieked. 'I'd hate him if he burned even a horse-thief!' I stamped and struggled frantically to escape, but his grip was as powerful as his words. Only when I kicked his shins viciously did he loose me. I ran clear out to the barn and hid myself in the hay. After a while Mama came and tried to talk me out of the unholy rage that filled me.

'There, there, dearie! Everything's all right. You just don't understand.'

But everything wasn't all right. Later in life she confessed that she hadn't thought so either, and admitted she'd worried a lot in her younger years about God's sending sickness and dooming people to eternal fire. There was no comforting me at the time. I was filled with wrath against such a God. And I wanted to help make people well even if He did mean them to be sick, though I shuddered at thought of what hell-fire it might bring upon me when I died.

God became to me a stern, white-whiskered old tyrant Who sat upon His throne high in the sky and spied disapprovingly upon my every movement. I feared him more with every breath I drew. I imagined Him devising some particularly awful malady for me — something infinitely worse than carbuncles. I'd seen Wiltz McKnight, a neighbor suffering from dropsy, sit helpless in his chair, looking like some terrible balloon. The hired man said they had to cut holes in his legs to let the water out. What if I should be punished that way? Daily I watched my legs to see if they'd begun to puff up. At night I dreamed of the doom hanging over me in this life and the next. I was too healthy and normal a child to be obsessed by such thoughts all the time, but they were always in my subconscious, waiting to clutch me in the dark when I went to bed.

If I'd talked about it in saner mood with Mama, she'd probably have helped me, but I couldn't bring myself to speak of it again to her. Yet there was a sweetness in her companionship which took some of the sting from this unhappy worry. She loved the night and the out-of-doors. Many a time she held me close as we watched the evening star appear or the moon come up, huge and brilliant, over the edge of the prairie. Often we walked a little way to the big cottonwood tree to see the night sky through its swaying branches. There was a sort of awesome comfort in the feeling of *safeness* I had with her in this familiar and beloved world about me, which, for the time at least, sheltered me from the wrath of God. For to me there was nothing of God in this Nature of

KANSAS HOMESTEAD

which I was as much a part as were the sweet grass-scented prairie breezes, the tawny hills and the infinite skies. This I loved with deep-rooted fervor. God I hated.

I shall never forget one Thanksgiving Day in the stone house. It was cold and windy and several hundred Indians had camped on the place the night before, on their way to distant unoccupied prairies to hunt buffalo. When we'd heard they were coming, Papa and Ike Bush buried all our extra foodstuffs in a cave they kept ready for that purpose. The Indians never molested settlers, but they demanded food as long as there was any in sight. Mama was sick when we woke that morning. She hadn't been well lately. Grandma and Aunt Mary had taken Willie with them to spend a few days with Aunt Ri Herren, Papa's youngest sister, who'd come with her husband to take up land the year after we did. A Mrs. Stuart, one of the neighbor women, had come to help Mama.

Ted and I had just finished breakfast when Mama called us to her in the bedroom. She told us God was sending her another baby and that we could help her most by doing everything Papa asked us to do.

We were greatly excited. There were too many Indians around for us to go out-of-doors to play, so when Papa told us we'd better go upstairs, we did. I knew the facts about babies, little pigs and calves and colts coming into the world, but I'd never known there was any suffering with it. Nothing could ever erase from my memory the horror of that morning as we listened to Mama's smothered cries and groans and sometimes an agonized scream, sharp and terrible, 'God help me!'

We buried our heads under a feather bed during these paroxysms of pain and whispered fiercely to each other the things we'd like to do to God for making her suffer this way. This was 'chastening,' evidently. He must love her a lot from the amount He was giving her. Ted had never had anything of my feeling toward his Maker, and at first was shocked by my irreverent statement of what I'd like to do to Him, but listening to Mama was enough to make him join me wholeheartedly. Our hatred mounted steadily. Sadistically we gloated over the 'chastening' we'd like to return. We'd brand Him in twenty places, Ted suggested. And push the red-hot iron clear through to the other side of His body, I added.

But after a while everything was still. We listened, afraid to breathe. What if God had taken Mama as He had Mrs. Gavin? I rushed to the stairs in panic, and just as I started down we heard a thin little wail. The baby! I heard Mrs. Stuart say, 'It's a boy.'

But Mama —! My heartbeats choked me. And then we heard her laugh! 'Well, I guess I scared the Indians away that time, all right.'

After a time Papa came up and told us to tiptoe downstairs and go out to the bunkhouse, as the Indians had left. Pretty soon he'd come out and get us and we could see the little new brother we had.

'I don't want to see any little new brother that God sent!' I yelled. 'I hate everything He has anything to do with. I'd like to burn His face off with a black pot!'

'Keep still!' Papa commanded, shocked at my sacrilegious outburst. 'Mama would feel terrible to hear you saying such wicked things!'

With hatred tearing into the fiber of my very soul like sharp teeth, I went out to the bunkhouse with Ted. He called in the dogs to keep us company, also the cat and Browny, the bantam hen whose leg Ike and I had set when the cow stepped on it. Ted said we'd better not talk that way any more, or maybe God would punish us. But I couldn't forget. I lay on my face on Ike's bunk, trembling with the shock of it all. I had been so sure for a moment that Mama was dead —! In a moment I would see her again, feel her arms around me. When Mrs. Stuart came to tell us that Mama wanted to see us, I leaped up, wild to be on my way, but Ted wouldn't go. He crawled under the corncrib where he had a hideout and refused to budge for hours.

As I stood beside Mama, I was amazed to see that she looked about as usual, except that her cheeks were very flushed. She smiled at me radiantly. I leaned over to kiss her.

'Mama,' I whispered, 'what makes you so happy when you were so hurt?'

'I'm like you were after your carbuncle hurt so, and Papa lanced it. Don't you remember how good you felt when that awful pain was gone?' I nodded, and she pulled me close. 'Let me show you the baby.'

I stiffened. 'I don't want to see that baby of God's!'

Quick understanding smiled through the momentary bewilderment of her face. Her eyes twinkled. 'I'll tell you a secret, Lora, if you'll promise not to breathe it. God didn't send this baby. I got him myself!'

What infinite relief! 'Let me see him, quick!'

Mama uncovered his tiny red face. 'Hold your arms. Mrs. Stuart will let you have him for a minute.'

* * *

Ike Bush was my champion in everything, right or wrong. I was very proud of the way he called me 'Doc.' One night when he had a severe chest cold he came in to be doctored, and Mama told him he'd have to have a mustard plaster. He protested stoutly. Not for the Virgin Mary herself would he allow one of those things to touch his hide. He'd seen what they did to one. But when I ordered him to behave himself and put one on, he finally gave in.

'What you say goes, Doc. But you'll have to make it for me yourself.'

Under Mama's supervision I concocted a most formidable one. We tied it on Ike — amid much protesting on his part — and sent him to bed with orders not to remove it unless it got to burning badly. Poor Ike! He walked into the kitchen the next morning with the skin of his chest bulged out like a cheese bag. He said he'd slept so soundly he hadn't felt it blistering. Mama wanted to let the fluid out, but Ike, with a great show of concern, said he thought it was so serious a matter that only a nurse should be trusted with it. I felt most important, even though I knew they were joking, when Papa, with grave face, heated a large darning needle and handed it to me, and Mama told me to open the blister 'close down to healthy skin,' according to instructions in Doctor Jackson's book.

I felt badly about that blister, but Ike's cold was broken. I believed him when he declared he'd have been a dead cowpuncher if he hadn't got the congestion out of him that way. I've told many a lumberjack a variation of that statement in later years to get plasters on chests — making Hippocrates undoubtedly very restless in his grave on occasion.

Across the wheatfields from us was our nearest neighbor, Matt Hermas, the music-master, who was a bachelor. Mama sent Ted and me to his place one day on an errand. She had given me a new handkerchief she'd just hemmed from a bit of muslin. 'For goodness' sake, don't forget to use it if you need it,' she'd admonished me.

Matt was sitting on his woodpile whetting his scythe when we arrived. As we talked, suddenly the keen blade slipped and I saw the cap of his forefinger fall backward and hang by a mere ribbon of flesh. The blood gushed out sickeningly. I remembered how Mama had pressed dangling flesh back into place and held it tight with bandaging when our dog got his foot caught in the mowing machine.

'Put it back on!' I cried. 'Hold it tight!' I whisked my unused new handkerchief out and bandaged it. 'Now get turpentine to pour on it. Mama used it on our dog.'

Sweat stood out on poor Matt's face and he flinched as I poured the stuff over his finger. We decided we'd better get him to Mama right away. She'd have bigger bandages and know what else to do. We took a short cut through the tall wheat. Matt held his hand high above his head and stepped in march time as he sang at the top of his voice, 'Die Wacht am Rhein.' Ted and I were much impressed with such spirit. Mama pronounced our work well done and said the finger ought to heal nicely. Which in time it did. Matt gave me a little pig as reward.

We children had been taught to sit horses as soon as we could walk, but Mama didn't let us out of sight of the house alone, for fear of Indians, in spite of the fact that this country was pretty well settled up then, and Indians rarely came through it. One of my earliest recollections is riding on Ike's horse with him. I covered hundred of miles with him rounding up cattle, inspecting fences, cutting out a fat young steer for beef or a wild range cow for dairy purposes.

One very dry summer, when the grass was too short and scorched to feed as many cattle as Papa had — he'd taken a lot to raise on shares in addition to his own — he decided to move the herd to better range. A friend of his had a homestead some hundred miles west of us, and a sod house which he said Papa might use as headquarters for the herders. A hundred miles was a long way when one drove cattle and grazed them on lands along the trail. We were greatly excited when it was decided Mama and we children were to go along.

The big wagon box, with its overjet and strong bows and cover, was packed for the trip. A camp stove called 'Number Seven' was taken along, and bedding and essentials. It was a great thrill to set off. Ike supervised the cowhands. He usually rode ahead, located a waterhole for the next night's camp, and rode back to report. Papa, sitting forward on the high spring seat like an old-time stage-coach driver, his foot on the brake — Ted and I beside him holding on for dear life — would crack his long whip over the four horses. He didn't touch them. It was only to speed them up. The wagon bounced and jolted, and Mama, sitting behind with the two youngest, would almost lose the baby off her lap.

When we were settled in camp, we would wait for the herders and cattle to catch up with us. The heat was terrific at times. Papa always did the cooking when we were camping, and when the oven was heated for biscuits, he'd have to keep as far away from the stove as he could, making only dashing runs to see if things were cooking properly. Milk soured, butter ran in grease, and bread fell into crumbs. All this I bore and still had fun, until the unhappy day down over a cutbank when I didn't have any *Toledo Blades* or other paper, and substituted a couple of nice clean leaves. Too late I discovered they were poison oak of a variety unknown to me before. The result made me pretty sorry for myself for some time.

The country was alive with prairie chickens and antelope. Off in the distance most of the time one could see herds of buffalo feeding. Wolves were thick and coyotes ran out of almost every draw we approached. We reached the new cattle range eventually and Mama set up housekeeping in the sod house. The men divided the herd into two parts and each was driven to grazing land where a waterhole was within convenient distance. There the men made camp. Tents were set up with guy ropes and pins securely fastened to withstand wind, and were ditched all around to drain off water in rainstorms. The men slept on the ground.

Twice a week we would drive to the camps with supplies and food Mama baked for them. One afternoon we were delayed in getting started to one of the camps. The moon would be full that night and Papa said it would be easy enough to find our way, as he had driven there often before. But it began to cloud up. We found ourselves hours later in the blackest night imaginable. We rode endlessly in the direction Papa thought we should be going, but we didn't get to the camp. Finally Papa said we'd have to stop for the night right where we were.

He reached for the lantern which always hung under the seat, but it wasn't there. He stopped the team and he and Mama called as loudly as they could in case we were near the camp and they might hear us. We listened. No response. We called again, Ted and I adding our voices. And listened again.

'There! They're answering. Over ——' Papa broke off. The horses snorted in quivering alertness. We clutched each other in fear, for the sound that came out of the darkness was the long-drawn howl of a wolf. Another answered. Another and another. Was a pack on our trail? They wouldn't attack people in a wagon, we'd heard, but they'd make short work of a team on the prairie.

'I reckon we don't stop!' Papa's words were light, but there was sharp undertone beneath them. But before the words were out of his mouth there came up from the ground that terrifying dry, clacking sound which warns, 'Rattlesnake'! From every side it came. In front, behind, fairly under the wagon. The horses plunged wildly and Papa laid on the whip. It sounded as though the very wheels were wound round with the horrible snakes. I had visions of one being thrown into our laps. We had evidently run into a prairie-dog town where snakes were thick as flies in the holes.

It was no place for frightened horses. If one stepped into a hole he might break a leg or his neck, with the others on top of him. There'd be no chance for us if we should be thrown among rattlers and under the feet of galloping horses. Once one of the rear team stumbled and Papa let out a cry that I knew was more prayer than oath, skeptic though he was. My heart almost popped out of my mouth. If he went down and Papa had to cut him loose with rattlers all around —! But he regained his stride and galloped on. A moment more and we had left the hissing menace behind.

Papa drew up the horses to slower pace. The wolf howls were fainter now and seemed to be moving far away from us. I drew in a deep, shuddering breath of relief.

'I know where we are now,' Papa said. 'Ike spoke of a prairie-dog town not far from camp, which was full of snakes.'

He made a sharp turn to the right and we all began calling again at the top of our lungs in chorus, and the baby began to squall lustily, so we had real volume. It was only a few minutes until we saw a tiny speck of light swinging back and forth. That would be Ike with his lantern. Never was a gleam in the dark more welcome.

When we reached the camp by the waterhole, we could make out the dim forms of cattle lying around the tent in a close circle. Mama wanted to sleep in the wagon, as she didn't relish going to bed with that many cows, but the wind had come up and was blowing hard. Lightning flashed close and sharp cracks of thunder sounded storm warnings. Papa insisted it would be safer to be in the tent in a high wind. A well-anchored tent on the prairie has withstood many a blow when even a sod house has been damaged or tumbled over.

Papa and the men examined the horses carefully to see whether they had any snakebites — luckily they hadn't —

and then carried our stuff into the tent. We'd no sooner got it inside than the big fireworks began. The sky would fairly rip open and the thunder shook the earth. I was peering out from under the tent, watching, when I heard another ominous sound. Horns clashed against horns as frightened cattle struggled to their feet. There'd be a stampede if they weren't stopped! But already the men were out circling them with horses and dogs which knew every trick. Rain came down as though it were a regular cloudburst. Above its din there rose a strange moaning sound. The herders were 'cow-singing.' Why frightened beasts were ever calmed by such dismal music was always a mystery, but they were. Even now they began milling. They were so close to the tent that sometimes they tripped over the guy ropes. As we huddled together around Mama and the sleeping baby, I had hideous visions of the tent flattening out and the herd trampling us to death, but it was anchored firmly and protected us as adequately as though its walls had been five-foot thicknesses of stone. The inside light shining through the canvas was a safeguard in itself, Ike told us later. After what seemed endless time, the herd quieted down and we got to sleep.

The morning was glorious. We sat around on tarpaulins, and through the open side of the tent the sun shone in on cowhands still soaking wet, who steamed in the warmth and smelled to heaven as we ate hot cakes and dried apple sauce.

'Ike, tell me' — I broke into a discussion of rattlesnakes — 'is it really true that a chew of tobacco tied onto a rattlesnake bite will cure the person?'

'Shucks, Doc!' He grinned at me. 'Who'd ever want to waste a chaw of good tobacco on a cowhand that'd let a rattler get the best of him? I don't think no one ever thought it wuth trying.'

But that very day he tried it — on his horse. He'd ridden over to the place where the cloudburst had struck heaviest and found it had torn out part of the prairie-dog town and washed snakes down a draw for miles. A rattler had struck from a bush and bitten his horse's leg. Ike immediately slapped a 'chaw' of tobacco on the spot and tied it tightly with his red bandana. The pony's leg swelled badly and he refused even bread and sugar all that day, but the next he was better and recovered shortly with no lasting effects. I've always wondered whether it was the quid or the bandana or faith in the tobacco that cured him.

The summer was a happy one for all of us in spite of poison oak and snakes and storms. There was a big roundup and the men who owned the cattle Papa was grazing on shares came from as far as the Missouri River. Some of them had never sat a horse before and were a never-ending source of amusement to the herders. Once one of them called Ike a 'cowboy.' Ike whipped out his revolver, his face livid.

'I'm wonderin' if my hearin's gettin' bad on me. I thought I hearn you call me a cowboy!'

The man quailed visibly. 'I — I never dreamed it was an insult!'

Meanings of words might vary widely according to localities. To our herders the term meant that picturesque outlaw in silk shirt, flowing tie and wide hat, who slept in his boots, shot up the town, and killed a man at the drop of a hat. Time, of course, removed the stigma, and it came to stand generally for the men so popular in Westerns, fiction and screen.

I have no recollection of the homeward trip except that Ike started to ride in the wagon with us, while his pony trotted along by the side of the team. Mama wanted him to take off his spurs and he didn't want to, as he might see something out on the prairie he'd like to chase. Finally Mama shooed him out and told him he'd better ride his horse. I was glad, because it meant I would be out riding with him a lot.

One day when we'd been home for some time, Ike came riding in to tell us that Granny Jedding, the old Tennessee hill-woman homesteading east of us, had gone to bed with her pipe lighted and flipped hot ashes in her eyes. What, he wanted to know, did the doctor book say to do for burned eyes?

Mama promptly made and strained a jug of tea and Ike took me on his pony behind him and delivered me and the jug at the Jedding home. Every fifteen minutes all afternoon I put fresh cold-tea wet packs on the inflamed eyes. By the time Ike came for me in the early evening, the swelling was almost gone. Granny said she felt as good as though she were 'tootled' on good old Southern rye. I felt the same way, I imagine, and went home feeling I was a real nurse.

But thought of that day's ending still brings a tightness to my throat. The sun was just setting as we came in sight of the stone house in its grove of box elders. Ike reined up his horse and pointed to the sun. There was a tenseness in him I'd never seen before.

'You know, Doc, every day the sun goes down on thousands of good men of your Pappy's kind. If you meet up with a bad man oncet in a while — well, mebby he's jest a cowhand anyhow. In every bunch of ponies there's always an ornery one. But that needn't make you scairt of the rest of 'em.'

I leaned back against him contentedly. 'They all ought to be like you, Ike.'

For a moment he hugged me up against him. Then without a word he gathered up the reins and we galloped on.

That night after chores were done, Ike came in where Mama was baking cookies. He stood leaning against the kitchen table, twisting his hat around and around, self-conscious and awkward as I had never seen him before. Mama handed him a hot cooky to break the ice, since he was obviously trying to say something that was difficult to get out. He munched it without his usual gusto.

'Them's mighty good biscuits, Mis' Wood. I — you see ——'

Mama handed him a couple more and smiled encouragingly at him.

'You've been mighty good to me, Mis' Wood. I aim I don't deserve it.' He hesitated. His lips parted as though he had more to say, but the words didn't come. He stared at the floor in silence a moment, then whirled and bolted out the door.

I bolted after him. Something was wrong. 'Ike!' I called. 'Wait for me!'

I overtook him at the bunkhouse and caught his arm,

numb with fear. His pony stood there before the open door, reins down. A blanket roll was tied behind the saddle. The dim light fell on the pony's white forelegs and the star on his forehead and gleamed faintly on the bridle trimmings.

'Ike —! You're not going away?'

'Yep, Doc, I'm a'goin'. I ——' He broke off as I threw my arms around him with an anguished wail. 'Look Doc —!' He lifted me up. He had never shown any sentiment for us children, just played with us, entertained and watched over us. But now, as he pressed his cheek against mine, he gulped as though he were trying to swallow something too big for his throat. 'I'm not goin' fur, Doc. Look!' He pointed up to the Big Dipper. 'I'll never go so fur I won't be seein' the same ol' Dipper an' stars an' moon you'll be seein'. An' wherever Ike rides, honey, you'll be a-ridin' with him.'

His cheek was wet. I was terribly frightened. Never before had I seen a man cry. He put me down and swung up onto his horse. Without a glance he was off, leaving me heart-broken. Dry-eyed but screaming, I turned and ran to the kitchen.

For weeks after Ike went away, Papa tried to find some trace of him, or some reason for his going. If the other cowhands knew, they never so much as hinted. We all grieved for him. Endlessly I worried over why he had left in such a hurry. It never entered my head that he might be keeping well out of reach of the law. To me he was a hero and beyond suspicion. The mystery was never solved. A hundred times I imagined I saw him riding down the long hill between the pasture fence and bottom land. He'd have his hat stuck on his horse's head, trimmed with an eagle feather or a bunch of flowers, and he'd be singing some cowboy song of endless verses. I'd hear him say, 'Feel in my pocket,' as he used to when he brought a little rabbit or a baby snake for us to turn loose on the prairie. But he never came back.

There was a popular song Mama and Ike used to sing before he went away. It began with the words,

> 'Oh, bury me not in the deep, deep sea,
> Where the wild, wild waves will roll o'er me.'

Once when Ike had gone to take cattle to the summer range, he picked up the words of another song sung to the same tune. It was called 'The Cowboy's Lament.' And ran,

> 'Oh, bury me not on the lone prairie
> Where the wild coyote will howl o'er me.'

But he couldn't remember all the words of it. About a year after Ike left us, Mama received a poorly written letter from him out in Montana. In it was a copy of the entire 'Lament.' His letter was full of longing for us, but he didn't say why he had gone away. Only that he could never come back. He mentioned each of us children by name and said to tell Doc he could still see the Big Dipper. And that he'd never again get such good nursing as I'd given him. That was the last we ever heard.

The loss of Ike Bush brought to me as deep grief as I have ever known. My one consolation was the thought that he believed in me and that some day I really would be taking care of sick people all the time. Nightly I prayed for his safety. Even God, hard as He was, must see the goodness of Ike and not harm him.

To keep me from brooding too much over him, Mama took me with her whenever possible, when she cared for sick neighbors. By the time I was ten years old, I was able to help her in emergencies and accidents. I could make mustard plasters, bread-and-milk poultices, and knew how to treat colds and croup. I helped bathe infants and give injections. (We'd never heard of 'enemas' or 'compresses.') With every scrap of cloth I could find, I bandaged something, even broken broomsticks. I was thrilled and happy when my patients got better, utterly miserable when they did not.

This neighborhood nursing was a heavy burden for Mama, with the demands of her family and home. So it was a joyful event for us one day when a man drove up to our house and introduced himself as Doctor Borst, and said he and his wife were locating at Smith Center. This was a small town which had grown up some ten miles from us. Doctor Borst was a tall, thin, overworked-looking man with kindly eyes. He glanced at the few doctor books we had, volumes worn from much hard usage, and asked who read them. He was much amused when I told him I did. But when I told him I knew what would cure chilblains, he looked at me with real interest.

'What treatment would you prescribe?'

'Poultices of fresh cow manure,' I replied. 'One of our herders had terrible toes all last winter. They were awfully swollen and black. He howled like a dog because they burned and itched so much. The old German up the creek made poultices out of cow manure and put them on, and before long he got well.' I remember vividly how the doctor's face went serious when I asked, 'Is it the smell that cures them? Cow manure smells like spirits of hartshorn, so I put some hartshorn on my chilblains and they were cured too.'

Doctor Borst explained that spirits of hartshorn and manure smell alike because they both contained something called 'Ammonia.' That it was made in Egypt centuries before there were any people in this country. It had been named for the Egyptian god, Amon, and was useful for many things. This understanding man opened a new world of knowledge for me. Seeing how earnest I was about nursing, he brought me books and medical charts. It was a thrilling moment when he first explained about the internal organs and showed me a chart of the human skeleton.

One day old Scott, our pet horse, out on the range with a herder, ran through a prairie fire and came tearing home with his saddle blanket ablaze. He bolted into the sod stable and set fire to the straw in the roof. Before we could rescue him, he was so badly burned Papa said he would have to be shot. But we children begged so tearfully for his life that Aunt Mary said she'd undertake to care for him. He was trussed up in a shed so that his feet escaped the ground and we all helped nurse him.

For nine weeks I was up at daylight every morning to run out to the shed to get things ready for Aunt Mary to do the dressings. I stayed with the horse all day unless forced away, feeding him, giving him drinks, keeping flies off him, raking the ground clean of manure. At first, the dressing of those burns was a terrible thing. His flesh fell off in great patches and he groaned and cried like a human being. As I think of it now, I can't understand why Papa didn't shoot him in spite of our protests. Night after night Aunt Mary and I stayed out with him until late bedtime, just to keep him company.

But at last the day came when he could be let down on his poor scarred legs. Little by little he gained strength and in time he was really well. Old Scott was an important member of our family for many years after.

We had a valuable colt sired by our thoroughbred stallion. One morning, Papa, who often teased me about my doctor books, asked me if I could find anything in Doctor Jackson's *Home Treatment and Care of the Sick* to do for a colt. He said, in a modest whisper, 'He's all bound up. I've given him oil and everything, but it doesn't do any good.'

We went behind the granary where the poor puffed-up colt lay. His eyes were turned back and he seemed to be unconscious. We held a consultation.

'Let's give him an injection,' I suggested.

'That's what Mama said, but we haven't any equipment big enough.'

I studied a moment. 'How about a gun barrel and the funnel?'

Papa laughed at me, but I ran to the house for a bucket of warm suds, and Papa got the barrel of a shotgun and the funnel. He sat on the colt's hind quarters and we carried on. When the colt was about ready to explode with so much water added to his already bursting sides, he made one last tremendous effort, floundered to his feet, and the treatment was successful. He tore down the creek bottom, getting smaller and smaller with every jump, and Papa and I lay back on the ground and almost split ourselves laughing.

Papa was strictly honest, a good neighbor and an excellent provider, and I am sure he loved his family, but he was nervous and exacting, impatient and quick-tempered. He thought it a sign of weakness to show any sentiment or emotion. But this colt incident seemed to crash down the bars which had separated us and I had never before felt so close to him. For days, every time we looked at each other, we'd burst into gales of laughter, which no one else could share — not having seen that colt. For the first time I felt close to him. And the bars were never put up between us again.

Many years later, when he was old, one of his horses kicked him and a blood clot formed at the base of the brain. Things which happened after this accident were remembered only a few moments, but everything else in his life before was entirely clear in his mind. This colt episode we laughed over many times in those pathetic years when he lived entirely in the past. When things got tense and Papa's ire was up because I wouldn't let him go into traffic alone, or do any of the things unsafe for him, the skies could be cleared by asking, 'Well, Papa, what about giving the colt a colonic irrigation?'

Life was pretty wonderful and interesting those early days on the Kansas homestead. My early resentment over the 'chastening' of a cruel God and His terrible injustices was short-lived. A strange experience changed everything for me.

Throughout the year we had lyceums of sorts, drawing for entertainment from our local talent. In the summertime a favorite meeting place was the natural amphitheater of our stone quarry. Papa was noted for his repertoire of recitations. He memorized poetry and prose endlessly. The poetic rhythm and noble language of his readings always stirred me deeply. I would listen to Papa give the 'Gettysburg Address' or 'Build Thou More Stately Mansions, O My Soul,' and then go and try to do them exactly as he did. I was always spouting lines far beyond my comprehension. Before I was ten I'd been in several declamation contests, and still have earrings I once won as a prize. As I grew older, I memorized *Evangeline* from cover to cover, and on one occasion gave as much of *The Lady of the Lake* as our lyceum head would permit.

But it was before I was capable of such mature offerings that this strange experience came to me. One evening in early summer we were having a big meeting in our stone quarry. People from miles around were there as we settled down after the picnic supper. It was a fine evening with a beautiful sunset and I loved it all — the gaunt stone quarry, stark against the sky, the sweetness of cottonwoods mingling with the damp of the creek, the crickets in the dry grass, the peaceful hills.

But my heart was not at peace, for the old hatred of God was rankling anew, stirred by a recent hell-fire-and-damnation sermon I had heard.

Papa and I were both on the program, well toward the end. I had been letter-perfect in my recitation for weeks and was sure I'd make a good impression. The sunset glory was faded and the evening star extraordinarily bright by the time it was my turn to climb to the wagon box which served as stage.

Confidently I began the first verse,

> Twinkle, twinkle, little star,
> How I wonder what you are,
> Up above the world so high ——

My eyes fixed on the evening star. It enthralled me with its beauty. I stared at it as though hypnotized, forgetting to go on. Its unearthly brilliance seemed to grow brighter, to shine all around me, shine all through me.

'"Like a diamond ——"' Vaguely I heard Mama's promptings, but I was transported to another world. The nameless need long clamoring in my childish mind — to know — *to know* — was suddenly satisfied. I was aware of a new God. Not the cruel God of the circuit rider, but a Presence, like my mother's presence when I was away from her, a love like her love, in spite of my being bad.

Papa startled me out of my revelation by swinging me down off the wagon with a none too gentle grasp. Mama, arm around my shoulders, hustled me over toward our wagon to hide her mortification.

'What in the world was the matter with you?' she demanded. 'You didn't even try to go on when I prompted you — just stood there staring up at the sky as though you'd lost your wits! How could you forget?'

I was tingling with the glory that filled me as I looked up

into her face. 'Forget —? What did I forget?' For the moment I had no memory of my recitation.

'I'm awfully disappointed in you, Lora!' She looked as though she were going to cry as she frowned at me.

'What are you sorry for?' I hugged up close to her. 'Mama — ! I've found out about God!'

I must have been a trying and unsatisfactory child. She shook me a bit in exasperation. 'Don't talk that way. Come on. Help me to pack up our things.'

I have never been able to explain that experience, but all down the years have come moments when I recaptured that sense of clear understanding and inspiration. A burst of music, a pattern of leaves on the ground in moonlight, wild geese flying over, a spring of clear, cold water in a bank, a tall conifer against the night sky — a hundred things — but most of all a brilliant evening star will bring it all back to me.

Somehow, I feel I started from there.

CALIFORNIA

CALIFORNIA

WHEN I WAS TWELVE YEARS OLD, we moved into a little house in Jewell City for the winter. Mama was going to have another baby and she wanted to be near a doctor. Doctor Borst had left recently. Papa could ride back and forth to the ranch to keep his eye on the men there. Mama had made all arrangements, but with the same sense of humor which has characterized my sister Florence all her life, she decided to arrive ahead of time.

The ninth of April was a bitter, snowy day. Papa was in Missouri delivering a span of pacers for the horse show. Ted was spending the night with a friend. In the evening after the younger children were in bed, Mama and I got out all the baby clothes for me to see again. This time it would surely be a girl. I had three brothers. With my own money, won as prizes at the County Fair for baking the best bread and cake and winning a footrace, I'd bought a baby buggy. I spread a dress and cap in it and began imagining how beautiful my baby sister would look when I took her for an airing.

'I hope she'll like her buggy, Mama. I wish we didn't have to wait any longer.'

'Don't wish that!' Mama looked uneasy. 'The way I'm feeling today I'm afraid it's coming too soon. Papa's a long way off, remember. I wouldn't want ——' She broke off, consternation in her face. She caught at a chair and leaned over the back as though she were hurting terribly. 'O, my goodness!' There were beads of perspiration on her forehead when she straightened up. 'Quick, Lora! Get Mrs. Connelly — tell her to send Art for the doctor. Run!'

'Is the baby coming now?' I was shaking with excitement.

'I'm afraid so. Hurry!'

Art was the deaf and dumb son of our nearest neighbors the Connellys. He talked with his fingers and all the children of the neighborhood had learned his language. But since the doctor probably wouldn't understand him, Mrs. Connelly sent a note along. She wrote only, 'Come at once, please.'

It happened that Art's aunt had been expecting a baby any day the last two weeks, so when the doctor read the note, he thought Art had brought it from her. He hustled the boy into his buggy, whipped up the horse, and took off in the opposite direction from our place, to go to her farm. Art protested, but the doctor didn't register what all his gesturing was about, so intent was he on beating the stork. Art wasn't any too sure himself when he got to thinking about it. He'd been wakened from sound sleep to carry a note to the doctor and he began to wonder if after all he might have been mistaken in thinking it was Mrs. Wood who needed help.

Meanwhile Mrs. Connelly and I carried on alone. She had delivered several women and no doubt did just as well as a doctor under the circumstances. Whether or not any blessed last-minute chloroform was administered in those days, I can't say. But I do know Mama never had it with any of her six children.

I heated water and sweet oil and got the baby's things laid ready. I put clean linen and Mama's nightgown to warm. When the paroxysms of pain would twist a scream from her lips, only the thought of that other time when she laughed so soon after the baby came made it possible for me to bear it. The stark grimness of it nauseated me, but here was real challenge. No doctor — but Mrs. Connelly was not alarmed and I must stand by to help as a nurse should.

If only it would end — this long-drawn-out misery! 'Mama, did I hurt you so much when I came?' I asked her once when she breathed easier for a moment.

She smiled ruefully. 'You took the longest time of any of them, honey. All day and all night ——' She gripped my hand comfortingly as she saw the unhappy tears spring to my eyes. 'But you were so *worth* it, darling!'

She smiled at me bravely between pains, until they came so fast that there were no betweens. 'It won't be long now,' Mrs. Connelly assured me. 'She's doing fine.'

I shuddered. If this were fine, what must things be when they were not? At the end the room swam dizzily around me at intervals, but I fought my weakness grimly. If Mama could stand so much, I mustn't fail her.

At last with a queer little animal noise, half cry, half cough, the baby was born. 'It's a girl!' said Mrs. Connelly. I watched, fascinated, as she worked. I held the blanket ready and in a moment my tiny sister was handed over to me. By the open oven door of the kitchen stove, I applied warm oil to her small body, then wrapped her in a soft blanket and cuddled her in my arms. It may have been something maternal that burned in me, it may have been the miracle of birth, or it may have been the nursing instinct brought at last to a sort of fruition, but whatever it was lifted me to ecstasy. And when I took the baby to Mama, after she had been made comfortable among her snow-white sheets and pillows, and she pressed the little thing close to her breast, I knew she, too, felt something very special and wonderful and triumphant.

We stayed on in Jewell City for several years. The ranch, on a share basis, was making good, and Papa's ability and experience in building made him so good a carpenter that his services were in constant demand in the fast-growing town. My youngest brother was born there, two years after Florence's advent.

But Papa had long had a malady not listed in Doctor Jackson's *Home Treatment and Care of the Sick*. Our hired girl, Hannah Peters, insisted she had inherited chilblains from her father. I had inherited from mine an itching foot — with itch extending to the knee. On the ranch every fall when the hay was stacked, the wheat in the granary and the corncrib filled, Papa had always begun to talk of other localities more desirable. I'd get out our old geography and we'd pick out places we'd like to see. Here in town he felt the same urge.

About this time Papa's sister Maria and her husband, Sam Herren, moved to California at the height of the land boom there. Uncle Sam went into real estate business and Grandma and Aunt Mary sold their homestead and went out to join them. Immediately they wrote back that carpenters were scarce and that fortunes could be made in real estate overnight if one had a little money to invest.

This news brought on in Papa an attack of itching foot so acute that all Mama's 'prevention and home treatment' failed to cure it. Papa had his heart set on California. Mama was most unhappy about it. It grieved her to think of selling the homestead. The stone house in its box elder grove, the garden plot and fields, every tree planted with their own hands, every building raised stone by stone — to her it was a sanctuary and shrine. And never again would she find such friends as these neighbors.

'But you'd never have to worry about cyclones out in California,' Papa guilefully informed her. 'They never have them.'

He knew her dread of those terrifying nights when she mustered her half-wakened brood from their beds and raced them down into the ever-ready cyclone cellar. After much debating, she reluctantly consented.

Preparations for that exciting journey stand out vividly in my mind. The ranch with its stock was sold. Our furniture was shipped out to Aunt Mary, who was to have a house ready for us when we arrived in Pasadena. We left the bigger part of our clothing behind — fur coats, heavy knitted stock-

CALIFORNIA

ings and caps, woolen underwear and flannel-lined overshoes. We were going to a land of perpetual sunshine. We would be able to eat a whole orange apiece at a time, instead of just the little sections of the delicious fruit Mama doled out to us at Christmas. There would be palm trees and mountains and the Pacific Ocean at the end of the journey.

We left for Kansas City on a combination freight and passenger train. On emigrant trains, such as we would take from there, no bedding was provided for the sleeping-cars. Emigrants carried their own bedrolls. There were eight of us and we looked like some expeditionary force. We carried our food in a brand-new washboiler. That was Papa's bright idea, and so humiliating to Mama that she could scarcely raise her eyes at first for fear she would see people laughing at us. Sensitive Ted, sixteen years old then, was so ashamed he refused to eat at first.

It was night when we arrived in Kansas City, where we were to change cars for the California train. Our train was to leave early in the morning. The noise and confusion of the station, the portion of the city we could see from the huge arched windows and open doors, filled us with wonder and delight, all save poor anxious Mama, who bedded us down on the floor of the waiting-room with other emigrant children. All night she sat beside us, shooing away the rats that scampered and scurried around and over the sleeping forms.

Somehow we managed to get settled in orderly fashion on the train the next morning. Ted sat as far from the washboiler as possible and kept his eyes glued to the window. The small children sat in one bunk on the neatly folded bedding. And then, with a long, wailing whistle that sent joyous thrills through me, the train began to jerk into motion, while the last 'All Aboard!' was still echoing through the train shed and corridors.

At first, I could scarcely tear my eyes away from the swiftly unreeling panorama outside the windows, but after a time I began to look over our fellow passengers. Midway of the car was a large and untidy woman with a huge pompadour. As I was going into the toilet about noon, she brushed by me, her hand over her mouth and obviously sick at her stomach. Wanting to be helpful, I assisted her as best I could by holding her head, and got nicely messed up for my pains. But she was pretty bad, so I stood my ground. That rigidly molded pompadour of hers had fascinated me, but now in her violent retching it suddenly collapsed as the stuffing shot out into the toilet seat. To my amazement I saw the 'rat' was a big roll of greenbacks held firmly with rubber bands. I retrieved it just in time.

In the section back of ours was a swarthy, tremendously big man who eyed us smilingly and eventually came to talk to Papa. One expected his voice to match the rest of him and boom out of his chest like that of an auctioneer. Instead it was a thin falsetto, and so squeaky that Papa plainly showed his surprise. The big fellow leaned close to Papa's ear and explained in an aside, 'I can't help talking this way. I'm a eunuch.' I overheard his statement and intruded myself at once into the conversation, much interested.

'What's a eunuch, Papa?'

'Hush!' There was such finality in Papa's manner as he glared at me that I never dared reopen the matter. It took me a year or so to find the word in the dictionary, since I was always looking under the letter U.

I had none of Ted's squeamishness and thought the food tasted as good from the washboiler as any other way. Mama's home-made bread was wonderful, and after sizing up the other children in the car, I smugly decided we young Woods were much superior. We had better clothes and we certainly behaved much better. I was proud of Papa, and to me, Mama, with her fair skin, soft gray eyes, and hair wound around her head in two braids, looked beautiful and distinguished. I compared her to the woman of the money, whose greasy, taffy-colored hair was piled up on top of her head in an ugly mass that looked for all the world like a buffalo chip. She had a whining little boy who ate peanuts incessantly and drooled licorice from the corners of his mouth. She scolded him every time she spoke to him. Mama, holding the baby in his long white dress, had only to lift her brows to check

Leslie when he licked the window-pane or quiet Florence when she sang too loudly.

My brother Willie was a pal of the conductor's in short order, and before we were two hours out was calling all the trainmen by their first names. There was a coal range in one end of the car, where emigrants could cook their food. Papa filled the oven with potatoes to bake and told everyone in the car to have one when they were done. I can smell them yet, and taste the home-cured ham that went with them. Everyone warmed up to everyone else before night and Mother started them singing. The colored porter joined in too. His voice was beautiful and you could hear it above all the others.

It was a great adventure. Nothing I have ever done since has seemed quite so grand. Only my ardent desire to see the Pacific Ocean and pick oranges off the trees reconciled me to the end of our magnificent journey. Fulfillment began with our first glimpse of palm trees and orange groves, and the sight of the Sierra Madre Mountains overwhelmed us. We had never seen mountains, never dreamed they could be so high, so massive. For the first time Ted forgot the humiliating washboiler and gaped, wide-eyed, at the gigantic wall.

Later, when I saw the ocean for the first time, it was a bit disappointing. It didn't seem any wider than our six-hundred-acre pasture back in Kansas. It seemed to run uphill. Looking at its roughness, I skeptically doubted that Jesus ever walked on the sea. I had prayed every night since first seeing pictures of ships at sea that I might one day go to the ocean. Now I felt that my prayers had been poorly answered. But the mountains made up for any lack.

At the very foot of these mountains, in Altadena, we moved into the tent house Aunt Mary had furnished for us. These houses were nicely constructed with double walls, good floors, many windows, and shingled roofs. They were a product of cheap and quick housing in those boom days. Papa bought a horse and buckboard so we could have transportation, and we were very comfortable and happy in our new home. And how we ate oranges!

It was on an all-day trip to San Pedro not long after we were settled that my dream of the ocean was suddenly realized. For a long time I watched a ship coming in from sea. At first there was only the mast, which grew longer and longer. Then the body of the ship grew from a thin line to a huge hulk. By the time this ship and others had landed, loaded and departed, I was ashamed of my first reaction to the ocean. Awe-struck and trembling with excitement, I watched a large sailing vessel which was lying in the harbor. I saw the canvas run up, saw the huge sails belly with the wind, and saw the clipper go racing to catch the sun before it dropped out of sight. From that day the sea got bigger every time I saw it. Already California was not enough adventure. I must go down to the sea in a ship sooner or later.

Mama rejoiced daily in California's calm sunshine. It was wonderful to feel that never again would she have to dread windstorms. It was infinite solace to her for the things she'd left behind. Secretly I grieved for those danger-spiced nights when we rushed out into the tumult, with wind whipping our nightclothes around our bare shanks and hindering our flight, while vivid chain lightning stabbed through the racing green clouds. Oh, there was excitement and worth-whileness about those Kansas years.

And then one night California betrayed itself to Mama. Out of those Sierra Madre Mountains there roared a storm far worse than any we had ever experienced. With a blast of wind-driven stones deadly as bullets, and dust that blotted out the skies, the gale struck the tent house, ripped off the roof, and swept it away. We thought our last moments had come, but Papa shouted to us to get out into the tent standing beside the house. It would be safer where there were no beams and walls to fall on us. The terrific gusts were interspersed at intervals with brief periods of calm. In one of these lulls we hustled out of the house into the tent, carrying with us crackers and milk and water as well as bedding. All through the night we older ones stood braced against the tent poles. In the short breathing spaces Papa dashed out to tighten guy ropes and drive tent pins deeper into the ground. Long streamers of torn canvas from the tent house whipped in the gale, friction-generated sparks snapping from their frayed ends.

It seemed the most endless night I had ever known, but dawn came at last and the gale began to die down. When we could safely investigate, we found nothing left of our tent house but the floor. The organ and range were still standing, but all the other furnishings, pictures, dishes, and beds were literally scattered to the four winds. Grandma's pictures and some other things were found by grape-pickers in a vineyard a mile and a half away. One wall of the tiny barn was still intact. The buckboard was turned over against it. The horse stood untethered, too frightened to move from his feed box. It was the worst windstorm in the life of the oldest inhabitant. Scarcely a house escaped some damage. But houses there were not built to withstand tornadoes as they were in the prairie country.

Papa assembled the scattered harness, righted the buckboard, and finally got the horse hitched up. He took Mama and the smaller children out to Aunt Mary's place. Her house was a tiny, hastily constructed boom-time cottage which seemed safe enough, in spite of the fact that it had reared up on its foundations during the storm and settled down again in a lop-sided manner. Papa and Ted put up our tent close to the house. We older children still hunted over the fields around our demolished home, salvaging our clothes and household goods from among the crushed yellow poppies: a shoe here, a stocking there, a frying pan half-buried in the sand, some things torn to shreds, others intact as though they had just been spread out on the grass to air. It was days before we gave up the search.

Then, when at last we got down to the business of living in another house, a new disaster overtook us. All six of us children came down with scarlet fever at the same time. It was a bad time for poor Mama, but Aunt Mary and Grandma helped. I was the first to recover and, with red-rimmed eyes and blotched, peeling face, waded into the siege side by side with Mama. My determination to become a nurse was steadily increasing. The three middle youngsters came through all right, but Ted had badly infected ears and the baby went into pneumonia. How many times Mama had ridden through cold and snowdrifts on black winter nights to nurse without a doctor's advice. She had brought many another mother's child back to health, but now all her faithful following of a skilled doctor's orders left her nothing of her last born but a picture and a curl of yellow hair.

The California boom days have never been featured in picture, song, and story as the Gold Rush days have been. They were not so colorful and dramatic, but were far more tragic. Papa, with thousands of others, made down-payments on land, expecting to resell at big profit before the second installment fell due. But the real estate bubble, expanded to the limit, burst overnight. One couldn't give a town lot away. Unable to hold on to any of his contracts, Papa lost everything. And he couldn't make a living as a carpenter when there was no longer demand for building. He managed to salvage enough from the financial wreck to buy a good span of horses and a wagon, and for several years he trucked and freighted and did everything that came to hand to keep the family in necessities. Mama kept boarders, but the profit was small. Ted, still not old enough to vote, made a secret marriage with a woman eight years his senior and left the state. Willie, now grown into a husky, sixteen-year-old 'Bill,' went to Montana to herd sheep on a ranch belonging to a great-uncle of ours.

After a time we moved into Los Angeles. The house was old and shabby and dismal. Mama and I arranged our furnishings to look as attractive and homelike as possible, then stood and looked at each other hopelessly. One could live in a tent for a short time when it was part of the program of acquiring great wealth, and look upon it as a vacation that was really fun. But this —! We were going from bad to worse fast.

'Well, Mama' — I tried to sound cheerful — 'no one can call us "stuck-up" now!'

'We look like the scum of the earth!' I think it was the first time in my life I'd ever heard Mama sound bitter. She was utterly discouraged for the moment. 'I belong with Mrs. Gavin — cutting out shirts with a butcher knife. Well, one consolation — Papa will soon be wanting to move again and we might get a better house. Certainly nothing could be worse!'

'What about that wild plum you used to make into jam — instead of eating it raw? Can't you — ?'

'This isn't a plum, Lora. It's green persimmons — a hayrack full of them!'

But the mood passed, and after a while she was her courageous self again, ashamed of weakening before me.

It was in this dreary period of my life that I first met Emory Hughes. Mama sent the children to the Sunday School of the nearest church, a Methodist one, and I joined the young people's group, feeling lonely for friends of my own age. It was there I first saw Emory. He was president of the Epworth League and was a man of twenty-five at least, I judged. I was much impressed by a quality in him which we would today call 'sophistication' — a term unknown to us then. He was slight and well-set-up, with a high forehead and dark, shining hair. His eyes were brown and full of humor. He told me, the first time he walked home with me, that his parents had come from Wales to Maryland before he was born. He had much of the charm and social grace of Southerners I had known and I was thrilled beyond words when I learned he'd been clear around the world on various sailing ships.

I exhibited him to the family with great pride. Papa looked him over and was at first inclined to be skeptical of those adventurous tales of far ports. But when he found from outside inquiry that Emory was a skilled draftsman in sheet metal and making good money, he accorded him more respect. He lived just a few blocks from us, 'batching' with a friend who'd often sailed with him. When I told him I wanted to be a nurse, he declared he was one of sorts himself, often caring for male patients at the County Hospital. I could be put on as assistant to a nurse, he said, and so get good experience. He wanted to be a doctor some day. Our interest in healing was mutual, but unlike me, he was dubious of ever attaining his goal.

'Ships and far places lure me too much,' he said one day as we sat on a park bench near the edge of a pool and threw bits of lunch to the swans. 'I'm always wanting to break away and go to new places.'

I felt warm understanding for him. He had shipped out on freighters several times, and he painted pictures of Hawaii and South Sea Islands which filled my landlubber soul with yearning.

I told him how disappointing the ocean had been when I'd first seen it. 'But now, when I go down on a dock and see ships and fishermen's nets and cargoes being loaded, and breathe in the waterfront smell, I love it more each time. Some day I'm going to travel.'

'It'd be a wonderful honeymoon trip — over to Hawaii.' The smile in his brown eyes embarrassed me as he moved closer.

'I imagine it might,' I replied matter-of-factly. 'I want to see the Pyramids, too, and the Amazon and Westminster Abbey. Some day —! But first I'm going to be a nurse.'

'Why pick such a hard life?'

'Because I like it. And I'll make good money besides to travel around on. Do you know that the nurse the doctor sent to help right at the last, when our baby had pneumonia, was there only two days and she charged *three dollars!*'

Emory shook his head. 'That's a lot of money. But think of all the things you could see just tramping around, in the time you'd spend training.'

'That's all right,' I laughed. 'You can walk and swim your way around the world if you want to. I want something better. Some day I'm going to have a horseless carriage like the one we saw on the street the other day. See if I don't! Imagine going three times faster than a horse and not having to bother with pasturage or oats for it.'

'Do you mean to say you'd ride around in a silly thing like that?'

'Certainly I would! And what's more I expect to see the

day when they'll have flying machines that will fly around the world!'

Emory laughed so long and loudly that the park policeman strolled over to see what it was all about. When Emory told him, he slapped his leg and roared too.

'Go on and laugh!' I flared at them. 'People laughed at the idea of a steamboat, remember. You fellows ought to have been on hand to rotten-egg Edison when he was working on his inventions. I notice you ride on the cable cars. Two years ago you probably laughed at that idea too. I'd like to see you sentenced to stick to old horse cars forever!' I was good and mad.

The depression of the early nineties was well on its way. As the last days of high school came nearer, Mama and I were at our wits' end to know how to buy material for my graduation dress. I hadn't a stitch that would do. I had to look my best, since I was to deliver the class speech at the opera house where the exercises were to be held. In one of the stores there was some beautiful cream-colored cashmere I'd long coveted, but it seemed as unattainable as the moon.

'It would make just exactly the sort of dress I want,' I lamented to Mama one day.

'If we could only sell enough of our chickens or ducks, you could have it.' Mama frowned speculatively. 'But there's just no market for them right now.'

Each day, as I helped feed that flock of unwanted fowls, hope of my dress became more remote. And then one morning, when we were out in the chicken yard, a man stopped at the fence and asked if the ducks were for sale. He was a meat broker, he said, and he would take all of them if they could be dressed and ready for delivery the next morning. Mama hesitated. Papa was out of town at the time and she'd never been able to cut the head off a chicken in her life.

I jumped in with a lusty 'That will be fine! I'll see that the ducks are all ready for you. Would you leave a deposit?'

He would. With a pleased bow he took the receipt I wrote and left. Mama wilted down on the chopping-block.

'Lora, are you crazy?' she wailed. 'Who's going to chop the heads off those ducks?'

'I am!' I grabbed up the axe and flourished it.

She eyed me with mingled admiration and revolt. Mama's chickens and ducks and turkeys were all pets and she could never bear to have one killed. She got up and went into the house, closing the door against the sound of coming slaughter.

I'd killed many a chicken, but when I laid the head of that first duck on the block, I knew this was going to be a very different matter. A chicken is always too scared to move, but that duck's head slithered around like a snake's. I raised the axe and brought it down where the neck should have been. It made me sick when I saw I had cut off only the bill. I swung again. The head should have been cleanly severed, but in horror I saw I had only hacked the flesh. But my third attempt was successful. Every instinct in me rebelled, but thought of that cashmere dress kept me from throwing down the axe. After a little bloody practice, I had better luck getting the axe squarely on the neck. But I was a limp and nauseated executioner before those twenty-two heads were off. Mama came to help me then, and we dipped the ducks in a firkin of scalding water and rolled them in grain sacks so that the feathers would come off easily.

'You'll feel better if you have a good hot meal before you begin dressing those ducks,' Mama said. 'What would taste good to you?'

'Anything but fresh meat!' I roared at her. 'I never want to see meat again as long as I live.'

'How are you going to stand a surgery? Maybe you'd better not try to go on and be a nurse.'

For á moment I wondered if I had.

All night we worked. Day was showing in the east when the final pinfeather was out and the ducks properly dressed.

'Why *dressed*,' I snorted to Mama, 'when they are so thoroughly *un*dressed!'

Mama had always insisted that coffee retarded the growth up to the time one was twenty at least, and so we never were allowed any as youngsters, except on Sunday morning or some special occasion. And then it was greatly diluted. But this morning's breakfast was memorable. Mama told me I could have all the coffee I wanted. I took it strong and black. I needed it.

The price we got for the ducks was eleven dollars. It was riches. As soon as the store was open in the morning, I was on the spot to buy the long-coveted goods for my dress. Seven yards of it, with silk cords to braid into a girdle and three dozen buttons to sew down the back of the basque. Mama spent the morning cutting it out and then began its creation. I helped her in every way I could, loving every stitch of it. I have a cabinet photograph of myself in it, a round-faced girl with high cheekbones and a pompadour. I've always wondered why my youthful photographs made me look so melancholy. My eyes in this one seem deeper-set than usual and have an expression of peering around for something lost.

When graduation night came, I scarcely recognized myself in the well-stayed — and uncomfortable — elegance of that cashmere dress. The high, stiff collars of that period, fastened in the back, were boned well up under the ears, and were separate from the waist. To prevent slipping and gaping, they were firmly anchored to the neckband in the rear with 'beauty pins.' It was only after I'd delivered my oration and received my diploma that I realized my neck was hurting more than even such a collar justified. I couldn't sit still with the pain and tried to move the tight thing into more comfortable position, only to find that in putting it on I'd pinned through a fold of skin. I'd been so excited up to that point that I hadn't felt it!

* * *

While the financial situation in California was no better the next two years, for me, at least, they were not unhappy ones. We had clothes and food and friends. I traipsed around the country with Papa at times, perched high on the wagon seat when he hauled hay or freight from one location to another. We both loved camping. I have rare memories of sitting beside a little fire in some arroyo along the road with our black coffee pot and lunch; I was always allowed coffee when I was out with him.

The sand was hot, but never too hot to suit me. The wood fire smelled of eucalyptus and the odor of sage lay heavy in the air. Rabbits by the dozen darted from cactus clumps. I never wearied of lying flat on my back on the sun-warmed earth, to look up into the soft clear blue of a sky where eagles always soared. Life was good.

Once late in the fall, Papa and Uncle Sam took me with them on a hunting trip up through the San Fernando Valley, through the Sagus Canyon out beyond Lancaster to a place in the hills known as Seven Springs. There were still traces there of an unsuccessful experiment in mail transportation — the old trail of the camel train which was planned to carry mail between Salt Lake City and Bakersfield. While the men were out after deer, I prepared the food for the next meal or lay dreaming in the shade of the wagon if it got too hot.

I had seen a lot of Emory in these years. He wanted me to marry him, but I was unwilling to commit myself. He was a charming and likable companion, witty and kind, but while I was fond of him, I was determined to let nothing interfere with my becoming a nurse. It had shocked me once when Emory told me he always gambled every Saturday night.

'Of course, if I had a nice little wife to support, I wouldn't risk losing money that way.' He smiled at me. 'But I spend three nights a week and all day Sunday at church, what with ushering, singing in the choir, and leading the Epworth League, and I get a big wallop out of a game of poker down at Jack's Place.'

I bothered mildly over this, but was much more concerned over how and when I was going to get my nurse's training. The first schools for training had been established in New York and Boston some eighteen years before, but west of Chicago real training schools were few and far between. Most of them were nondescript religious institutions, mostly Catholic, and one had to subscribe more or less to their rigid code. Unfortunately, I had been raised in an atmosphere opposed almost cruelly to Catholicism in any form. The few doctors with whom I had talked advised me to go to any hospital where they would take me in, learn to be a practical nurse, and forget all about my diploma. But I wanted something more than a chance to empty bed-pans, scrub, and break my back lifting and managing delirious patients, or old drunks brought in from the gutter.

So, as I sat in the desert, looking off over the Joshua trees into the blue distance, I said aloud so all the horned toads could hear, 'No! I don't want to marry Emory. Some way, God, help me to become a trained nurse yet!'

And then Fate, in the person of Great-Uncle Jeremiah, took a hand in our affairs. Only a few weeks after the camping trip, a letter came from him, asking us to come at once to Montana to join him on the sheep ranch where my brother Bill had already gone. He offered Papa a share in the business and made it sound most worth while. From Bill's letters we knew the ranch was about thirty miles from the little town of Glendive, that the log house on the small creek was pretty crude, and that the stables were dirt-roofed and the sheep pens in cutbanks. And there were no neighbors for miles around.

The thought of such a change appalled me. How could I go bury myself in such a place? It would mean giving up my ambition to be a nurse. On the other hand, how could I stay behind with no funds on which to live?

Emory's insistence at this point that he could not let me go out of his life, that he loved me so much he would never be happy unless he could help me get the training I so much wanted, and that it was sheer folly to go where I could never get it — all these things bearing down upon me, when my mind was so torn and confused, weighted the scales in his favor. I decided to stay.

There was little time to think. Papa was chafing to be off at once. He and Mama were not enthusiastic about my marrying, but they did not oppose it. Like most schoolgirls, I had imagined that some day I should be romantically in love and that life would become the thrilling thing love-stories would have us believe. But deep in my heart was vague resentment that I was preparing for my wedding day and had experienced none of it. But Emory was wonderful to me. Maybe it would come after marriage. And so I put on the cream-colored cashmere, which was still doing duty as my 'best' dress, and stood with him beneath the arch of smilax and heliotrope Mama had hastily constructed, to make my solemn vows.

Emory had bought a four-room cottage. A scarlet climbing rose covered the porch and it was clean and pleasant. Mama tried to seem happy for my sake when she saw us established there before they left. They ate their last dinner with us. When the time came to go to the train, she pulled me out in the storeroom and held my face close to hers.

Once I had seen a coyote caught in a trap and the dogs were worrying it. It looked up at me in a way I'll never forget. Mama's eyes had that look now. I had been so busy with my own affairs that I hadn't realized until that moment what torture this going away to Montana without Ted or me meant to her. A day's round trip by wagon to the nearest neighbor, a log shack, wind and thunder storms and prairie fires and accidents, and no doctor within thirty miles — it wrung my heart to realize her dread of it. I had so much to say I could not even say 'Good-bye.' I saw the word form on her lips, but she made no sound. Then Papa's voice reached us, hurried and impatient. 'Come on, Molly! We'll miss the train.' And they were gone.

For the next few months I took some training in the City Hospital and was then sent out by Associated Charities as a district nurse and investigator. There was no pay for this service, nor any prestige. Just plenty of hard work and experience.

The very first case that came up for investigation was my nextdoor neighbors, the Princes. They had been in need for some time, and Emory and I had helped as we could. This was the peak of the great depression, and the very day I was assigned to their case, the Los Angeles contingent of Coxey's Army started to march to Washington, D.C. We stood on the porch watching them go by, their small packs flung over their shoulders. It seemed as silly and ineffectual a gesture as man could ever make, but in my secret heart I wished I were going along — at least to the city limits of the national capital. It would be fun to make coffee in a tin can and sing 'Sweet Adeline' around a campfire.

As we watched the last stragglers out of sight, Mr. Prince appeared to see if I could go over to his wife, who'd been feeling sick all morning. They were a shiftless couple, but gave themselves many airs. She was a pasty little person with white eyebrows, an emaciated body, and a face showing lines of pain and patience. She had a knee infection and had been hopping around on one foot cooking the meals, if they had anything to cook, until I secured a pair of crutches and a wheel chair from the Associated Charities. She liked the wheel chair and would sit in it for hours, dressed in her shabby best and cheap jewelry, reading dime novels and imagining herself in the rôle of some great lady.

'Just fawncy, my deah!' she would say, sticking her little finger in the air as she drank tea I often took her. 'Just fawncy!'

There was a little boy four years old. It is indicative of her whole mentality that she named him 'Hero Noble.' Mr. Prince had been given the staunch name of Daniel at birth, but his wife renamed him 'Percy Archibald,' using the full name every time she addressed him. Some men are stout, some corpulent. Percy Archibald Prince was just plain fat. His forehead slanted back to the vertical line which came up from the medulla oblongata. They met in an angle in the vicinity of the occiput. Mrs. Prince told me his head was that way because his mother, before he was born, had been frightened by a gorilla in a zoo.

In the memory of any who knew him, Percy Archibald had never worked much. When I asked him once what sort of job he thought he was best fitted to do, he replied indignantly, 'I don't want no job. I want a position.' But in the end he took a job we found him and things seemed to be going fairly well for them until Mrs. Prince took this turn for the worse. When I went in response to his call, I found her in great pain, with a fast pulse and high temperature. I had her brought over to our house and sent for a doctor. After a few days she was taken to the hospital. I went along while Percy Archibald took care of Hero Noble.

The hospital would scarcely be recognized as such in this day of marvelous equipment. There were six beds, kitchen, and surgery on the second floor of a store building, with no elevator, no X-ray, and only a crudely improvised sterilizer. It was found that Mrs. Prince's condition called for the amputation of her leg above the knee. The clever young surgeon who was to perform the operation was keen on anatomical research, and he asked me, as we were getting ready, if I would mind bringing the amputated leg over to his laboratory and research room for analysis. He had some calls to make before he could return. I was eager to be identified with the profession in every way and told him I would, feeling very important over the assignment.

It was my first surgical case, and I felt pretty unsteady before we were through. It was afternoon before I could leave Mrs. Prince. She was quite hysterical after the anaesthetic wore off and began to worry, as soon as she was conscious, about what disposition to make of the severed leg.

'Why, Mrs. Hughes —!' she wailed. 'That leg —! Since it got so swelled up, it was almost a third of my body.'

'I know,' I soothed her. 'I'll take care of it myself just as soon as I can get away. But you'll have to quiet down or I can't leave. Think of your husband and Hero Noble. You want to get well fast for their sakes.'

She clasped her hands over her flat breasts in a dramatic gesture. I could see her fancying herself in a martyr's rôle. 'I shall brace myself against the iron of fatality,' she declared.

A leg severed above the knee is not a thing to wrap easily into a neat bundle. I used half a dozen *San Francisco Examiners* before I felt halfway hopeful that the blood wouldn't soak through. It wasn't a great distance to the laboratory where it was to be left, and since no cars ran that way, I walked. The package got weightier and more awkward to handle every step. My keenness to co-operate in scientific research lost its zest as I plodded along, trying to keep my mind off the leg. I told myself sternly I must develop the professional hard-boiled attitude of the nurses and doctors I had observed.

But I was horribly self-conscious. I imagined everyone I met stared at me. They'd believe me an axe-murderess disposing of the body in sections, if they guessed what was in that package. Then I began to wonder about Mrs. Prince. I remembered stories of people who'd suffered tortures in amputated members because they were buried in cramped position or dumped wrong side up. An old coal miner I knew suffered chilblains every winter in both feet, though one of them had been left behind in Wales years before. And there was a neighbor who'd lost one finger. How often I'd seen her start to polish the nail on it! What might Mrs. Prince feel if her leg were carved up for research?

I dismissed it as foolishness and walked faster. I was certainly glad to reach the laboratory. As I walked up to the door, I silently vowed this was the last leg I should ever agree to deliver in person. I heaved a vast sigh of relief as I grasped the handle of the door. I turned it. It was locked. I almost battered the door down before an old fellow, mop in hand, came to open it. I stepped inside and asked for the surgeon.

'Oh, he's went, ma'am. Called to 'Frisco. Won't be back for several days. The other feller that wears a white nightshirt, he's went too.'

I explained about the leg and how the doctor had asked me to bring it to the laboratory

'I don't know nuthin' about it.' The janitor stepped back. '"Tain't none of my business. You'll have to take it some place else.'

'No! He asked me to bring it here. I've carried it around long enough. It isn't my leg, you know!'

'"Tain't mine neither. I won't have nuthin' to do with it.'

'You're janitor here, aren't you? Surely you could dispose of it for me. Put it in an ashcan some place.'

'You mean just dump it down some'ers? You can't do that, lady!'

'Can't I?' I retorted hotly. 'Show me the can!'

He looked at me in outrage. 'Look here, lady. That ain't decent. You go wrap that leg up in flannel and put it in a box all nice and straightened out and bury it right away.' He opened the door, and I knew I was dismissed.

But I just couldn't go out with that leg again. I threw it down on a chair by the door and turned to dash from the place. But the old man was too quick for me. He grabbed up the leg and fairly threw it at me as he blocked the door.

'You take that leg out of here! I won't touch it for a million dollars! I gotta do my work. You bury it proper or it'll sure bring you bad luck.'

Why I didn't leave it on the doorstep and run I don't know. But I found myself out in the street with it again. I was good and mad. 'A great nurse you've turned out to be,' I told myself. I turned off the street into an alley.

There were plenty of trashcans here. I crept up to one swiftly and was trying to pry loose a tight lid, when a glance down the alley's length discouraged me. Women stood in doorways, talked over fences, hung up washings. Men were unloading things, were delivering milk and coal. Children played everywhere. A girl carrying kitchen refuse hurried down the back walk toward the very can I was trying to open. I crouched low behind the hedge and sneaked on down the alley. A white-uniformed nurse putting a bundle about the size of a newborn baby in a garbage can —! Who wouldn't yell for the police if a severed human leg were found among the potato peelings? I came out on another street just as a streetcar clanged around the corner. I ran and signaled it. If I could get into the less populous suburbs, I might be able to ditch the thing unobserved.

I clambered up the steep steps and dropped into the first seat vacant. My nineteen-inch bundle was awkward and I eased it down beside me. The strings had slipped and the newspapers were loosening. I saw the top was showing damply red. I hated that leg. It had kept me awake nights before it was off. and now I couldn't get rid of it.

CALIFORNIA

I was startled by sudden movement behind me. Something growled close to my ear, and I turned to see a pop-eyed poodle standing in his mistress's lap, paws on the back of my seat. He thrust his nose over my shoulder and sniffed suspiciously.

'Sit down, Toto,' a voice entreated. 'Don't be a naughty doggie.'

But he declined to sit down and yapped shrilly. I shifted and tried to cover my bundle better. The woman pulled the little beast down, but in a moment he was up in my back hair again, whining frantically. Everyone turned around to see what the fuss was about, and it was evident I was the cause of the dog's outburst. He growled protestingly in the direction of my package.

A man across the aisle whispered excitedly to his companion and they both leaned forward, staring at the thing I was trying to hide. It was then that I saw protruding, through an advertisement of Lydia Pinkham's Vegetable Compound, five pallid toes! It was a terrible moment. But Lydia's placid face, with its parted-in-the-middle hair waving on either side, looked serene and confident. She gave me courage. I snatched up my bundle and, holding my head high, marched down the aisle to the door to escape.

I was in the street again. I'd heard that a cat could be cured of killing birds by tying a dead one around its neck. I wondered what sin I'd committed, that I was saddled with this leg. But when I saw where I had landed, I had a bright idea. There was a blacksmith near-by who attended our church. He was a pious soul who never missed a meeting of any sort. Privately we called him 'Glad-I-realize,' because he always gave the same testimony whenever he got up in meeting. 'Brethren and sisters, I'm glad I realize and I realize I'm glad that Jesus saves me.'

I turned my steps toward his shop. Surely he would help me. As I passed the park which bordered the street, I saw a friendly-looking policeman standing at the entrance. I stopped and told him my trouble. He wasn't a bit moved by a woman's leg, off or on, he said, but it just couldn't be dumped down any old place. That he knew.

'I had a buddy oncet,' he told me, 'and when we was ridin' the rods the train jerks him off and runs over his hand one day. Lucky we was in the yards at the time. We runs him to the hospital, him bleedin' like a stuck hog. When they lets me see him later, he begins complainin' about his wrist and fingers. Says the hand is bent backwards and the pain is gettin' worse and worse. To humor him I says I'll go find his hand and fix it comfortable. So I goes back to the yards and after a while finds the hand raked up in a pile of trash. And sure enough, just like he says, the hand's all bent back. I gets a section hand to dig a hole in the sand, and not havin' a han'kerchief by me, I takes off my vest, lays it smooth in the hole, and puts the hand on it nice and straight. When the section hand sees what I was doin', he throws his shovel and runs.'

The policeman threw back his head and laughed at the memory.

'So I shovels in the sand myself, and just as I got done, Number 36 comes boomin' in. That was the train we'd figured gettin' out. Well, I went back to the hospital, and my buddy's layin' there with his eyes half-shut, comfortable as you please. "You done it, didn't you?" he asks. "I knowed when you got them fingers straight. It was just before Number 36 come through. Thanks, old man. It's a big relief. I'll do the same for you some day."'

I tried not to show too much impatience as the policeman told his story. The leg weighed more every minute, but I was becoming convinced I'd have to do the right thing by it.

'I can't do nuthin' with that there leg now,' he went on to say. 'I can't leave the beat. But if you'll stick around 'til I'm off in an hour, I'll take and bury it proper and your woman'll never be worried with no pains in it.'

I was anxious to get back to the hospital and on home from there. I thanked the policeman and told him I'd be back if I couldn't get rid of it sooner. I was confident the blacksmith could help me. The blacksmith was shoeing a horse when I got to his place. I put down the leg on a block of wood and waited until we were alone.

'Glad-I-real — er — I mean, Mr. Perkins, I've heard you say many times how glad you were to be saved. How'd you like to save me?'

'I don't know what you're driving at.'

'I have a woman's leg in that package. You'll save my life if you'll bury it for me out behind your shop.'

'A woman's leg!' He repeated it several times, and then bent double laughing at what he thought was a good joke.

'Here — I'll show you.' With a few gingerly peels I laid bare the lower part of it.

The smith turned the color of weak tea. He looked around nervously to be sure no one was looking in from the street. 'Say, now, I don't know the joke, but you take that thing away quick. I ain't no cemetery!'

No amount of arguing would change his mind. He made it evident that I was most unwelcome. I tried as best I could to rewrap the thing again and went back to the park to find my genial policeman. He was there, and his relief with him. Each was munching an apple turnover from the bakery across the way. My policeman stuffed his mouth with the last portion and relieved me of my burden. I noticed the toes had again worked into view. Grinning, he held it up for his friend to see.

'Mother of God!' gasped the relief, and dropped his turnover to the ground.

I was free. I fled, calling back over my shoulder, 'Thanks! Thanks very much!' I must catch the car before the policeman changed his mind. He might hand me back the leg!

It was late when I got home. I was tired and hungry, but I was dying to tell Emory of my experiences. I opened the door to find the Princes, father and son, very much in possession. Percy Archibald opened up on me before I'd crossed the threshold.

'I've just been tellin' Mr. Hughes here that my wife should uv never had 'er leg taken off. If you'd-a kept 'er home and looked after 'er proper and built 'er up fer a few months, Nat're would uv cured her.'

'Look here, brother' — Emory turned on him in disgust —

'if Nature intended doing anything for that knee, she'd have shown some signs long before my wife wore herself out with it.'

Percy Archibald glared at him, and snatching up Hero Noble, sailed out of the house without the supper he'd undoubtedly come to wangle. Emory and I looked at each other and laughed.

'Reckon it must have been a hyena and a couple of rattlesnakes, as well as a gorilla, that frightened his mother,' declared Emory.

'What's to eat?' I asked.

Mrs. Prince made a good recovery, and in time the Associated Charities bought her an artificial leg. She got around very well with it, but often complained of her amputated leg being cold.

'If you'd only wrapped it in a nice woolen bat or something, I'd have been so much more comfortable,' she told me accusingly one day. I'd never told her the adventures of that leg.

'You ought to be mighty glad to have it cool for a change,' I replied. 'Don't you remember how hot and feverish it used to be? Now with summer coming on again you'll be mighty thankful on warm days that your leg isn't wrapped in wool.'

'I suppose so.' She sighed heavily. 'But I do think you might have got a lot in the cemetery. It could have had Christian burial. I'd like to know it was lying at peace, waiting for the rest of my mortal clay. As it is —!' She sniffed reproachfully.

She spent hours on my porch sewing and complaining. Hero Noble rode up and down in a cart made of her old wheel chair. But there was one compensation.

'This does make such a handy pincushion when I sew,' she smiled up at me one day, as she stuck pins into her expensive cork knee.

I find the memory of the next two years of my married life so full of heartache that I cannot bring myself to set down here more than a brief outline of the events. My husband's health began to fail during the second year. The depression still continued. With the loss of his position when his employer went into bankruptcy, Emory's condition grew worse, and he was soon unable to do anything at all. I gave up my training and took piecework in a cannery, which paid well. With our vegetable garden and canned fruits we could get through the winter. And then I found I was pregnant.

Knowledge of the added burden this would bring so aggravated Emory's condition that his mind was affected. While I struggled with unending nausea, he talked gloomily of killing himself. The doctor assured me that with him this was only a form of hysteria, and would pass. But I hid our revolver in the storeroom where I was sure he couldn't find it.

When the *Maine* was blown up by the Spaniards in Havana Harbor and we were plunged into war, Emory felt more than ever useless. He knew the Islands and was greatly excited over Dewey's brilliant victory in the Philippines. We couldn't really afford a daily paper just then, but he had so few compensations that I paid for one anyway. He read it from front to back.

'I'd like to be over there fighting those bastards,' he repeated endlessly.

At the end of the longest nine months I ever knew, my baby daughter was born. She was a tiny, fragile thing, and never very well. Emory was devoted to her and seemed more himself after her birth. He spent hours telling me what he'd do for her some day. But all my yearning care could not save her. The day she died, my husband's mental grip on things seemed to break and he was worse than I'd ever seen him. When we returned from the funeral service, he declared that he never again would set foot in our house; that he was going to take ship and sail around the world once more. He begged me to consent to the sale of our home, and to go down to Honolulu where the need of nurses to help in the terrible typhoid epidemic among soldiers was so great.

He had no reason in him, so everything we owned was

sold. He assured me that he would be more himself after a long sea voyage, and that if he were alive after a year, he would join me then in Honolulu.

But he did not join me there. For years he wandered wherever his fancy took him, restless and never content. Often I didn't know where he was for long periods of time. At last the mania to escape the responsibilities and the dissatisfactions of life which had stalked his poor mind for so long became irresistible to him, and he committed suicide.

HONOLULU

HONOLULU

IN ANSWER TO A LETTER OF INQUIRY to Presidio Army Headquarters, I learned that an army nursing unit was being organized, but could not sail for some time. So far, any nurse going abroad for service would have to do so at her own expense. Undoubtedly, the letter stated, with so little help and an epidemic raging, the doctors and officers of Honolulu would welcome my services. I could enlist later.

Within a week my arrangements were all complete. Los Angeles was a sleepy town then, more popular as a health resort for 'consumptives' than for pleasure-seeking tourists. Property was cheap. After settling all the bills for the sickness and burial of the baby, I had left only a meager two hundred dollars.

I had seen in the paper that a boat — I think it was the *SS. Columbia* — was going to the Hawaiian Islands on an excursion, sailing from Seattle. The fare was ridiculously low. So was the railroad fare. It would cost less to go to Seattle and take advantage of the cheap rate than to sail from San Francisco. Reservations were made. I arrived in Seattle twelve hours before schedule, but the ship wasn't in the harbor. I waited. And waited. At the end of two weeks, when I'd spent far too much of my precious funds for board and room, word came that the vessel was tied up in litigation at the dock in Honolulu, with a cargo of bananas rotting in the hold.

Then the steamship company advised me that the *SS. Centennial* had been chartered for the run. She was a dubious craft, condemned on account of her boilers, but the owner and master of the ship considered her safe enough. However, to protect the insurance company we were informed that those who sailed on her did so at their own risk. The company would refund the passage money of anyone not wishing to make the voyage. Two hundred had made reservations for the excursion, some coming from as far as New York. At the last only thirty-five took passage on the substitute ship.

I had long dreamed of 'going down to the sea in ships'; the very smell of a tarred rope on the dock at San Pedro had always thrilled me and set me longing to embark. Now, when that dream was about to be realized, nothing seemed to matter. I wanted to feel excited and find life good again. I wanted to look forward eagerly to the moment when I'd stand with pounding heart and catch my first glimpse of the tropical islands. Emory's stories of Honolulu had made things very vivid to me. Pineapple and sugar plantations, strange fruits and flowers, sunset from the Pali, the wonderful fish markets, grass huts and natives. I'd longed to hear the native songs, to take in my fingers a warrior's cape, made of the feathers of the Mamo and Oo birds. I'd wanted to see the sudden tropical downpour and hear rain on banana leaves. But now, as we drew slowly away from the dock and the waving handkerchiefs grew dimmer and dimmer, I felt nothing. I was still numb with the shock of what I had gone through.

The master of the ship was big Captain Whitney. His wife, who always traveled with him, was known as 'Little

HONOLULU

Captain.' They were a pair who, in his own words, 'roamed the seven seas and a few lakes just for the hell of it.' I learned that he was rated a very able captain. But since shipowners had come to frown on captains' wives sailing with them, he took command only of vessels that had no restrictions. He declared he'd rather steer a scow around the world with the Little Captain along than 'be Master of a Noah's Ark.'

Our crew was picked up on the waterfront on a half-day's notice. 'A tramp crew on a tramp steamer,' declared that happy-go-lucky sailor, George Clemens — later captain on Puget Sound waters. There were only four women passengers. The food served was good, and since I was not seasick I attempted deck sports of all sorts. The officers and crew and passengers toppled down bars of traditional ship's etiquette and we mingled together like one big family. Captain and Mrs. Whitney took a helpful interest in everyone. They had made several trips to Honolulu and once spent ten weeks there 'landlubbering.' When they found out I was going to nurse in the Army, they said they knew the very person I should contact. She was a nurse, a Mrs. Jennie Edwards, who had a row of bedroom cottages to rent.

'It isn't very far from the wharf,' Mrs. Whitney told me. 'Most likely she'll be around when we land. Everyone comes running to the dock when a boat is sighted. If she's not there, here's her address.' She scribbled a note on a card.

I was most grateful for the information. It gave me a sense of security to know of someone who'd know how to approach the matter of getting into the Army. I must have been more tired than I knew, for it seemed to me I slept half the time at first. The weather was perfect and the sea calm the first six days. Then things began to happen. The engines broke down. There were masts on the ship, but there were no sails. The wind freshened to a gale. Black clouds scudded across the face of the sun and the craft groaned and bucked like a wild horse. Every loose thing rolled and bumped dangerously. When there was any lull, the sound of the repair hammers rang up from the engine room. The gale lasted twenty-four hours. Then came dead calm with huge swells that lifted the ship up and sideways to tremble on the crest of the wave and then plunge crazily down again. I did not know until afterward the peril of a ship without power. The calm lasted three days. It was a joyous moment when the throb of engines once more ran through the old tub. We had a dance and much champagne.

After sixteen days at sea we reached the Islands on a glorious morning when their black cones lifted in sharp outline against a brilliant sky. It was just as Emory had pictured it. Harbor, palm trees and flaming flowers, rows of grass huts, brown boys diving for coins; throngs of people, native and foreign, all in white, waiting on the dock as the Hawaiian Band played. Passengers crowded the rails, thrilled and excited. But I stood there knowing only a sense of absolute unreality.

There was but a single wharf then. Though small compared to those of the present, it more than took care of the ships which docked at the port of Honolulu. The arrival of any craft, especially mail or passenger boats — the *Australian*, *Alameda*, or *Mariposa* — was a high spot in the lives of the inhabitants, I found out later. But the docking of such a vessel as the SS. *Centennial* was occasion for a fiesta.

Somewhere back there beyond the palm and mango trees soldiers might be suffering and dying, but here the band played, friends waved and called to friends, and the natives sang in welcome. As we filed down the gangplank, women in holakus hung leis of flowers around the neck of each of us. It was just as well I didn't know what a maelstrom of sickness and death was to engulf me even before the carnations of my lei began to wilt. My courage might have failed me.

Mrs. Whitney went down the gangplank before me. 'There's Jennie Edwards now!' she cried as we stepped on the dock. A slender, well-groomed woman rushed forward to embrace her.

'Where in the world did you blow in from?' she inquired. There were kindness and animation in that tanned face in spite of its tired lines. 'I thought you were in Seattle waiting for the *Columbia* to go back — if she ever does. I understood the Captain was to master her on a big excursion.'

Mrs. Whitney explained briefly, then turned to introduce me. 'Mrs. Hughes is a nurse. She thought you might use her over here.'

'A nurse! My dear, you're a gift from heaven!' Jennie Edwards took me in charge. 'I'm certainly glad to see you. We're frantic for help here.'

Other acquaintances crowded around Mrs. Whitney, so Mrs. Edwards and I took a horse-drawn taxi for her place. I had never before seen so many taxis of that sort as were at that dock. The houses along the way were low, one-story buildings, almost hidden in flowers. Bananas and strange fruits I'd never seen before were ripening on trees. The tropical air was heavy with a scent altogether unfamiliar.

Mrs. Edwards's house had a broad lanai and was set in the midst of lawn and trees and massed tropical shrubs and flowers. Across the way was a park where she said the Hawaiian Band played in the evenings. Her renting cottages, single-room size, were hidden around in the shrubbery. I took one of them and soon had my belongings unpacked. The most impressive thing in the cottage was the mosquito netting gathered on a hoop over the bed. It covered the entire bed like a tent and could be tucked in on all sides.

'All beds in the Islands have these nets,' Mrs. Edwards told me. 'Except some of the sick soldiers' cots. I hope you have a strong heart. If you haven't, you won't be able to endure the suffering you are going to see. The military setup here was not prepared for such an emergency as this typhoid epidemic. We lack equipment of all sorts and the milk supply is inadequate. We haven't a tenth of the nurses we need. Before the Islands went Republic we formed a Red Cross Chapter here. My sister, Ethel Vernon, and I are charter members. We often laugh over some of our experiences. Our first-aid station was a room which had housed a kindergarten. We borrowed screens for partitions. There were only two doctors until Major Davis came with the New York Volunteers.'

'What about the hospitals now?' I asked.

'There's only an improvised one. It's halfway out to

Waikiki Beach in a grove of algaroba trees. It was a skating rink once, but when that failed, the building was used for storing hay. We moved the hay and equipped it and a bungalow next door as best we could. It's known as the King Street Military Hospital. I have to go on relief there this afternoon, so you can walk over with me if you like.'

I marveled that anyone with rooms to rent and a house and boarders to look after, as Mrs. Edwards had, could have any time to relieve at the hospital in the afternoons. But when I saw her staff of well-trained servants I understood. Her housekeeper was a native woman, educated abroad as many of them were, following the pattern of their former queen, Liliukolani. Emory had told me that the queen was not 'an ignorant nigger in a Mother-Hubbard,' as one of the newspapers had once dubbed her. She had been educated in Europe, was a charming and gracious hostess, knew music and art, and spoke thirteen languages.

Late in the afternoon we walked down through the palace grounds to the hospital, where Mrs. Edwards turned me over to Major — not yet Major General — Leonard Wood. I told him I had come to nurse soldiers and wanted to enlist right away.

'There is no enlistment for nurses as yet,' he told me. 'You will have to go in under contract, at forty dollars a month and two rations a day.'

I signed the contract and was assigned to the bungalow.

'My orderly will go over with you right away. There's a medical student by the name of Poole over there in charge. He's a very capable fellow. Tell him what you want.'

What I saw and smelled as I walked over to that bungalow hospital haunts me to this day. On the ground under the trees close to the building lay dozens of soldiers stricken with the fever, waiting to be cared for. It was hot. Flies swarmed over them, and their faces were blotched and swollen from mosquito bites.

Inside the reeking building were rows of cots packed in as close as they could be put. The soldiers on them were so young — mere boys — that my heart ached at sight of them.

HONOLULU

Some lay with fever-flushed cheeks and parched lips, picking with unsteady fingers at their sheets. Others, emaciated, their stricken white faces dripping great drops of sweat, lay with half-closed eyes sunken in their sockets, stupor giving them temporary relief from intestinal cramps. The stench was nauseating.

A young man in an untidy white duck suit looked up from the patient he was attending as I stepped over to him.

'Are you Doctor Poole?' I asked.

'Not "Doctor" yet!' He pushed back a lock of uncombed hair. He was well built and handsome in spite of his unshaven face and dirty clothing. He was too tired to smile. 'They just call me Poole around here.'

'I'm Mrs. Hughes, a nurse from the States. I just got in this morning.'

'A nurse!' He stared at me, his eyes lighting. 'Did you say a nurse, or am I hearing things wrong?'

'I've just been assigned to this bungalow. When shall I go on duty?'

'How soon can you be ready?'

'Give me an apron. I'm ready now.'

'Now —? Good God! Come with me!'

We went to a partitioned part of the building where soldiers' uniforms and surgical aprons hung.

'Here, take off your dress and climb into this. When you're ready, I'll tell you what to do.'

On a long table in the center of the room were piled supplies in shocking disorder. 'Mill around among this stuff and see if you can get enough together to make bedside notations,' Poole told me. 'We need charts on the wall above each cot. Here are the thermometers — these mouth, these axilla. Here's solution in these glasses for disinfectant. Don't battle with the delirious ones just now. Here's cotton and a pencil.'

And so my work began. I kept three one-minute thermometers going at a time, counted the pulse and asked and answered questions. To those who were conscious and fearful of not recovering, I'm afraid I gave more assurance than I really felt. There were forty beds in the bungalow and only one lavatory. A Kanaka orderly and Poole had been the only ones on duty for some time. At night a native man and his wife, both well-trained, took charge. In the morning Poole and the orderly came back and all four worked together to get the patients cared for before the night nurses went off duty. But what meager treatment and comfort could four nurses give to those forty suffering and dying men!

Without food or rest I worked that day, forgetting it in the need to get the patients bathed and their linen and beds changed. They were so desperately needing it. I drew the sheets over the faces of two who died. They were immediately removed and two on the ground under the trees were brought in. Night dropped without twilight. We lit kerosene lamps and immediately the humid night grew hotter. I grew so faint I felt I just couldn't go on, fatigued and hungry as I was. And then suddenly there rushed in clean fresh air, fragrant with the odor of flowers and wet soil. And a welcome sound through the open windows. The patter of rain on banana leaves — just as Emory had described it to me. The cool air braced me immeasurably and I knew I could stick it out until the relief nurses came on duty.

Poole walked home with me. I was grateful for that, as I'm certain I might have been lost in the confusion of trees and shrubbery in a strange place. On the way we passed a native house where an acquaintance of Poole's lived. They had been having a luau — native feast — and Poole insisted we should go in to give me some idea of native food. Mostly raw fish and poi. Poi, Emory had told me, was a gray mushlike mixture made from taro meal and allowed to ferment. It was supposed to be eaten with the fingers. I saw fruit and cakes piled high as well.

'Come on,' Poole urged me, when I hesitated, wanting nothing so much as bed, tired and bedraggled as I was. 'We won't stay long. It will interest you.'

'But I can't eat poi off fingers that smell as mine do,' I told him, aside. 'I scrubbed and disinfected until I nearly took the hide off, but they still smell horribly unclean.'

He snapped off a twig and took out his knife, grinning at me. 'I'll whittle you a paddle. Come on.'

The host was a big fat Kanaka. His wife was a little fat Portuguese. They spoke good English and were most hospitable in their reception of me. Their house was like the average dwelling of the whites. All the better class of natives aspired to abandon their grass houses and own one of these homes with the best furnishings possible, Poole told me. Most of the women wore the native holakus, but the men were in the thin white shirts and white cotton trousers of their foreign brothers. Everyone on the Island seemed to wear white. When I commented on the laundry bills that must entail, Poole laughed.

'The Chinese tailors will make you a dress — furnishing the material — for fifty cents. And they'll launder a whole bag of soiled ones for fifteen cents, so it's not much of a problem to keep immaculately white — unless you work as we've been doing in the hospital lately, with no time to change.'

The feast was spread on a table in the yard, under cover of a roof of poles and grass, reeds, and huge leaves of the banana and other tropical trees. I had no appetite for the raw fish, but I did like the poi, which tasted like the mulled buttermilk Mother used to make in Kansas. Our stay was very brief. We were sleepy.

Music came faintly to our ears as we walked along a heavily wooded stretch of road: haunting sort of music, with throbbing rhythm that beat on the senses with insistent demand. I stopped short, fascinated by the tone quality of those native instruments and voices.

'Hula hut back in there,' said Poole.

'Hula? So that's the way it sounds! I'm certainly going to see a performance before I leave the Islands. The primitive dance — not the censored one. My husband spent some time here and he told me about them.'

'So you're going, eh?'

'Yes, I am. And it must be pure quill. Will you take me?'

Poole puffed on his cigar in silence a moment. Then he laughed — an odd sort of laugh. 'Evidently your husband didn't see the real thing, or he was too much of a gentleman to tell you what he saw. You'd never ask a man to take you if you knew. But I'll take you if you insist. I'll make an opening in the side of the grass hut so you can watch without anyone seeing you. Then I'll leave you there while I go somewhere else. I only ask that you never tell who escorted you.'

'Is it really so vile as thát?'

'Vile —! The first one I saw, I threw up my dinner.'

'The first? So you went back other times?'

For a moment he glared at me. Then he laughed. 'Matter of scientific research. Doctors have to understand lots of unpleasant things.'

I might state here that I never saw the 'pure quill' variety.

It was late when I got to my room. There was a plate of fruit on the stand by my bed, short fat red bananas, mangos and papayas. The bananas were juicy as peaches and better than any I had ever dreamed of. But the other fruit — to me it tasted like turpentine or something suggestive of hospital smells.

The days ran late into the nights, and the nights ended too soon in other days. Endless suffering and inadequate effort. There was no romance, no glory. Only heart-breaking defeat, dysentery, delirium, and death. I can hear valiant Melvin Wells gasping out, 'Don't waste time on me, I'm going to die anyway. But don't forget — write mother — I wasn't afraid.' And the Fischer boy from New York — he did pull through, in spite of those hideous days and nights of delirium when he begged to have the hot iron pulled out of his side and something cold put on his head.

I believe the hardest thing for me was the inability to say some word that would help the ones entirely conscious, who knew they must be going to die. They didn't want to die. They weren't afraid to fight it out on an open field or on a ship, but it was inglorious to lie here week after week. One protested bitterly, 'We're rotting here like rats in an alley!'

There was an English noblewoman living in Honolulu at the time, who used to come often to visit the ward. She was a devout Anglican and always brought inspirational and church literature for the men. Looking through the things she had left one day, I came across a picture which caught my interest and held it long as I looked at it. It was that of a young man as magnificent-looking as I've ever seen. He was in clerical robes and his name was Stanley Wilkins. His was a face, virile and finely molded, that seemed fairly to glow with the passion of serving his fellow men. In his eyes was the look of one who might just have witnessed the Resurrection of his Lord. The lines beneath, telling of his recent ordination, stated that he had been an all-round athlete at Oxford and an outstanding boxer and cricketer. He fascinated me. Here was a man who combined so many rare qualities. I put it in a drawer I had commandeered for my own use.

One day I was doing my best to help a lad who was afraid he was going to die. He jeered at belief in a hereafter.

'That Sunday-School stuff is all right for women and kids, but not for fellows like me. I'm no sissy!'

I went and got the picture of Stanley Wilkins. 'You wouldn't say this chap was a sissy, would you?' I smiled down at him. 'All kinds of athletic honors — yet he believes so much in God that he's devoting his whole life to help others to believe in Him. He doesn't think religion's just for women and kids.'

The boy stared, as fascinated as I had been. 'Gee, he looks like our swimming-coach at home. And he sure was great.' The likeness seemed to mean something. That face would inspire anyone. A new look came into the boy's bloodshot eyes. 'Could I keep this awhile? Maybe Johnny — when he wakes up —— He's been bitter about things. This might help him.' The boy went to sleep with it in his hand.

Strange thing about that picture. Even on a piece of paper the faith of that man reached out with power. It did help this boy. And it helped Johnny to die with hope. And it helped many another sick and desolate soldier. They came to ask for it as though it were a sacred talisman. They didn't want to go soft. But this man wasn't soft. And he believed in God.

The nightmare weeks fell wearily into each other, and we worked with a feeling that there was no escape ever again for our minds or bodies. But at last there came the day when a transport landed thirty-two trained nurses! A cluster of buildings had been organized into a new hospital unit known as the Buena Vista, and all the patients who could be moved were taken there in ambulances. Two soldiers near death were left in the bungalow and I was detailed to stay with them through the night — or as long as they lived. The main building of the old King Street Hospital had been cleaned and made ready for the nurses.

For several days I had been so tired that every level spot, floor or sidewalk, tempted me desperately to lie down and rest. The day before the nurses arrived, I began having chills and ached terribly. I was afraid to take my temperature for fear I had fever. But now, alone in the place with a dying patient on either side of me, I knew I had it. My knees at times almost buckled under me and things often began to whirl dizzily.

A few soldiers went by on the walk, singing, 'Just break the news to mother . . .' They were right under our windows as they sang the lines. 'Oh, tell her not to wait for me, for I'm not coming home.' I remember how glad I was that the poor boys dying there couldn't hear them. They wouldn't wince as I'd seen others do at that song. I was beginning to shake with chills and things were getting hazy when I looked at them. One of the doctors came in to see how things were going. I had to ask him to excuse me and staggered into the lavatory in an agony of cramping. I faintly remember toppling over on the floor, but from then I know what happened only from hearsay, as I did not regain my senses for three weeks.

My first conscious thought after those weeks was pleasure in the fact I was lying down. It was so utterly comfortable. Then I saw a strange nurse bending over me, and at the same time saw a lizard climbing up the mosquito netting above me. The nurse saw the lizard at the same moment and, being new to the Islands and not accustomed to the friendly, creeping things, she let out a terrific screech. I laughed so heartily that another nurse dashed in, thinking I was delirious again. I was bewildered to find how long I'd been ill. It was strange to be so weak. But it wasn't many days before I could be bolstered up on pillows, and after a while I was strong enough to hold a magazine.

I found I was in a small cottage, one of the hospital units, with shrubs and flowers banked around it. The Fischer boy whom I had nursed, able now to walk around after weeks in bed, fairly camped on our lanai, always ready when the nurse needed time off or when she had to help in the other building. He read me the newspapers and guarded my bed net zealously to keep away lizards, scorpions, and centipedes. It was a great day when he brought around a wheel chair and the nurse put me in it. I just about lived in that chair. It was adjustable so I could flatten it out for sleeping. Tom Fischer wheeled me around the grounds and brought my tray at mealtimes. Jeff, the cook, sometimes smuggled me out a cup of Roman coffee — though I wasn't supposed to have any kind. Mrs. Edwards came now and then and often sent rare home-cooked things by her maid, Toma.

Convalescing soldiers, many of whom I had nursed in the King Street Hospital, would gang around my chair in the shade. To them I was just another soldier who'd fought a hard fight. Tropical typhoid fever was tough as any other enemy force. Together we dreamed and planned only one thing — getting home to the U.S.A.

The typhoid was lessening now and facilities were adequate. No longer must sick men lie dying on the ground for want of beds. Surely after a while I would be able to go home. And then came a day I shall never forget.

My clinical chart had always hung on the wall well out of my range of vision. Patients are not supposed to know their case history. One morning, by mistake, it was left on the table by my bed. I had been consumed by curiosity to see it. After all, I was a nurse myself, and I wanted to know what I'd been through. There were pages of notations: 'Temp. $103°$ — $104°$. Pulse 130. Very weak — thready — irregular.

Delirious — coma — delirious.' Hemorrhages in appalling numbers. We had no plasma then, no blood transfusions, no intravenous treatment. These notations were the usual thing in typhoid cases that were fatal. I should have been dead, but somehow I had survived.

But there were other notations which threw me into panic. 'Hypo. Mor. Sulp. ¼ grn. — Hypo. Mor. Sulp. ½ grn.' Over and over again. Even the very night before, 'Codeine (by mouth) ¼ grn.' I put the sheaf of papers back on the table. I lay very still, full of such fear as I had never known. How long did it take for drugs to get a grip on one? The few morphine addicts I had encountered in district nursing in Los Angeles had been enough to give me an abject horror of the habit.

That evening Doctor O'Malley came into the cottage with a big bottle of liquid medicine. 'Hello there!' He greeted me heartily. 'I see you'll be out surf-riding before long now.'

'I'm floundering around in deep water right now.'

He looked at me sharply. 'What's the matter?' I couldn't speak for a moment, groping for the right thing to say. 'Whatever it is,' he assured me, 'this new medicine will fix you up all right. I'm discontinuing the white tablets you've had at night to make you sleep. The nurse will replace the dose each time with sterile water. It wouldn't be wise to stop the tablets too abruptly. Let your nerves adjust gradually.'

'I'm not going to take one drop of medicine from that bottle!' Hot rage welled up in me. 'Now or any other time. You've been giving me morphine!'

'Well, what of it?' His voice was impatient. 'You had to have it at first to control those hemorrhages. Then the delirium and restlessness. You're down to a small dose of codeine now. Nothing to get excited about. Be a good kid and do what I say. You're making remarkable progress and in a short time you'll forget all about drugs.'

'But I'm telling you, Doctor O'Malley, I will not take the stuff again, liquid or solid. I'll do anything else you say, but ——'

HONOLULU

'All right! All right! You just think you won't. But you'll be glad the bottle is here when you change your mind.'

An alcohol rub, a cup of hot milk, and a little white pill was about all the attention I had been needing of late at bedtime. But that night there was no little white pill. 'I won't let it matter,' I told myself. 'I'll go to sleep and forget it.' But no sleep came. Only a steadily increasing restlessness.

'About time for a little spoonful of that medicine, Hughesy, don't you think?' The night nurse came and smiled down at me.

I tried to be calm. 'I'm not going to take it.' But I couldn't calm myself. I shook as with chills. I grew hysterical and cried helplessly. The nurse pleaded with me to take the medicine. Then Doctor O'Malley came in again and scolded me heartily.

'Give her a hypo right away whether she wants it or not,' he told the nurse as he left. She brought the hypo.

Then I did go to pieces. 'Take it away! Take it away!' I screamed until they heard me clear out in the main hospital. They must have thought some soldier had been drinking 'swipes,' a liquor made from the palm. It made you good and drunk to begin with, then for three weeks after, every time you'd take a drink of water you'd be crazy drunk again.

The nurse sat patiently by me for a while, needle ready. Then she started to slip away. 'Don't go!' I cried, the thought of losing that relief was unendurable. 'I'll take it!' But when she came back, I knew I must hold out — a little longer. I prayed for strength to resist it. All night I fought, alternately spurning the drug and begging for it, until the nurse was almost beside herself. But the long night ended. Exhausted, I watched the first rays of the morning sun fall across the flamboyants by my window. I had not licked the enemy yet, but I had defended my position. The fear of the night faded and I saw, for a moment, a brilliant star above a stone quarry; silent and strong, it upheld me. I had lost forty-five pounds during my illness; I could sit up only a little while at a time, and I was too weak to stand on my feet at all, but my will power still held. I never took morphine again. But the thing was not banished. Many times I struggled half the night with that all-consuming restlessness. But the indescribable need gradually lessened and at last I knew I was safe.

On a red-letter day Mrs. Edwards came to the hospital, her face all animation, bringing one of my dresses with her. She had exciting news. I was to be dressed and go in the wheel chair down the street to see the parade. It would be a big one, for this was a momentous occasion. The Army had brought a horseless carriage to Honolulu and it was to be exhibited.

My dress hung about me so loosely I felt I must look like a scarecrow. But it was fun to wear one again anyway. Tom Fischer and some other boys pushed my chair and those of other convalescents, and Mrs. Edwards went with us. We arrived early and enjoyed watching the crowds while we waited. It was a most thrilling moment when the Hawaiian Band came stepping down the street. They were followed by all the soldiers able to march, who acted as escort for the resplendent officers who followed. An Army band was next in line, and then came the wonderful horseless carriage. It was ingloriously drawn by six big Army mules! At the moment of entering the triumphal march it had refused to start under its own power. Perhaps the voyage to Hawaii had jolted loose some of its internal workings. The local blacksmiths were baffled and didn't know how to repair it. But even at that it was one of the most exciting events the city had ever witnessed, not excepting the celebration when the Islands became a republic, or the festivities which followed the advancement of Major Wood to Major General. For me, even at worst, it was satisfaction. I'd always believed in horseless carriages.

Another event helped make that a memorable day. When I returned to the hospital, there was a letter from home to which everyone had contributed. There was even a letter from old Wash, the sheepdog, signed with an outline of his paw which Florence had done. There was an urgent command from her. 'Hurry home and help me weed onions!'

Mother wrote that Bill was getting married and they were turning the ranch over to him. They'd sold the sheep at big profit and had bought an orchard tract in western Montana. There were a good house and barn on the place and it was close to a school. In a town not far distant was a large hospital with nurses' training school. I read and re-read that letter. Things were beginning to shape anew for me. I knew a deep gratitude.

Three months after I had fallen unconscious on the floor of the old King Street Hospital, a company of convalescents and nurses — I still in my wheel chair and unable to walk alone — sailed on the *SS. Australia* for San Francisco. My leave-taking would have been entirely joyous had I known at the time that Jennie Edwards was eventually to return to the States and remain my good friend down through the years. The epidemic of typhoid had been broken and most of the nurses had sailed for Manila.

The voyage to San Francisco was a thrilling and wonderful one to me. Because of the aftermath of fever, it had been a long time since I had had any solid foods. I was heartily sick of slops. My poor nurse on the trip was so seasick right from the start she couldn't get out of bed. She said she hoped she'd die and didn't care in the least if I did, so I was happily left to my own devices. When the steward came in with the elaborate menu card, I didn't waste any time looking at the pictures on the cover, but just checked Number 1 Dinner from soup to fingerbowls — champagne, Roman punch, and all the rest of it. There were no serious results such as might have been expected, for by the time I had merely tasted everything on the tray and had two cups of coffee, I felt full to bursting and had to leave most of the food regretfully uneaten.

Not a meal did I miss after that. My nurse missed nearly all of hers. I was out on deck in a steamer chair most of the time, while she was too ill to be up. During the eight days of our voyage, I gained ten pounds and she lost fifteen. I declared I was all for sailing around the world as soon as I got well, while she, poor wretch, swore she'd never, as long as she lived, set foot even on a ferry. It was most ironic that I should be sent home from long-dreamed-of Hawaii without even starting to see it. To have been in Honolulu, yet have seen nothing of the Islands —! But I had been ill a long time and it would be wonderful to see my family again. Montana was unknown territory to me, but where they lived was home.

After we landed in San Francisco, we were taken to a nursing home for convalescents in Presidio. The building had once been the sexton's house in a cemetery. It was a shabby place with poor plumbing and lighted by kerosene lamps. Gravestones, like loose old brown teeth in the face of the hill, reached out to nibble at the very doorsteps. When I was able to be up and around, I learned to walk again by holding to the tombstones, staggering from one to the other, feet braced apart like a young colt's as I struggled for coordination of muscle and balance.

When I was able to walk without holding on to anything, I was given my discharge. We had a celebration that afternoon. Soldiers, officers, nurses, the milkman and the garbageman, the Chinese cook, the boy who did up our rooms and the Japanese boy who mowed the lawn, all ganged around tables piled with food and drinks. We hadn't chairs enough to go around, so sat on cots and boxes and nailkegs as well. All of us from Honolulu had suffered in some way or another. Some of us had been together for months. And most of us were going home soon. It was a most hilarious party, yet there was an element of sadness in parting after all we'd shared so intimately. We knew we'd probably never see each other again.

'I suppose you'll be taking the crack train out of 'Frisco tonight with the rest of the discharged nurses and boys.' One of the soldiers looked at me enviously. He was chafing to get back to New York, but was still on crutches and under treatment.

'Indeed I'll not. I'm taking slow old Stop-at-every-station-and-like-it, Number 3, in the morning.'

'But why? You've got a lot coming to you, you know.

Elegant chair car, observation car, and in your case a stateroom and no end of attention.'

'I know, comrade. But I've worn out a couple of timetables figuring how to see Mount Shasta, Mount Hood, and Mount Rainier by daylight. I've dreamed of them for years, and I'm not going to be cheated by whizzing by them in the dark, as I did before. I was in Seattle for days waiting for the Honolulu boat coming over, but I didn't catch even a glimpse of Rainier on account of rain.'

'So the Islands haven't won you away from the States?'

'No. Nor have the States won me away from the Islands. Maybe you can't believe it, but when I was sitting in a wheel chair there at Buena Vista Hospital, in such a wealth of flowers and lush ferns and shrubs and palms, I longed for the desert at times. And now when I get up into the Montana mountain country, I'll probably begin pining for the sight of open water and the feel of a ship coasting into the trough of big surges. The more I travel, the more I crave it.'

The next morning a few of the boys and nurses went down to the station with me in the Army hack and I took the slow train. If ever selfish personal prayer were answered, mine was on that trip, since for the whole way the sun shone by day and the stars by night. There were no clouds nor fog.

It was evening when we came in sight of Mount Shasta, glorious and lofty in the sunset. 'Isn't it magnificent?' I exulted to the grouchy spinster across the aisle from me.

'I can't say I see anything to it,' she sniffed. 'What's there to get excited about in a pile of rocks with some snow on them?'

The porter heard her comment. He lifted his eyes as though to defend both the mountain and me. Then he turned to her reproachfully. 'Lady, Ah's been goin' up an' down this road eight years. An' ain't no time Ah ever sees that mountain that somethin' inside me don't git down on its knees an' say, "O Lawd, how wonderful is Thy wu'ks!"'

Forests and lakes and the mighty Columbia. Beautiful Mount Hood and then Rainier, more breath-taking and wonderful than anything I had ever seen. Puget Sound and the rugged Olympics and Cascades. Daily I thanked God for such an America. Some day I'd come back to this country to live, I told myself. I loved the mountains and streams of Idaho and western Montana and the zest of the air as it got higher and dryer. It was the morning of the third day when we approached the town that was to be home to me. We'll call it Riverton, though that's not the name on the map. A great valley stretched wide and flat between foothills on one side and snowcapped peaks on the other. Two swift rivers flowed through it and creeks emptied into them from every canyon. The town looked clean and prosperous and I liked it immediately.

When the train came to a stop in the station, Leslie's strong arms lifted me down the steps. There was the family, a little older, beaming and happy, to welcome me home.

MONTANA

MONTANA

As we drove through town in the family carryall, I was amazed at the crowded streets. 'How many people live here, anyway?' I asked. 'This looks like a city.'

'There's a circus in town — Barnum and Bailey,' my young sister informed me. Her eyes were wistful.

A circus! The family never missed one. It was the only event which unbent my austere father to light-heartedness. But I had no money. How was the family fixed, I wondered.

Papa caught my eye and shook his head at the question he must have seen in my face. 'The last installment on the sheep isn't due for a month yet and buying this new orchard tract has taken everything we have. Leslie's saving every cent he makes to take him to the University. Don't look scared. We're getting along fine. With the crop of apples we're getting this year, my credit's good anywhere. We have plenty of food and clothes and everything, but no money on hand. We'll have to make it up another time.'

So we laughed the circus off. To be together was enough celebration for one day.

I was delighted with the new place, which lay in rich bottom land, some five miles out of town. There were twenty acres of beautifully cultivated fruit trees; the house was comfortable and the outbuildings good. Already Mama had masses of flowers blooming around the porch and fences. It was wonderful to walk through rooms which held beloved, familiar things of my childhood. Alone for a moment in the downstairs bedroom they'd given me, I walked over to touch the little old chest of drawers that had held clothes for so many babies. My own baby, Emory, and the last few hectic years all seemed somehow unreal as I felt the warmth of my family enfold me once more.

Just before we were to sit down to a good chicken dinner, Papa came in with excitement twinkling in his eyes. He had been gone for several hours.

'Get on your best bibs and tuckers,' he ordered. 'We're going to the circus tonight!'

'The circus?' we cried with one accord. 'How can we? We're broke!'

Papa washed his hands at the sink and came over to Mama, towel in hand. She was dishing up mashed potatoes. 'Molly, Bess got out of the pasture and into wet clover. I found her all swelled up twice her size, dead as a nit.'

I thought Mama was going to drop the potatoes. 'Oh, Jasper! What'll we do for our milk and butter now?'

'Well, our neighbor Dolman happened to be down there when I found the cow. He'll sell me a fresh one. I'll put a new roof on his barn in pay.' He pulled some money out of his pocket. 'Dolman helped me skin the cow and he bought the hide. So we'll take the foreign nurse to the circus.' He grinned at me.

'But Jasper, I don't think Lora's strong enough to go,' protested Mama. 'She's tired after ——'

'Of course I'll go to the circus!' I cried. 'Even if it's on a slab!'

It was a grand splurge. Undoubtedly it would have been

more sensible to have spent the money on something practical, but down the years we might easily forget tons of meat and potatoes, while the thrill of that night still wakes pleasure in us.

After all these years of hospital, Associated Charities, private and Army nursing, I seemed as far as ever from signing R.N. after my name. But I was determined to have a diploma. The Army nursing had taken terrible toll of my health and I wasn't able to work hard enough to get money for training school. But a dose of castor oil led up to a way of achievement.

Papa had a half-acre of Bermuda onions coming up through as handsome a patch of weeds as ever man tried to subdue. They had to go, so in heavy overalls and blazer, up with the sun, kneeling or sitting on a gunnysack of straw, I began on the onion patch. I rested often, lying full length on the warm ground in the sunshine, loving the deep flawless blue of the sky and the green of foothills lifting to the mountains. I grew hungry as a bear and gained strength and flesh amazingly.

One day a neighbor woman came running across the field to me. She said that her little son was sick. The doctor had ordered a stiff dose of castor oil and assured her the boy would be all right. But he refused to swallow the stuff. Battle with him as she would, coaxing and using force, he was too much for her. Since I was a nurse did I think I could get him to take it? I said I'd try.

I found the boy whimpering, his nightclothes and the bed showing messy evidence of the conflict. The mother poured out the ordered dose in a spoon. I leaned over his chest, grasping his nose tightly so that he had to open his mouth to breathe. Before he knew what was happening to him, he had swallowed the oil and found a piece of peppermint candy in his mouth. I joked with him until he laughed and we got along so well that when he did not respond to the castor-oil treatment, but developed an intestinal infection, the doctor called me on the case. With the mother's help I was able to see him through to a good recovery.

In the nineties, before State registration for nurses was instituted, a nurse went on twenty-four-hour duty in private families, often washing and baking for a sick housewife, besides caring for the children. I had a long siege of this sort of thing after I was able to do regular work again. To be able to snatch short vacations between cases meant salvation to one. To get clear away — to mountain trails, campfires by rushing streams, pine-bough beds under the stars.

But time made me skeptical of vacations. Too often I escaped only to land right in the middle of another case. At Calaveras National Park once, a little boy was stricken with appendicitis near the hotel where I was registered. He was camping in a tent with his grandfather, while his mother worked in the hotel kitchen. The attack came on very suddenly in the night. I saw at once he must have immediate medical and probably surgical attention. The mother insisted the boy be carried to Stockton, where their family doctor lived. It was as near a place as anywhere the little fellow could get hospitalization. One of the forest rangers begged a team and wagon from a rancher, filled the wagon box with hay, and I put all the covers they had on top of that to make a bed for the boy. Another ranger joined our outfit to help if needed. It took two days to get to the hospital. The efforts to keep cold packs on the child, the bumping of the wagon over rocky roads, the mosquitoes and deer flies, and the useless, hysterical mother were hard to endure. But worse was old Grandpa, who showed his gratitude by getting amorous and trying to paw me.

But we got the boy to Stockton in time and the doctor took him over. The mother declared her gratitude knew no bounds. To show it, she didn't repay the six dollars I'd given the rancher for his team and wagon. She said she was stonybroke, but she would pray for me all the rest of her life.

And well do I remember that rare fall day in Montana when I got down from the stage by the side of a Bitter Root Valley road, where two youngsters were waiting for me with saddle horses. They were Hugh and Grant, sons of my friend Sarah, who had a ranch back in the foothills. I had come for a month's freedom from hospitals, doctors, and telephones.

Sturdy Grant tied my duffel sack on a pack-horse and put me on a trim bay mare. He mounted his roan and little chattering Hugh rode beside me on his pinto.

As we came in sight of the ranch house, the younger boy raced on ahead to tell his mother I had arrived. And then suddenly I saw his horse stumble — a gopher hole probably — and Hugh was thrown. When I came up to them, the child lay in a little heap, with the pinto lipping him gently in sympathy. His leg was broken and the shin bone stuck out through the skin. While Grant galloped to the nearest telephone four miles away to summon the doctor, I arrived at the house with the screaming Hugh in my arms. And my vacation had begun! Valiant Sarah! She didn't swoon or wring her hands.

While I prepared a hypodermic to lessen the pain, Sarah stood beside the frightened, bloody Hugh and shook him gently. 'Did your father howl this way when he broke his leg?' she demanded sternly. Her son bravely bit his lip. The fight was on for all of us. For sheer nursing fortitude, the test is a ten-year-old boy with a compound fracture. But the weeks passed and in time he was as good as new.

Many of these emergencies seemed to have a comet-like tail of compensations, flinging little meteorites of happiness, gratitude, and friendship down through the years. Only last Christmas, Hugh, grown a little gray in his long years in the Forestry Service, straight of limb and strong and clean, came to visit me. In his khaki-clad arms he carried a florist's box of extravagant length.

'Don't tell me you've ordered my coffin!' I exclaimed in mock consternation.

'Your "niffoc"? Well, hardly!' We laughed, remembering our game of reversing the letters of words. It had baffled all the children that summer he'd been recovering from his broken leg, and had afforded him much fun. It touched me that he hadn't forgotten.

On that same vacation trip I incurred the everlasting gratitude of that excellent person, Aunt Connie Thurston, whom I visited now and again. She ran a cattle ranch up the creek above Sarah's, and added to her meager income by keeping summer boarders. Teachers and office girls they were, mainly, and some society-fagged females. Her husband, cadaverous Uncle Micah, worked harder at doing nothing than anyone I ever knew. When the boarders were out, he prowled about their rooms, pretending to dust their furniture and singing lustily, 'W-i-t-h the blowing of the horns and the beating of the drums!' and always in mind the hope of unearthing a stray piece of candy or sweetmeat. No sweets were ever safe from Uncle Micah. Fresh doughnuts or cookies vanished before they cooled unless Aunt Connie stood guard or hid them. Once when I went up to the place, I had taken along some fruit laxative I'd made of dates, figs, and senna leaves, which I'd molded, rolled in powdered sugar, and packed neatly in a candy box. Along in the early evening the second night there, I left the porch where I'd been talking to Sarah and went up to my room to get this concoction to show her. I found the box completely empty. I laughed grimly to myself, knowing Uncle Micah's failing. I strolled out in the back yard to reconnoiter. Results of such a dose should be immediate. And they were. From the direction of the three-holer far in the rear I heard agonized groans.

'Connie! Connie! For God's sake —!'

I called her and we both rushed out. Uncle Micah was lying outside behind the raspberry bushes. He was the color of turnip greens and sweat poured off him as he writhed in senna cramps. In spite of the first aid I administered, he passed out several times before the doctor arrived in answer to Aunt Connie's call. The doctor said the patient would soon be all right and that I had done everything necessary, except, perhaps — this aside to me with a suspicion of a wink — giving him a physic. I suspect he knew that would have been the end of Uncle Micah, and I suspect he wouldn't have cared if it had been. Everyone knew the doctor had been in love with Aunt Connie since her pigtail days, when their families came to Montana overland in covered wagons.

One morning after Uncle Micah was quite himself again, Aunt Connie and I sat on the back porch, watching his half-hearted efforts at the woodpile. She turned to me, laughing. 'Well, thank goodness, so far Micah's not done any more snooping. Maybe he's cured!'

'Aunt Connie, how did you happen to choose Micah instead of the doctor?' I asked.

The laborer surrendered to his inertia, wiped his brow, picked up his customary single stick of wood, and started for the house. But he sang as he walked up the path, roaring at the top of his lungs with zest astounding in one so limp. 'W-i-i-t-h the blowing of the horns and the beating of the drums —!' With him, the energy which might have gone into work was conserved for song. There was fond pride in Aunt Connie's eyes as she looked at me.

'The doctor couldn't sing,' she chuckled.

I remember another vacation time I planned for myself, but before I could get away Doctor Benson appeared one morning in a terrible hurry. I'd worked a lot with him.

'I'm glad I caught you. I have a call from Number 2 Camp, up the Blackfoot. Some logger. Pneumonia, I imagine, from what they told me over the telephone. Can you hop along?'

'Ay, ay, sir!' I replied.

We were soon on our way. Roads were not what they are now, and the automobile was just coming into practical use. It was far from the easy-riding conveyance of today. Several times as we hurried along I bounced up and hit the top of my head on the top of the car, but the doctor didn't slow down.

We found one of the lumberjacks, Matt Brent, mortally stricken with pneumonia. His co-worker, O'Toole, had stayed by him all night, holding him up so that he could breathe more easily. The doctor did everything he could, but he knew it was vain. He left instructions and me with them. All night the faithful O'Toole hung over Matt, while other loggers peered in the bunkhouse door to see how things were getting along. About three in the morning Matt died.

When my duties for the deceased had been finished, the cook made coffee and sandwiches and the men and I sat around a greasy table in the mess hall, making arrangements for the funeral. It was sympathetic O'Toole who managed everything. Brent was not a Catholic, so O'Toole said he must have a preacher, and flowers and music and a write-up in the papers. The lumberjacks made up a purse and those who had any money left over from their last spree in town emptied their pockets. Those who hadn't asked for an advance. In the morning when the 'dead wagon' came up for Brent's body, I rode out with it and carried along enough funds 'to bury a banker in iligant style,' as O'Toole instructed me.

The day came for the funeral. They expected me to be there, so I went. It had been well advertised. Loggers who had never seen nor heard of Matt Brent before got a day off on pay to attend. A couple of drinks all around loosened their emotions. They wiped their eyes on the back of their wrists, tapped each other on the shoulder, and nodded their heads at some recounting of the virtues of the dead man.

The chapel filled, but no O'Toole appeared. It would never do for the service to proceed without the chief mourner. We waited. And waited. At last, just as the impatient minister decided to get on with the ceremony, in came O'Toole, dressed in ill-fitting new clothes from top to toe, and thoroughly soused. For a moment he surveyed the scene uncertainly, then walked down the aisle, lurching from side to side like a sailor in a storm. He paused only when he stood before the altar and swept the floor with his hat in a bow to the minister. He would have fallen if the Reverend had not supported him. I rushed over, piloted O'Toole to a seat, and sat down beside him.

He slumped down and sat in a stupor through most of the services. It was when the minister began eulogizing the virtues of this diamond in the rough, Matt Brent, using the very words O'Toole had told me to write for the speaker's guidance, that the drunken man came to life. He listened for a moment and shifted uneasily. Then he pulled himself up on his feet and pointed an unsteady finger at the minister.

'Yer Honor,' he bawled out thickly, 'excuse me fer contempt o' court, but it's a damn lie! That ol' son of a bitch in the box there, he owed every damn man in camp. He was the ——.' I jerked him down in the chair. Before he could get up again to remonstrate further, the minister motioned to the soloist to take over. If the lines of 'Asleep in Jesus' were sung with less muted effect than usual, there was a reason. But the song soothed O'Toole. The pallbearers carried the expensive, flower-blanketed casket out to the hearse, and the people filed out. I shook O'Toole, but he was dead to the world. The last I saw of him he was leaning forward, arms folded on the back of the seat in front of him to pillow his head, sound asleep in the empty chapel.

'Speaking of vacations,' said Doctor Benson one hot day when he and Mrs. Benson and I were cooling our feet in a canyon creek after a picnic lunch, 'there's a spot on the shore of Salmon Lake I want you to see. It's perfect for our two tents. And there's a telephone at the ranger's station, so I can keep in touch with the hospital. It's ——'

'Is it wild?' I interrupted.

'Good and wild.'

'Uninhabited?'

'Yes, except for a few trappers and the forest ranger. As soon as Mrs. Flinn's baby comes, we're off. What do you gals say?'

Our response was unanimous and enthusiastic. The Bensons and I often tramped around together. Sometimes we went light, carrying packs and sleeping on piles of leaves or well-lapped fir boughs, and loving it. Though Mrs. Benson insisted the ideal way to enjoy hardships was in luxury.

It was the middle of August before Mrs. Flinn had her baby. At that the doctor might just as well have been in Little America, since the infant was born in a huckleberry patch where the Flinns had gone for a day's outing, twelve miles from a medical man or hospital. It was their eighth child and they came riding into town with it wrapped in Mrs. Flinn's petticoat. 'Shure it was fartunate there wasn't two of 'em, for Flinn had nuthin' but one tiny piece of sthring an' a jackknife to perform it up proper like a midwife.' She laughed as she thought of his efforts.

It was sunset when we arrived at Salmon Lake. I'll be satisfied with heaven if it's as beautiful as that place. We pitched our tents on a level stretch of shore beneath evergreen trees which were low-limbed and sheltering. With our bed rolls unwrapped, a campfire grate set up, we were at home. We ate supper and then just sat in thrilled silence while the glory faded and darkness came. There was no moon. It was a night when stars had their own shining way.

It seemed utterly lacking in appreciation to go to bed and lose any of it. I left my tent flaps opened wide to the starlight and cool fragrance of pine-scented mountain air. But I slept almost instantly. I was waked by a sound so unexpected in this remote spot that I could scarcely believe my ears. Men's angry voices raised in drunken argument, stumbling feet on the gravel of the shore. At first I couldn't make out what they were saying. The Bensons woke and we speculated uneasily on what was happening.

Doctor Benson got up and peered out into the starlight. 'Two drunks — coming this way along the lake shore.'

I wondered if they'd try to murder us. And then we caught the drift of the argument.

'I say it was Lord Bacon. You say it was Shakespeare. By what authority —?'

'I don't give a damn for authority. I say what I please. All men are created equal, and first, to thine own self be true. That's why — (hic!) — I couldn't be a priest. What priest could —?'

The doctor went out to investigate. The men greeted him in surprise. They said they were trappers who had a cabin on the upper end of the lake. They'd been to town on a semiannual toot and had got off the logging train at the crossroads as usual. They'd left their canoe tied down here somewhere when they crossed the lake going out, but had been hours trying to find it, as they admitted they were too 'tight' to remember where they'd tied it. I listened to their voices wonderingly. Theirs was cultured speech, in spite of the alcoholic slurring. Why were men of this sort up here in the wilderness, trapping for a living?

The doctor brewed them some strong coffee and as soon as they learned there were women in camp they were most apologetic. They finally located their canoe just around the bend from our camp, and headed home. They laughed when the doctor expressed fear of their drowning themselves in such a state. 'We never get so drunk we can't swim!'

We speculated a lot about them the next day. Superior-looking fellows, both of them, the doctor told us. We had no idea the mystery would ever be solved, but that evening about sunset we saw a canoe cutting across the lake and two finely built, well-shaven, and perfectly sober men came up and introduced themselves as the trappers who'd disturbed us the night before.

'I am Jules Anton,' said the taller of the two, 'and this is Mack Trevor. We didn't know what luck you'd had fishing, so brought these along.' He held out a fine string of trout.

'And this,' said the one called Mack Trevor, 'is a mess of jackrabbit. We thought you might relish a bit.' His eyes twinkled so wickedly as he handed me a heavy package that I tore off the wrapper to investigate. It was as fine a haunch of out-of-season venison as I ever saw.

'These Salmon Lake jackrabbits grow to amazing size!' I grinned at him. 'Regular Paul Bunyan bunny!'

'Quite,' he replied. 'It's the free and untrammeled life up here.'

All evening we lounged around a campfire built down on a rocky point of the lake shore. We studied each other with frank curiosity. Jules Anton was too tall for his breadth, loose-jointed, angular. His hair was darker than red, and his eyes, under bushy brows, were wet-brown, spotted, changing and restless. I felt alertness in them, as though he suspected some danger lurking always behind him. His face was narrow, his nose tilted slightly upward and his mouth was wide.

Mack Trevor was built perfectly to scale. He was very

dark and his brilliant black eyes never moved from one while he spoke. At first his calmness disturbed me, made me almost afraid of him. Yet his every thought and mood shadowed his face. His mouth was sensitively cut and a little weak, not at all in keeping with the rest of his strong face.

I made coffee over the campfire when darkness came and Mrs. Benson brought down sandwiches and a chocolate cake we hadn't cut into yet. The men fairly wolfed the cake.

'I always have had a sweet tooth,' declared Mack, 'but Jules doesn't bake.'

'Tell us about yourselves,' I urged, after they were filled and smoking in content. 'How do men of your sort happen to be living away up here as trappers?'

Some pent-up emotion in them seemed to find freedom in our companionship. They talked of themselves freely. I listened in amazement.

Jules Anton was an unfrocked priest. From childhood his parents had urged him into the Church. 'They were ambitious. Thought I might be a cardinal some day! I began as altar boy and finally took orders, but I never had any enthusiasm about it. I wanted to be let alone to roam through the woods and climb mountains and go fishing. I broke my vows after a year and was excommunicated. It left me in a bad state of mind for a few years and I hoboed around, not caring much about anything. Then I met Mack and we hit it off and decided to leave men behind and take to the wilderness. So here we are!'

Mack Trevor had been a doctor. 'Drink got me,' he said slowly. 'My wife left me. After one of my patients died on the operating table — I'd been drinking and it was my fault — I was barred from medical practice. One night, utterly discouraged, I struck out on the railroad track along the river, hitting for the trestle over the falls. I fully intended to end things. Then down the bank I saw a little fire. A man was over it, cooking mulligan in a tin can. He hailed me and I stopped to talk to him a minute. That was the first time I saw Jules. He had some whiskey and I guess he saw I needed something. Then he made me eat with him, and we got to talking. It was wonderful to find someone who didn't condemn me. When the fire died down and the chill began to creep up from the river, Jules and I rolled up in the same blankets and went to sleep. We've been together ever since.'

I thought long of those two after I went to bed that night. What a waste of manhood —! And yet, as I drifted off to sleep, full of the deep happiness mountains always gave me, I wondered if it were.

When they left camp, they had exacted a promise from us to have dinner with them the following day. We were up early and started on the five-mile hike around the lake to their cabin. We took along some sandwiches, as we knew we'd be hungry and were dubious about bachelor cooking. We knew the kind — gummy sourdough bread, beans and bacon, and a tough old rabbit or half-cooked fish. When we were on the last lap, with only a narrow strip of water between us and the little island on which they had built their cabin, we stopped out of sight in the trees and fortified ourselves.

The island was not more than fifty feet off the mainland in one place. Across this strip the trappers had built a sort of drawbridge. Anyone wanting to get over to the cabin would have to swim or shout for service. It enabled the men to put out of sight any 'jackrabbit' or a skin that had somehow, unlawfully, got itself into the drying shed. The game warden told us he often had a good feed of 'rabbit,' but that they never killed unless they needed meat.

As we approached the bridge, they were watching for us and let it down. We were escorted over with a flourish. The cabin was a good-sized log structure and its interior a revelation. Bunks were built in, one above the other, to save space. Before an ample cobblestone fireplace stood a table made from a section of four-foot fir log, sawed crossways and mounted on sturdy legs. The broad surface was sandpapered and polished. Skins covered the solidly comfortable home-made chairs and seats, and other skins lay on the floor. There were kerosene lamps, books in great numbers on built-in shelves, and such little hand-made conveniences as would have delighted many a housewife. They had created things themselves and they took pride in it. They had towels of flour-sacking, and on the neatly spread bunks the gray army blankets were capped by sheets of the same material. Though Mack told me on the sly that they never slept in them, just kept them for show and an occasional guest who might come that way.

I insisted on helping Jules with the dinner, but he took me by the seat of my corduroys and collar and flung me up on the top bunk. From this vantage-point I had good opportunity to observe our hosts in a more intimate way than I had before. Firm as the strongest trap he ever set was the mouth of Jules Anton. You'd know at a glance that he would make furniture painstakingly, with pegs of wood, while Mack, perhaps, would drive a careless nail. Mack's entire erect, muscle-and-sinew being personified unity of strength, save for that weakness of the mouth. I marveled how this man in his middle fifties could debauch himself periodically for years, and still seem so physically fit. But I learned in talking with him later that it was only once or twice a year he went on a real 'bender.'

While taking in the details of the cabin, I noted a square of unsoiled wood on the door, with tacks in the corner of it holding shreds of cardboard, as though something had recently been torn down. It was Mack who produced the card before the morning was over. On the crumpled piece was written, in the literary style of Benjamin Franklin, an oath signed by each trapper, swearing that no woman should ever be allowed to cross their threshold. Jules had torn it down that morning just as we came in sight. It was a prized possession of mine for years.

The dinner was served in odds and ends of dishes. Prizes in baking powder or cereal packages, utensils from abandoned logging or mining camps, tin cans improvised into gravy boats and cream pitchers, jelly glasses and commercial food containers. The food itself was delicious. There was tasty salt-rising bread of the texture of angel-food cake. There were tiny green onions and watercresses with vinegar and real olive oil, four 'rooters' or grouse, with dressing and gravy, corn on the cob, freshly shelled beans cooked with hunks of salt pork, and wild blackberries with brown sugar. The joke was on us for wasting space previously on sandwiches — not that one could possibly suspect it, from the way we stowed that meal.

Jules said he'd never learned to bake pie or cake, since in the monastery at Saint Pierre's, where he learned to cook, they were allowed no such delicacies in their practice of self-denial.

I count that afternoon as one of the most unusual and interesting of my whole life, listening to three such well-read students of religion, medicine, and philosophy in a wilderness camp. The time went all too fast. When we reluctantly prepared to leave, they said they would take us across the lake. Jules could take the Bensons in the large canoe and Mack could take me in the tiny one.

There was a heady scent of leaves and fresh water, of acrid rushes in the shallows and spicy evergreen. The wall of the shore line stood black against the night sky, with a silhouette of tall trees on the promontories. The brilliance of the stars and their reflection in the water made a soft, eerie light.

'How'd you ever happen to find this heavenly spot?' I asked.

'Jules and I found it when we were prospecting. Thought there might be gold up here. We didn't find any, but we found something just as valuable, maybe. So we took up a claim and began trapping. Means a lot of tramping, but living out-of-doors is good for one.' He paddled in silence for a moment. There was something different in his voice when he spoke again. 'I've got back some self-respect — not too much. I go off the deep end once or twice a year. Get the stuff and don't try to fight it. Just drink, and to hell with it! But I hope you'll never see me like that.'

As he paddled down the lake, Mack told me stories of campers and happenings around the lake. One was particularly dramatic, of a young fellow insanely in love with a girl whose family was camping with his. He told Mack the girl had encouraged him and then laughed at him when he asked her to marry him. He declared if she refused him again he was going to take her out on the lake in a boat and drown her and himself as well. 'I hadn't the slightest idea the kid was in earnest,' said Mack, 'but that's exactly what the fool did. Here in this very spot. They never found the bodies. Sort of bottomless here.'

A bluff rose darkly above us. The other boat slipped silently out of sight. I shivered, thinking of those two bodies in the deep water below us. And then, seemingly from the black water, rose a sound to curdle the blood. Laughter — brittle, cackling, mirthless. I leaped half out of the seat with the shock of it. The canoe rocked dangerously.

'Hey, sister!' Mack yelled at me. The hideous sound was dying away. 'Are you trying to repeat the act? This is a canoe, remember. And that was only a loon.'

'I know, Mack. Silly — but they always scare me.'

'You know,' he said, after a time, 'right now I feel as though I'd never take another drink if you asked me not to. You ——' He broke off and laughed shortly. 'But don't do it. I'd probably break my promise.'

'I've had patients who promised — after they'd been in the hospital with delirium tremens.'

'Did any of them ever keep their word?'

'Only one. He died in the taxi on the way home from the hospital.' I had spoken jestingly, but somehow we didn't laugh.

'Lucky dog!' said Mack. 'At least he died sober, which gave dignity to the occasion. With me now, I'll likely —— Sometimes I wonder why I don't put a bullet through my head and end things decently. Why the devil —?'

'Stop talking like that!' I made no attempt to hide my disgust. 'You and I've seen babies born abortively — starting life a step behind the line. Who knows but that we will begin again, some other time or where? I'll be darned if I want to land in another existence in an abortive state. I'll stay right on the job and dig my ditch with my big shovel. If I turn in my tools too soon, I might get a teaspoon next time!'

'Say, I never thought of it that way. But you must have felt like quitting many a time, just the same.'

'I have not! Life is too interesting.'

'It ought to be.' Mack cut into the water with powerful strokes. 'Yes — it might have been.'

My hand ached in his grip as he told me good night when we stepped on shore. The Bensons and Jules were waiting for us. 'I'll never forget this day. Good night, sister.'

The days passed all too fast on this vacation. We saw our trappers often and hiked over many forest and mountain trails with them. It was with great reluctance that we bade Jules and Mack good-bye when our time was up. They came to see us off and we waved them a last farewell as the car began to climb up the hill from the lake.

'Two wasted lives,' mused Doctor Benson.

'Wasted, nothing!' I snorted. 'It's a wonderful way to live!'

At the moment I longed to chuck everything and stay. Trees and clear cold water and mountain air — I didn't want to go back to sickrooms. The hard family work in private homes, the rows of high narrow beds in a hospital with the never-ending hurry, long nights on duty, trays of shining instruments, smell of anaesthetics, the spatter of blood on a white sponge —— I blurted out as much to Doctor Benson.

He nodded understandingly. 'Just at the moment, girl, I agree with you. But a moment's short.'

Very short. Just at the top of the hill we came upon the young family in the buckboard. The woman, a child in her arms, was driving. The sick man leaned on a pillow, one bandaged hand propped high above his head. We asked if we could help. Unbound, the hand looked like a purple bag. Red streaks flamed angrily to the elbow. It started from a fish-bone cut, they said. The man was in an agony of pain.

'Blood poisoning,' said Doctor Benson.

The urgency of immediate treatment was explained to the couple. In a few minutes we had the man in our car, going full speed ahead, leaving the woman to drive into town alone. We tore along the rocky forest road, up hill and down again, ran recklessly through a herd of steers, took curves on two wheels. With the suffering young father beside me, all desire to abandon my profession vanished. I could scarcely wait to begin treating that hand.

We got the man to the hospital in good order. For a solid week, day and night, I did double duty; they couldn't afford to pay a nurse. That was a great fight. Hour after hour of hot compresses kept the thing from getting worse. But it didn't get better. At last the doctor said he was sure the hand would have to be amputated to save the arm. I begged for time — one hour more, even. I just couldn't bear to see that man lose his hand. The doctor said he'd wait until morning, unless the infection began to spread. If there was the slightest change for the worse, I must call him immediately.

Between treatments I slept in a Morris chair beside the patient's bed. Some time in the night a storm woke me. A thunderclap, which sounded as though the earth might be collapsing, brought me out of my chair gasping. My patient — ! It was a few minutes short of the time I'd expected to wake and see to him. Quickly I uncovered the hand to apply a fresh compress. I was almost delirious with joy at what I saw. The hand looked like a white bladder, from which the air had been expelled.

'Look!' I cried, as the man opened his eyes. 'We've got it licked! Your hand is getting well!'

He had not been able to move his hand without great pain, but now he lifted it a little, raised his head, and took a long look. Disbelief was in his eyes, then fearful hope. His mouth crumpled and tears swept down over his face. I felt an overwhelming weakness assail me. My legs gave way as I bent over the hand. I got the compress ready and sagged down on my knees to complete the dressing. I remember nothing else. Doctor Benson, called to the hospital on an emergency case before morning, came into the room to see how things were going. I didn't hear him. He often jokingly told the story afterward, how he'd left a nurse in charge of a desperately sick patient, thinking she could be trusted, but when he made his rounds he found the patient sitting up in bed and the nurse sound asleep on the floor! But it was a glorious ending to a glorious vacation.

I had many good cases after this and at last had money enough ahead to go to training school. The hospital board 'sat' upon my case and decided I should be allowed half time off the required three years because of my previous experience. That was wonderful news to me. At last I could realize my ambition.

* * *

But getting off was not easy. A dozen times I was all packed to leave for the hospital training school, when some doctor would insist I go on a case — just this once more. Nurses were scarce and there was lots of sickness. But at last the day came when I boarded the train to go to the big Catholic hospital where I was to get my schooling. Doctor Todd had told me a lot about his sister, who was Mother Superior in this institution.

'She puts up a glacial front,' he warned me, 'but don't let her bluff you. Underneath she has a rare sense of humor.'

He must have said mighty nice things about me in the letter he sent her, for when I arrived at midnight, Mother Juliana herself was there to meet me. I was overwhelmed with the honor. She was a majestic woman, but looked a little tired and old.

'You shouldn't have come down to meet me this time of night, Mother Juliana,' I protested. 'I could have taken a taxi out to the hospital.'

'You could have walked.' Her tone was icy. I couldn't see her face, but remembering her brother's description of her, I wondered if she mightn't be smiling.

She introduced me to the handy-man, Timothy, who came to pick up my luggage. He piled my stuff in the phaeton, slapped the reins on the old gray horse, and we jogged off through the quiet streets.

Mother Superior regaled me with accounts of the Sisters' Hospital. It was practically a new institution and she was proud of having built it up from the very foundations.

'We built the laundry first, and all lived there for some time. We ate our meals on washtubs turned bottom-side up, and put mattresses on the shelves to sleep on until our furniture came. We were given the smelter contract and were pushing everything to get the main building finished when there was a bad accident at the smelter. Dozens of men were injured. And we were supposed to care for them.'

'What in the world did you do?'

She laughed. 'We each hauled mattresses onto the floor of the main building. The windows weren't in yet and it was pretty cold, but we hung blankets over the openings and praised God for a roof. Most of the patients were burned, but many not too severely. We cared for the worst ones all night. Fortunately we had plenty of medical supplies.'

'I've heard it's the finest hospital in the State.'

'Yes, it is. But some day we'll have a bigger, better one. We're improving all the time.'

Presently we arrived at the hospital. It loomed, in the starlight, big and bare and imposing on the prairie at the outskirts of town. The door was opened by a tall, shy, very blond orderly whom the Mother Superior introduced as Tommy Ackerly. A small Sister, dark-eyed and arrestingly beautiful, came into the lobby and was introduced as Sister Sistine.

'She is helping tonight and will take care of you,' said the Mother Superior. Her manner was very curt. 'Come to my office at ten in the morning. Good night.' Without a smile she walked sedately down the long corridor.

Little French Sister Sistine had the most saintly face I have ever seen. She fascinated me from the moment I saw her. She gave me a cup of coffee and a sandwich in the big dining-room and then took me to the nurses' quarters, a great basement room with small high windows looking out on the stubble around the building. There were about twenty beds in it, separated from each other by curtains on wires. It was clean and neat and bare. The place was dimly lighted and the only nurses there were sound asleep, so after Sister Sistine bade me good night I crept into my cubicle as silently as possible and got myself to bed.

I was much interested in the girls on either side of me, who introduced themselves the next morning. Isobel Jarvis on my right was a dark, slender girl, strikingly good-looking and a bit reserved. Betsy O'Shay, on my left, was a trim, pert-nosed little person, warm-hearted and anxious to help me unpack or something. She took me to the Mother Superior after breakfast.

That dignitary looked me over critically without any warmth of greeting. 'Dress too short,' she said icily.

'Yes, Mother Superior,' meekly. 'That's why I want to lay it aside for a nurse's uniform. A long one.' Seeing the little amused puckers at the corner of her mouth, I ventured, 'One with a train.'

She got up out of her chair and put her hands on my shoulders. 'You'll get along all right, my dear. Acquaint yourself with everything you can on the second floor. You'll go on night duty there Thursday at seven o'clock.'

Though scared with the prospect of night duty in a strange hospital and all the responsibility it entailed, I was overjoyed. At last I was on my way to that diploma which was letter of credit in any man's country.

Isobel Jarvis was half through her second year of training and was very friendly to me until she learned that the Mother Superior herself had met me at the train. 'She's playing favorites, is she?' The girl's eyes were full of resentment. 'How do you happen to rate such attentions?' When she found I was going to be allowed to graduate after only a year and a half of work, she was outraged and would scarcely speak to me. She insisted she didn't see why any board should shorten my time, no matter what experience I'd had. I tried to make her like me in spite of things, but her animosity toward me smoldered, ready to break into flame at the slightest provocation.

Betsy O'Shay was quite a different sort and thought it wonderful that I should get my diploma so speedily. She was good-natured and full of life, in every way a normal person I thought, until I found she would have nothing to do with men, except as it was required of her in the hospital. She insisted she hated all of them. Later, when I knew her better, she confessed she'd had two unfortunate love affairs, and swore she was through with men forever.

It amused me that Tommy Ackerly, the shy orderly with whom we worked most, should be as aggressively a woman-hater. These two fairly bristled at sight of each other. For some reason Tommy exempted me from his aversion. I had been accepted as a kindred spirit and he even expected me to share his antipathy for my sex.

'Why should you like them?' he asked me. 'Look at that Jarvis cat. She has her claws in you every chance she gets. Jealous as the devil. Women haven't any scruples, I tell you.'

'Your mother was a woman, Tommy,' I retorted one day when I was tired of listening to him.

'That's just the trouble!' he flashed back hotly. 'My mother dumped me down at the gate of a foundling home and damned well never bothered her head about me again.'

Ordinarily retiring and uncommunicative, Tommy, aroused, was resourceful, defiant, almost aggressive. With ward patients, old people, children and charity patients, his gentleness was phenomenal. One day, in a more expansive mood, he told me he had been with the Franciscan fathers for six years, nursing sick boys in their school, to help get to medical school some day. To this end he was on duty as orderly. Sometimes it seemed to me he already knew more about medicine than some of the practicing physicians.

I liked him a lot. Being so closely associated with me on night duty, he came to talk quite freely to me of his ambitions and struggles to attain them. It was most amusing to see how Tommy and Betsy avoided each other. On the assumption that they did 'protest too much,' I decided they must really be interested in each other. At midnight we had coffee and sandwiches on the landing halfway between Betsy's floor and mine, so we could hear bells from either. On these occasions, those two bantered each other endlessly, and sometimes it was pretty sharply edged.

'What floor got the patient you just admitted, Tommy?' she asked him one night.

'Obstetrical case. Just in time, too, if you ask me.'

'What do you mean, just in time?' she asked, all innocence.

'If the ambulance hadn't cut corners she would have been too late.'

'Oh, she had a date, then? Dear me! Tommy, if I had a date with you, would you object if I rode in an ambulance, wearing your orchids?'

His face got red. He hated this teasing. 'I'd much prefer seeing you come in a hearse, with my orchids on your chest.'

Betsy giggled hysterically, delighted that she could annoy this tall male.

One of the nurses, a widow, had an apartment in town which she urged me to use on my days off. I liked to go there in her absence and cook meals for invited friends. Betsy and I often ate together. Sometimes I had Tommy when she was working. One night I invited them together. It took a lot of coaxing to persuade Tommy, though I knew he was dying for a home-cooked meal.

'What did you want to ask that brazen hussy for?' he protested. 'I hate her and she hates me.'

'Oh, come on, Tommy,' I urged. 'She's just joking. I shouldn't wonder if she were really very fond of you.'

'You're crazy! I'll sure be glad when we don't have to work together any more.'

But he came. We sat down to dinner in the midst of a terrific thunderstorm. We'd just begun our steaks when lightning struck a tree right outside the dining-room window. The blast fairly rocked the house; lights went off and livid little snakes of lightning darted hissing around the room. When the lights went on again, there was Betsy, the man-hater, all crumpled down in the arms of Tommy, the woman-hater. She clung to him, forgetting I was on earth, and he kissed her with unabashed relish.

They were married shortly after Betsy graduated. Then she went to work and helped Tommy through medical college. A few years later, when twin daughters were born to them, they nicknamed them 'Thunder' and 'Lightning.'

There were two encounters with Mother Superior I well remember. One happened on her birthday. She had been laid up with a broken leg and was just able to stand for the first time. The nurses thought it would be a nice gesture to take her a huge box of roses. She accepted the offering with a surprised 'Thank you.' But when she opened it, she looked sternly at me as though I had been the leader of a terror gang.

'How much did these cost?' she demanded.

Most of the girls were admittedly afraid of her. They drew off in nervous alarm. I stepped forward a bit stealthily, leaned toward her ear, and announced in a dramatic whisper, 'Not a cent. I stole them off a grave!'

Mother Superior was always nearer laughter than anyone knew. Her dignity vanished and she laughed heartily. She told us to go walk in the garden for fifteen minutes and then come back to the dining room. When we returned, she served us cake and wine and was very much the gracious hostess.

The other encounter was in the matter of a bread pudding. A rather untaught lay Sister had charge of the nurses' dining room. After each meal, she frugally collected every scrap of bread left at the plates. For weeks on end she had served us a concoction she called bread pudding. Sometimes there was a handful of raisins in it, sometimes a dash of spice, and once a dab of jelly on top, but more often it was just sweetened milk and bread scraps.

We nurses ganged up on the Sister. I put a metal slug in a thick crust of bread. The next day one of the nurses got it in her serving of pudding. I told the Sister we didn't want to eat the scraps from the plates any more, and she most indignantly denied the pudding was made from such. I was reported to the Superior and told to appear at class the next morning with an apology.

Doctor Swann presided with Mother Superior at class, which was the time our nursing difficulties were settled. My name was called. I stood up. Mother Superior's eyes twinkled as they looked into mine, but her voice was judicial.

'I believe you owe an apology for your remarks concerning

the bread pudding served at the nurses' table. What have you to say?'

I held up the slug. 'One of our nurses got this in her pudding. I confess to putting it in bread left at my plate. But as to an apology —! Mother Superior, I had nothing to do with the making of that pudding. If I had, I would gladly apologize for it!'

Mother Superior struggled for something to say or do that would preserve her dignity as disciplinarian. She turned to Doctor Swann.

'I think all these young ladies are equally guilty.'

'I agree,' solemnly.

'Doctor Swann, what would you consider a suitable penalty?'

'It is a serious matter,' the doctor pronounced. 'I recommend that every nurse be deprived of bread pudding for thirty days, Mother Superior.'

'Substituting apple pie,' she quickly amended. 'Class dismissed.'

* * *

Night duty was not heavy at first. So when Sister Sistine contracted a bad chest cold and was ordered to bed, I often had time to go in and sit with her after my patients were settled for the night. We quickly became warm friends.

She chafed at being away from the children's ward. She was in charge there and was wonderful with them. They all loved her devotedly. I had been fascinated by her understanding way of bringing a refractory youngster to terms. But she was so young, so talented and beautiful, that I wondered every time I was with her why one of her sort should have had her head shaved and put on the stiffly starched and uncomfortable headgear and voluminous skirt and cape of a nun. Why had she left home and lovers — surely she'd had many of them! — for this sort of life? One day she must have read my mind.

She smiled at me. 'Always you wonder, n'est-ce pas? I see it in your face. I shall tell you.'

I wish I could tell her story as she told it, with all the charm of idiom she used. But I know little French and I can't even approximate her accent. It was the tale of a young Parisienne, born to wealth and luxury, reared by a father of high rank, who lavished on his motherless daughter everything in his power. She had been educated in convent schools with others of her kind, and though the good Sisters talked much of the duty of the rich to the poor, these sheltered girls had little idea of real poverty or the depths of squalor and degradation in the city around them.

'My aunt took my mother's place and I was carefully groomed to make a proper début and marriage,' Sister Sistine told me. 'The girls talked a great deal of their older sisters' and cousins' gowns and jewels and conquests. It made us eager to get into society. I dreamed often of the husband I'd have some day, the magnificent establishment, the balls and soirées. But in the chapel at school or in the cathedral at Mass, these things would fade. For there, unbidden and a little frightening, something deep in my heart whispered that I should give my life to the Church. The longer I lived in the school with the Sisters and Mother Superior, the more I was impressed by the beauty of their lives. Sister Theodosia let me help her with the little children whenever I could, and I loved the work.

'But as the time for my début approached, nothing else seemed important. My ball was to be given at the home of my aunt and uncle. He was a wealthy banker and they had a most impressive place. For weeks we girls talked of what clothes we would wear and what men we would meet. So far we had known few, since we had not as yet been socially presented.

'At last the memorable night arrived. As the carriage waited to take us to my uncle's for dinner — we were going early as I wished to dress there to keep my things from being crushed driving over — I grew more and more impatient that my father was being detained. I was anxious to get off, but the minutes ticked by. Finally father sent word for me to go on with my maid and he would join us as soon as possible.

I hated to go without him, but the sun was getting low and I wanted to get dressed. Already I'd lost half an hour.

'"Tell François to take all the short cuts he can," I told the footman, as he tucked the robe about my skirts. "I'm in a hurry."

'"There is a way" — he looked at me hesitantly — "if Mademoiselle approves. We can cut off several miles. But it means going through slum districts."

'"Take it," I ordered. My maid was about to remonstrate. She was twice my age and hadn't much respect for my judgment, I'm afraid.'

Sister Sistine paused, her eyes remote and deep sadness in her beautiful face. 'On that ride I saw things I had never dreamed existed. For the first time I realized how sheltered my life had been, that I should have seen nothing of the suffering of humanity.' She shuddered.

'Every foot of the way took us into more frightful misery. Children, emaciated, cold, almost naked, begged with outstretched hands. Such numbers of them — crippled and misshapen. Pathetic little ones crouched against lamp posts or in doorways, shivering. Feeble old women, bent double, prowled in alleys picking up bits of wood in their bony arms. Old men tottered along the gutters, poking through refuse for scraps of food. I turned faint when I saw one pick up some bit, blow off what dirt he could, and put it in his mouth.

'My maid insisted on putting down the carriage curtains so that we needn't see the awfulness of it. But I insisted just as much that I wouldn't have it. One white-haired old man stumbled and fell almost in front of our horses. They swerved and reared to avoid stepping on him as he struggled to regain his feet. My coachman leaned far over and lashed at him before I could cry out to prevent it, then laid whip to the horses and swept us away from that spot.

'"François!" I screamed at him in horror. "Stop! You beast! You may have hurt that old man. Go back! I must help him."

'But I might as well have pleaded with the wind. Such anger as I have never known filled me. For the first time I

knew bitter hatred in my outrage.' Sister Sistine crossed herself quickly. 'I appealed to my maid, but she shook her head.
'"If you stopped in this dreadful place, we might never get out alive. And never with your jewels. Your father would be furious if we were so careless with you. These pitiful-looking beggars are nothing but professional thieves, most of them."
'"Not those poor little children," I protested. "I can't bear to have them cold and hungry when I have so much."
'"Your eyes will be all red and swollen if you cry," she reminded me. "Don't you remember you're going to your début? A nice sight you'll be."
'My ball —! At the moment those pitiful ones had far more reality than my ball or any of my past life. I sat in a daze all the rest of the way, filled with shame that such things were so near me and I had never done anything to help. My aunt was aghast when she saw me.
'"My sweet, forget these things," she admonished me, when I told her of my experience. "They're old as the world and there's little you can do about them. This is your night. You must be gay."
'I tried. I was young and I couldn't bear to ruin everything I'd so long planned. It was beautiful, that ballroom with its banks of flowers and palms and crystal chandeliers. All the girls in exquisite gowns, all the old friends of my parents, distinguished men and women come to see me make my bow to society, all the young men paying me compliments, the wonderful music — a few hours before I would have thrilled with joy over it, but now I was speechless and shaken. It didn't seem to matter. I could see only the hungry, suffering children, crippled and homeless; the withered old women and bent, vacant-eyed old men. I tried not to show how I felt, but as I danced, the things the men said to me might have been in a foreign language for all they meant.
'And then The Vision came to me.
'Over my partner's shoulder, out in the ballroom, high above the heads of the dancers, glowed a radiance. And there appeared in it the face of Our Lord. The crown of thorns

was on His head and drops of blood trickled down over His face. And in His compassionate eyes was love that surpassed any human love. And as He looked at me, I was filled with shame and horror for the blindness and selfishness of my life, for the luxury and jewels and idle pleasure. I pulled away from my partner as I gazed upward in awe. The bewildered young man touched my arm and spoke to me, but I pushed him aside and stood in adoration, my eyes on the face of Our Lord.

'And then He spoke to me. "Give thyself to no man. Thou, Thérèse, shalt be a Bride of the Church. Thou shalt serve my children, the poor, the sick, the hungry."

'And then the radiance faded and He was gone. I was filled with holy ecstasy. "Yes, Blessed Lord!" I whispered.

'My partner stared at me and crossed himself. "You have seen a vision —?"

'"Yes," I told him. "Our Lord has called me. I must go."

'We were undoubtedly a strange spectacle as we walked across the ballroom floor. It was an intermission between dances, so that guests were more aware of us than they would have been otherwise. I had but one thought — to get away, strip off my finery, and prepare for service. My partner, probably thinking I had gone mad, tried to stop me. People stared, but it didn't matter. I walked out like one in a trance. My aunt tried to cover my retreat from the guests and divert me, but I kept on. Just as I reached the doorway, my father came up the broad stairs.

'He smiled at me fondly. "Ah, Thérèse. I am here at last. Have you saved a waltz for me?"

'I shook my head. "I shall never dance again, Father. I am going home."

'I saw the quick displeasure in his face. He evidently thought, from my partner's looks, we'd had some difficulty. He covered the awkwardness of my bald statement by laughing. "Since nothing again can ever equal this, you think, you'll be content with nothing less? You are too romantic, darling. But if they will excuse us a moment, I have news to discuss with you." He offered me his arm, bowed to the staring guests, and guided me into a small lounge and shut the door.

'"Now," he turned on me angrily, "what is the meaning of such behavior at your début ball? You are making an outrageous spectacle of yourself!"

'My poor father! That was a terrible scene we had. At times he tried to be patient and gentle, as one would with an irresponsible sick child. Then he would storm and swear I was an imbecile to let such a neurotic whim overcome me. He called in my aunt and uncle to add their arguments, but I stood firm. I could not go back to the dance floor from the presence of The Christ. And so my beautiful ball went on without me, everyone pretending nothing was amiss. But the sensation grew momentarily, with every whisper. I left by a back stairway and my aunt announced that I had been taken ill.

'My father locked me in my rooms when we reached home, but before morning I escaped over my balcony and went to the convent. And I never returned. In time my father gave me the legacy which had come from my mother. With it and her pearls I endowed a home for orphan children. Later I was sent to Montreal, where I taught French in a convent school. When this hospital was being built, I was sent here.'

I drew a deep breath as Sister Sistine finished her story. 'Did your father ever forgive you?'

'In a way. But he grieved over it as long as he lived. He died a few years ago.' Tears filled her eyes. I knelt by the bed and kissed her on each cheek in the manner of the French, and she blessed me.

We sat silent, and I looked at her a long time, still wondering. 'Tell me, Sister Sistine, didn't you honestly ever regret your step? Wouldn't you have been happier if you had married and had a home and children? You could have done an immense amount of good with your money just the same.'

Her lovely eyes met mine levelly. They were clear and pure as a mountain spring. 'I am human. I shed many tears that first year. Even Our Lord was subject to temptation.

But individual happiness is not important. A deep and holy peace comes and a true happiness that the world does not know. I would not have had it different.'

* * *

Doctor Seymour was the two-hundred-pound head of the staff. He was fat and florid and startlingly blond, even to his brows and eyelashes and the hairs on his pudgy hands. He had a fat and florid wife who weighed ten pounds more than he. They were never apart when they could possibly be together, and other staff wives, a bit jealous possibly, insisted she went along to watch him. But they were congenial companions and knew how to get the most out of work or play.

At first I thoroughly disliked the man. He'd come into the dressing room when I was in charge nights, and tell stories and jokes that were disgusting. I thought him hard and very unsympathetic — until the night Tilly's baby was born.

Tilly had come from the Old Country to marry Pete. Somehow Pete didn't get around to it right away. She was Doctor Seymour's patient and her time had come. In a calm period between labor pains the doctor asked her kindly, 'Tilly, tell old popper — it takes the average woman nine months to have a baby. You've been married only four months. Pretty smart, eh?'

'Oh yah,' Tilly beamed at him. 'Oh yah. Ay know. But de papy he vas half made ven me and Pete get us marrit, an' Pete he nefer tolt me!'

I was amazed by the doctor's tenderness to poor suffering, homesick Tilly. He soothed her, babied her, mothered-and-fathered her, and evidently suffered, with her, every pain she had. At last he handed the lusty, yowling infant to the maternity nurse, and when the girl was made comfortable, asked me if I wanted to go take a look at the young Swede. He looked at the child a minute, then turned to me, his tongue in his cheek and his eyes twinkling. 'You know, that damn fat little red-faced brat is the dead image of me!'

My heart still aches when I think of Doctor Dundeen, who

instructed me in the giving of anaesthetics — in those days within the province of the trained nurse. I always think of him as the brown Scot. His hair and eyes and skin were brown, and he always wore imported suits of brown homespun. He was tall, thin, and scholarly, with cultivated taste in books, music, and poetry. He had a habit of singing snatches of old Scotch ballads at the most unexpected moments, when he was scrubbing up after an operation, dressing a wound, or even setting a bone. I've chuckled at him singing 'Scots Wha' Hae Wi' Wallace Bled' as he came in smeared with blood.

One day in the operating room he had just given a lumberjack ether and was handing me the cone to keep him under, when the patient's heart stopped beating. We worked with the man a long time, but there was no reviving him. There was another critical operation to follow immediately and Doctor Dundeen motioned me into the dressing room. He was so pale and nervous I thought he was sick. I was horrified when he handed me a bottle of cocaine and hypodermic, and ordered me to give him a shot. Any drug habit, we had been taught, was the supreme crime in Materia Medica. But he insisted. Said he usually gave it to himself, but he was too shaky to do it just now. I obeyed, utterly heart-sick. It was tragic.

The next day he asked me to go with him out to the smelter to see a man who was dying of cancer of the colon. On the way he told me he was suffering from the same thing. On his last vacation, he had been under the knife at Mayo's, and was now doing his work with a tube in his side. His time was limited and the cocaine gave him freedom from pain so that he might work as long as possible.

'You're older and have had more experience than the other students. You can help me in the surgery. And please keep this to yourself. I don't want anyone to know.'

All through the year I worked with him I felt I had never known such courage and self-sacrifice. He was a brilliant man in the very prime of life. Before my time was finished, he depended more and more on the shots. One day after he had taken the cocaine and was putting the finishing touches on his pre-operative sterilization, I noticed his hands were trembling badly. Close to him, so the others couldn't hear, I begged him to let Doctor Hemington, who had just come in, take over. He was not on the staff, but was a specialist. Doctor Dundeen hesitated a moment, then closed his lips tightly. 'Another shot — a small one,' he ordered. There was no time for privacy. The room was full. Pretending to be occupied with the sterilizer, I filled the hypo unobserved and then ostensibly tying his surgical coat strings, gave him a shot in the shoulder muscle.

He nodded toward the patient being wheeled into the operating room. His smile was whimsical. 'I've played chess with him for years. If I don't pull him through, I won't have anyone to play with when I retire.'

But that was the last operation he performed, as his condition soon forced him to give up his active work. I visited him and his charming wife often. Strangely, in the six months he lived afterward, he seemed little changed. He was able to attend our graduation exercises and hand out the diplomas. I was grateful for that.

I was at the end of my first week of night duty at the hospital when I met Doctor Fleck. I'd heard a lot of the brilliant urologist from the moment I arrived.

'He's the Mystery Man,' Isobel told me. 'We can't make him out. He's so spectacular you feel he ought to be a regular lady-killer, but women seem to bore him. He's dark and good-looking, with awfully tanned skin and dazzling white teeth. And his smile is devastating. But his eyes give you a grue somehow. You'll know what I mean when he comes creeping up on you like some jungle cat. He lived in the South Sea Islands for years and it did something to him, I think.'

One night, as I sat at the desk midway of the long hall, bringing my charts up to date, I chanced to look up — I swear I'd heard no footsteps — and saw a man moving down the hall toward me. From his dark tan and the litheness of his walk, I judged this must be the Mystery Man. He came up to the desk, appraising me dispassionately. And then, whether I amused him or not, he smiled at me. Isobel had been right. His smile certainly was devastating. My heart fairly turned over. But his eyes startled me as I looked into them. They were like deep holes with flames in the bottom of them.

'You're the new night nurse, I take it.' His voice was delightful in timbre. 'I'm Fleck. The nurses call me the Mystery Man, I hear.' His strange eyes burned into mine. 'Do I look like a mystery to you?'

'You know, don't you, Doctor Fleck, that all a nurse is supposed to say to a physician is, "Yes, doctor"?' I didn't know whether I liked him or not.

He regarded me critically. 'I'll give you leave to say whatever you feel like saying to me at any time. I'm shunned around here as though I'd brought back the bubonic plague from the South Seas. Maybe I'm lonesome. Don't you ever "Yes, doctor" me. That's orders. Remember?'

'Yes, doctor,' I said.

He took a step nearer and looked as though he were going to shake me. '"Yes, doctor! Yes, doctor!" Are you just like all the rest of them? Maybe that's all you *can* say.' He fairly glowered at me with those disconcerting eyes. 'Do you like to dance?'

'Yes, doctor.' I grinned at him.

He laughed this time. There was a quality in him that fascinated me. He leaned across the top of the desk. 'Would you like to —?'

A bedside bell buzzed. I rose briskly. 'Excuse me, Doctor Fleck. I dance to the tune of bells.'

He caught my arm. 'Damn the bells! You're crazy! Why should a woman such as you be a nurse? And why should a man such as I be a doctor? Why are we messing around with all this hideous business when life could be so beautiful? You'd love it down in the Islands where I've been. You were in Honolulu for some time, I heard. You know what I mean. Those warm ——'

I pulled away from him. From a doctor the discontent of those words tumbling over each other revolted me. 'I happen to like being a nurse,' I informed him, and hurried off. I'll certainly steer clear of that man, I told myself. He's bad medicine. I wonder if he really intended asking me to go dancing with him. Surely he hadn't. After all, he was married.

But there was no steering clear of Doctor Fleck. Night after night, when I was on duty, after the patients' bells had quieted, he would come to sit in the hall by my desk and talk to Tommy and me. Always he talked of the South Sea Islands. He spoke once of a nice little copra business he'd had there and again of doctoring the natives, and of a French priest to whom he was devoted. But usually one felt in his talk only nostalgic longing for the idleness of warmly lazy days.

Listening to him, the unpleasantness of my Army experience in Honolulu dimmed, and memories of the sensuous charm of Hawaii gripped me. I began to feel the pull of those luscious sunny days, of nights when moonlight and dreamy Kanaka music, exotic flowers, and fragrant ripening fruit blended into magic. There was witchery in his words. I began to long to hear soft-speaking natives in the shade of the lanais, to hear the sound of dashing rain on banana leaves and see the quick sunshine afterward. There were mail boats to Honolulu twice a week now, Jennie Edwards had written me. There were churches and libraries and operas. That fascinated me. But Doctor Fleck's remote atolls, where ships stopped just once a year and one went native and lost all desire for activity — I wanted none of that.

Interested though we were by talk which left us breathless, there rose in both Tommy and me antagonism to the thing this strange man craved. 'It's like dope to him,' Tommy said one night, after Doctor Fleck left us. "Dundeen told me Fleck had one of the most amazing minds of any of the medics around here, but this desire is destroying his will to use it.'

I never saw Doctor Fleck alone, but his attentions to me were open and undisguised. I was feminine enough to be flattered, but he embarrassed me and I felt I was being put in a very bad position. He came to seem more like an orderly than Tommy, being always around doing things for the patients to save me time and work.

'What about your wife?' I asked him one night when he'd been talking about how he longed to go back to the South Seas. She'd been ill a long time when he came to the hospital and had had no part in social affairs. They said she was as queer as he was. He seldom spoke of her and I'd never seen her. 'Does she share your enthusiasm for remote places?'

His intense eyes met mine in quick glance. 'She still can't bring herself to use a telephone unless it is absolutely necessary. And clothes —!' He smiled. 'One wears too many here. But she has made better adjustment than I have. You must meet my wife some day. You'll like her.'

It was about a month later that I did meet her — and danced with Doctor Fleck — at a benefit ball given by the Devorees. Mr. and Mrs. Devoree had arrived several weeks before and were living in a suite at the best hotel. It seems they had come from South America recently. He was making an extensive survey of smelting methods used in different countries, I heard, and was particularly interested in leaching processes. The smelter men all agreed he was a mighty smart fellow. Mrs. Devoree, charming, gracious, and beautifully groomed, was immediately welcomed by the town's socialites. They liked the glimpses she gave them of life abroad, in Rio de Janeiro, Paris, and London, and the delightful anecdotes she told of her French chef, English butler, and the German maids she'd left behind in New York.

The town had been trying for some time to raise funds for a park and recreation grounds, and the city fathers were much impressed when Mr. Devoree appeared at a council meeting one day and said he and his wife would be glad to give a benefit ball and turn over the proceeds to the park fund. They would pay for the hall, orchestra, refreshments, and all incidentals, and make a substantial gift themselves. He suggested tickets should sell for two dollars apiece, and his proposition was accepted enthusiastically.

The date was set and the ball widely advertised. It was to

be given in Odd Fellows' Hall, the only place in town with cloakrooms and serving arrangements, big enough to accommodate such a gathering. We all bought tickets, even though we were being escorted, since the cause was so worthy. Slag hounds from the smelter, who had no intention of attending, bought tickets by the hundreds. Their kids would play in the park and they were all for it. It was to be a swanky affair. An orchestra and caterers from Helena were engaged and the local florist was cleaned out with the flowers ordered for decoration. A number of town girls were hired and fitted with smart uniforms, to help the butler and two maids being shipped in to take charge.

Excitement ran high when the gala night arrived. I loved dancing, and the young druggist who was my escort was an enthusiast. We'd never seen a ballroom so lavishly banked with flowers. Mr. Devoree wore tails produced by masters of the craft and Mrs. Devoree wore a gown that made every other woman there feel like a blanketed squaw. The butler was superb and we enjoyed immensely the way he presided in the banquet room. Our host made a clever and witty speech of welcome, and turned over to the mayor a personal check for one thousand dollars as a contribution from his wife and himself.

It was well along in the evening before I saw Doctor Fleck. He was dancing with a woman so like him in finely cut features that I thought she must be his sister. He lifted a hand in salute when he saw me and steered his partner in my direction. What an extraordinarily beautiful pair they were, I thought, as they came up to us. I was amazed when he introduced her as his wife.

She smiled at me cordially. Even her beautiful white teeth were like Doctor Fleck's. 'I've heard a great deal of you, Mrs. Hughes. John thinks you're pretty fine. He's dying to dance with you. Might we change partners?'

My druggist relinquished me all too willingly, I thought, at the dazzling smile Mrs. Fleck gave him. And then Doctor Fleck's arm was about me and my hand was in his as we glided into the waltz. Dancing of that day was a most decorous performance. The gentleman put the palm of his right hand gently between the shoulder blades of his partner, while she laid her left hand lightly on his shoulder. Then, with space enough between them to accommodate a heating stove, they touched their free hands palm to palm at arm's length out in space, quite often pumping them up and down in time to the music. But Doctor Fleck didn't dance that way. He drew me disconcertingly close and we danced with an enchanting sense of rhythm that cast a spell upon me. I don't know how long it might have lasted if I hadn't caught the look I did in Tommy's eye as he swung by with a nurse. It brought me back to earth. The eyes of my superior officers would be upon me also. And those of the staff doctors and a bevy of jealous nurses. For weeks I had been pushing aside a vague fear of hospital reaction to the time Doctor Fleck spent on my floor every evening. Now, with horror, I realized we were being watched and criticized. I shouldn't dance with this man another time. But there would be an encore. What if I were discharged for unbecoming behavior?

I meant to refuse the encore, but somehow I was dancing again with the words unsaid. Only this once more. This was something so —— And then a woman's hysterical scream stabbed through the soft languor of the violins.

'Help! Help! We've been robbed!'

There was consternation among the guests when the woman shrieked, 'All the purses have been emptied on the tables in the cloakroom. My fur coat's gone — and so are a lot of others!'

There was a great rush to the cloakroom where the maids had so recently been in charge. They had disappeared. My purse had vanished — with some twelve dollars in it. The purse I valued highly, as it was a very handsome one, presented to me by the Army Medical Staff in Honolulu.

'Where's Mr. Devoree! Find Mr. Devoree!' voices were shouting.

The two policemen who had been keeping order among the small boys and curious out in front of the hall, came in. They had the butler in custody. He was so drunk he could scarcely stand. It was a stunned bunch of guests who realized some ten minutes later that the Devorees, the maids, and all the park money were gone. Only the local hired help, clearing away the tables, remained. Angry cries arose on every side from unpaid musicians, caterers, and florists. The mayor pulled out the check Mr. Devoree had so generously donated. 'One thousand bucks!' he moaned. 'And I'll bet it's no good!'

It wasn't. They never caught up with the Devorees. They had driven away in their own powerful eastern car. If they'd stuck to it, they'd have been easy to find, since such cars, the sheriff pointed out, 'were scarce as braids on a bald head. They must have driven like two hells — maybe twenty-five or thirty miles an hour!' The car was found the next day near a railroad station in Butte. A New York dealer claimed it later. They'd made only a small down payment on it.

When the 'butler' sobered up, he told a most convincing story, which the police verified. He'd been playing the rôle of English butler with a theatrical company that had gone on the rocks the week before. He was sitting in a saloon wondering where he'd get his next meal when Mr. Devoree found him and told him about a big party they wanted to swing, and hired him just for the swank he'd give it. The poor chap seemed an honest fellow and was so scared over being mixed up with a robbery that he was positively sick. Good old Tommy appealed to the Sisters at the hospital and the man was brought out and set to peeling potatoes and emptying garbage cans to tide him over. Later he developed into a successful gardener.

Mrs. Fleck called me a few days after the ball, to ask if I would come out and have tea with her some afternoon. I hesitated, but I thought it might help appearances to let it be known that Doctor Fleck's wife approved of me — for I had been more and more disturbed by his attitude toward me since the Devoree affair.

The Flecks had taken a house outside the city limits, with a sizeable garden and a hedge which shut out the bareness of the prairie around them. Although a recent frost had killed the blooms, I could see how vivid the garden's color must have been. These two seemed to need tropical background.

It was from Mrs. Fleck this first afternoon together that I gained insight into the relation of this pair. Doctor Fleck had talked endlessly of the Islands and the natives, but he had never spoken of why they had gone there. When Mrs. Fleck began talking of the country, I asked her bluntly how they'd happened to go to such a place.

'Didn't John ever tell you?' she asked, in surprise. 'I thought you knew about us. He says he's always talking South Seas with you. We hadn't meant to go there to live. We were shipwrecked. And we couldn't get away.'

'Shipwrecked?' I looked at her with new interest. 'Tell me about it.'

'We were on this cruise — John, his father and mother and I. John had just finished medical school the year before and had been practicing until he became very ill. It was for his sake, when he began to feel better, that we were on this cruise. His parents were my own uncle and aunt. They had adopted me when I was left an orphan in infancy, so John and I grew up as brother and sister. There was a terrible typhoon when we were near this inhabited atoll and the ship was wrecked on a reef. John and I were the only survivors. A native in an outrigger canoe rescued us, as we clung, half dead, to wreckage. He took us to Father Anthony, the old French missionary stationed on the island, and we lived with him. The only boat, which came to the island once a year, had just made its visit, bringing supplies and loading on copra. So we just had to make the best of things.' Her eyes were far away as she paused and smiled to herself.

'Wasn't it awfully hard to adjust to such a different sort of life?' I asked.

'At first we were so shocked with grief over the loss of our parents that we didn't care about anything. It seemed as though work — the harder the better — was all that kept us from going under. We'd lived so actively in the States that we didn't know how to relax. But after a while the climate makes you. It's a wonderful feeling when you get accustomed to it! We spent endless hours idling around, swimming, canoeing, fishing. We both began to feel that we never wanted to go back to the hurry and worry of the world we'd left. John grew well and strong. He'd never really liked medical work — going into it only because his father had been a doctor and insisted. He thought of returning to it with a sort of horror, and finally we decided when the boat came again we wouldn't leave.

'We gave first aid to the natives when they needed it, but there was practically no sickness on the island. After a while we built a house. It was Father Anthony who insisted that we must be married if we were to live together, since we were not really brother and sister. He laughed about it, but he was in dead earnest. He was so sweet and gentle an old man that we couldn't outrage him, so we agreed and he performed the ceremony.' Mrs. Fleck studied me intently. 'We'd always been fond of one another, of course, but, as you may imagine, there was nothing romantic in such a marriage. But we were happy enough. We stayed seven years. And probably would have been there yet if I hadn't developed a condition that required surgery. I was sick a long time, so we had to come back. Poor John! He's never been happy since. But that's enough about the Flecks. Let's have tea. And you can tell me about yourself.'

That was the beginning of Mrs. Fleck's attentions to me. I wondered about her often. Her friendship seemed genuine and she invited me time after time to visit her alone when I had hours off. She insisted on my calling her by her first name, Abbie. She had a name for me I couldn't pronounce, let alone spell. She said it meant 'belated blessing,' which at the time seemed senseless

There was no change in the doctor's attitude toward me when his wife was present. He was eager and attentive. And strangely, she seemed to encourage him. I became so embarrassed with the situation I determined one day never to go to their house again. I regretted the invitation I'd accepted for dinner the following Sunday evening, although I understood there were to be other guests as well. But this certainly would be the last. The man was too disconcerting for my peace of mind, and his wife's friendship made me uncomfortable.

When I arrived for dinner, I found there were no other guests. They made no explanation. The food was delicious, and I did full justice to it, in spite of being nervous over a subtle something in the air which I couldn't define. After we had finished, we sat by the fireplace and talked.

Doctor Fleck brought out a number of queer native instruments to show me. One was a contraption with two strings strung over a long-necked gourd. When picked, the strings gave out a most weird tone. He manipulated the thing a bit, then began some native air so monotonous it irritated me, and yet it was fascinating.

Abbie Fleck reached over and covered my hand with hers. 'My dear, this is most personal, but I'm sure you'll understand. John and I had you alone with us tonight because we wanted to explain to you our domestic situation. I've told you there has never been real, romantic love between John and me. For some time now there has been another and deeper interest in my life — a revival of an old attachment our Island experience interrupted. So I'm more than glad that John has found a greater interest as well.'

She looked at the doctor and smiled. He didn't speak. He didn't need words, with those eyes holding me, telling me things I didn't want to know.

'Our divorce proceedings begin tomorrow,' she continued, her tone pleasantly casual. 'I'm leaving here at once. This is sort of a farewell party for me. I just wanted you to know how fine and honorable I think you are. I'm sure things will work out wonderfully for all of us.'

My fingers dug into the arm of the chair. John Fleck leaned toward me, strumming some disturbing thing on the queer little instrument, and began to sing a native song. It might have been a love-song, or, for all I know, it might have been a chant they used in the Islands when they buried their babies alive. Whatever it was, I was revolted by it and by the smile on Doctor Fleck's lips as he sang the thing and by the hot flame in his eyes. The entire setup was somehow suggestive of a snake-charming exhibition I'd seen once. Was I being worked on by two witch-doctors? If this man hadn't been on the hospital staff and in a position to damage my standing as a student nurse, I would have told them off. I got to my feet, confused and shaking.

'I have to go. I promised to be back early.'

They protested, but I threw on my things. 'We're terribly disappointed,' Mrs. Fleck reproached me. 'We'd looked forward to a long evening with you. There are so many things to consider and I thought we could all be frank about them.'

Together they drove me back to the hospital. I was between them on the buggy seat, and her arm was around me. I was mad enough to bite her. I felt as though I had been convicted and sentenced before I'd committed a crime. Their calm assumption that they could arrange my life without consulting me made me furious.

John Fleck's arm held me close for an instant as he helped me out of the buggy. I pulled away violently, cutting short something he was whispering to me about 'tomorrow.'

All night I floundered around in my conflicting emotions. This strange man who had so fascinated me — was there anything of love in my feeling for him? And did he really love me? If he did, why had he humiliated me by leaving it to his wife to speak for him? Was it tribute to my sense of honor, her outspoken recital of their private affairs? Or, kind and seemingly honest as I had thought her, could Abbie Fleck be planning to name me in the court action to insure her own freedom? They'd been so cold-blooded about the matter — or were they only being sensible and dealing frankly with a problem? It seemed impossible that two people should be so egotistic as to believe I would meekly fall in with whatever they planned.

Round and round I went in the maelstrom of uncertainty. I was physically sick over the whole thing. I dreaded facing those burning eyes when I should go back on night duty again. When dawn came, I still didn't know whether I never wanted to see him again, or whether I wanted very much to see him.

But the problem was to be solved for me — sooner than I thought and far more drastically.

* * *

A nurse has little time for private life. The day after this incredible evening with the Flecks, I was plunged into a situation which demanded all my thoughts and energy and resourcefulness. John and Abbie Fleck had to be pushed clear out of my mind.

Isobel Jarvis had developed a virulent case of diphtheria. Since the regular County Detention Hospital was full of smallpox patients, she would have to be sent to the two-room shack used as a pesthouse, a block and a half from the County Hospital and Poor Farm, out on the edge of town. A nurse would have to be quarantined with her. The Mother Superior called for volunteers, declaring she would go herself if no one wanted to undertake it. I said I would take the case. It seemed a providential way of escape from Doctor Fleck. With daylight I had decided I didn't want to see him. He was interesting, but he made me uneasy all the time. Isobel disliked me thoroughly because she thought I'd had favors shown me in the training school, but maybe she'd get over it.

'The accommodations are a disgrace to any community,' Mother Superior told me. 'You will be shocked.'

It was noon when I reached the drab, isolated little house. An orderly had brought fresh sheets and towels and linens over from the County Hospital and hung them on the fence a few feet from the door of our shack. It had been thoroughly fumigated, but there'd been no time to clean it after the last smallpox patients left the day before. When I opened the door, the fumes of formaldehyde were so chokingly strong that I left Isobel in the carriage Mother Superior had provided for us. I'd have to get the place aired out. And cleaned out! The floor was covered with smallpox scales as large as a fingernail. The furnishings were simple. An old cook stove, a few cracked dishes, an apple-box cupboard on the wall, two cots and mattresses, a table, and a couple of chairs. No telephone. Water to be carried from a hydrant fifty feet from the door. A wire was run over the fence to the County Farm and a cowbell hung on the far end of it. When I wanted anything, I was to pull the wire and the orderly summoned by the bell would come to the fence and take the order or telephone to the doctor for me.

After I had the place in good shape and had Isobel in bed and quieted with a hypo, I made out a long list of needed supplies, summoned the orderly, and at a safe distance read him the list over the fence. He told me we were guests of the county and I might have anything I wanted in the line of food or necessities.

As I continued my scrubbing and cleaning, Isobel's temperature mounted higher and higher. Late in the afternoon, when the place was as clean as supplies and resources would permit, I sat down to rest in the open doorway. It was a pleasant enough prospect, with farm lands in the distance and a spur of low green foothills in front. As I sat watching a hawk circle high over the hill, a man came slowly up over the crest and headed down the slope toward our shack. He would walk a few steps, stumble and fall, get to his feet again and plod on, falling repeatedly. I thought he was drunk and went out to warn him away when he was a hundred feet or so from the shack. He was a small, dark man, very thin.

'Don't come here!' I shouted. 'This is a pesthouse. Diphtheria!'

But he kept on coming and waved a paper he carried in his hand. I could see his lips move, but could hear nothing of what he was trying to say. Then I saw that he was sick. By this time he was close enough for me to understand his painful speech. He said he'd been stealing a ride in a box car, but had got a very sore throat. The yard man found him and detained him until the county doctor looked him over. The doctor told him he had diphtheria and sent him to me with this note. The paper asked me to put this man, Max Something-or-other-I-couldn't-make-out, in a tent in the yard, and he, the doctor, would be out in the morning to see what had to be done.

Mentally I cursed the doctor soundly. But the poor fellow's throat was in an awful state and he was filthy dirty. I hustled him into my bed in the kitchen half of the shack and began giving him what aid I could. Both my patients were delirious before dark, and it began to look as though there would be no sleep for me. The orderly from the County Farm brought over a tent and cot and covers and put the tent up close to the shack. But since I couldn't hear Max if I put him in the tent, or couldn't hear either of my patients if I went there myself, I left him where he was and put a mattress on the floor for my own use, so that I could get a little rest between treatments.

After things were ready for the night, with a sheet tied loosely over each of my patients and fastened to the bed frame, so they couldn't climb out of bed in their delirium, I dropped down on my mattress to relax. It was the first moment I had had to think of myself. My mind was just turning back to the unfinished problem of Doctor Fleck when I was startled half out of my wits. A man appeared at the window on the hill side and started to climb into the room.

'Don't come in here!' I yelled at him. 'This is a pesthouse!'

'That's why I'm here.' He swung both legs in and sat on the sill looking at me. He was a big, rangy chap with a nice, homely face that looked as though it might have been chopped out of a solid block with an axe. He obviously was in the best of health. 'I'm sorry I startled you. I didn't dare go around to knock at the door on the other side for fear I'd be seen from the hospital. I'm Alan Jarvis — Isobel's brother. Just call me Al.'

'I thought you looked familiar. I've seen your picture daily on her dresser. But you can't ——'

'Yes, I can. I'm on vacation. I just got to town this afternoon. When I heard Isobel had been taken out to this damn place, I had a shot of serum and came out to help — without telling anyone, of course. I'm camping in a shack I found just over the hill. I'll come in at night when no one can see me, to help you. You can't handle a job like this alone day and night.'

There was a deep groan from Max's shaded cot. 'Hold 'em, boys!' he muttered. 'Hold 'em!'

I thought Al Jarvis would go through the roof. 'Jumpin' Jehu! What's that?'

I couldn't keep from laughing. I told him I was collecting patients rapidly and he'd probably be another on my hands if he stayed. But he insisted he was safe enough with that shot of antitoxin, that he had put food enough in his shanty to last a month, and that no one knew he was there but the watchman along that part of the railroad tracks.

I made coffee, and Al sat in the window to drink his. He was tall and slim and strong — all sinew and muscle. His brown hair waved back from a high forehead, and was so heavy it looked as though it were being borne up, like a helmet, by his large ears. His blue eyes could change disconcertingly from tear-filled tenderness to steely hardness. Heavy eyebrows bristled above lashes so long and curling they would have been the envy of any girl. Isobel had once told me her brother was known by the nickname of 'Old Granite.' It was certainly apt.

After he had finished his coffee, he ordered me out to the tent to sleep awhile. He said he'd take care of the patients and promised to call me if I were needed. I was tired all over and I sank down to sleep most gratefully. He didn't call, but I went in every hour or so. Isobel kept mumbling and tossing. When Al would speak to her, she seemed to know him and quieted down. But both patients grew worse. About daybreak Al brought in wood and water, emptied the garbage, and did everything he could, then took himself off over the hill before anyone should see him. Every night this was repeated.

And every morning the county doctor — he's dead now and if he has any star in his crown, it's not for anything he ever did for us! — came to stand outside the window a few minutes while I read the charts to him and reported on everything. He'd give me a little uncertain advice in a thick, stupid tongue — there was a lot of contagion around and he seemed to think he had to drink amply to hang on — and then he'd stumble out to his buggy and drive off. First he came in a car, one of the few around town. But it couldn't be trusted to get him safely home as an intelligent horse would, so he went back to the horse and buggy again.

Max was delirious only a day or two. Then we moved him out into the tent and gave him a cowbell to ring in case he wanted anything between my visits. His throat was still bad. He didn't regain his voice while he was in quarantine.

With Isobel it was different. For ten days and nights she hovered between consciousness and delirium and coma. Once I insisted the doctor bring a specialist for consultation. He did so and they agreed her case was so hopeless that all we could do was to make her as comfortable as possible. It was that day I learned Doctor Fleck was dangerously ill with pneumonia. His wife had left some time before and he was alone. I felt infinite pity for him and wished I might see him, but it was impossible, of course.

Al never failed me. We put everything we had into the fight for Isobel's life, not content to take the doctors' verdict as final. We got to know each other mighty well in those long vigils. One night, when even we had felt that the end was near, he called me about two o'clock, his voice shaking. Isobel had just awakened from the first natural sleep she had had in days and had called for me. I knew she had passed the crisis and would be getting well the moment I saw her. It was a happy night for Al and me. It was a long pull after that, but there was steady improvement. Al retired from night duty and came only to visit her after a time. His pal, Jock Gordon, was to join him soon and they were going on to Canada to homestead in the Grand Prairie country up in Alberta.

Whatever praise I had for being a good sport and doing my job 'all alone' should have been shared by self-sacrificing Al Jarvis. But his being there was a matter never discussed outside the four walls of our pesthouse.

Max and Isobel and I really enjoyed each other before the quarantine was lifted. Max, shorn of his black bristles, emerged as a personable enough man. His whispering voice gave him a secretive air, quite in keeping with the silence he maintained regarding his occupation and past activities. I wondered if possibly he had been a convict. But he was neat and helpful and made himself agreeable in small ways, we all played cards together, and I read aloud by the hour. Someone sent in a bundle of old magazines, some cheap trash, some religious tracts. I read them, anyway, cutting out parts I didn't like and substituting whole pages ad lib. for interest and dramatic effect. It was really fun.

Between times I cooked — and how we ate! The doors and windows had not been closed since we came to the shack except when I was giving baths or treatments. All of us profited by the bracing Montana air, warmed by the old cook stove.

Daily I asked about Doctor Fleck. He was in very grave condition, having had a relapse after the pneumonia had seemingly been conquered. I could imagine how he must be longing for the warmth of his South Sea Islands. But I knew he didn't want to go back alone. In our talks, I realized now, I had met his mood and understood the magic he had known. But he had not been justified in building me into the picture.

I had come more and more to compare him, with his sensitive shrinking from the difficult things of life, to Alan Jarvis. Al was something solid. He didn't yearn for a tropical isle where he could loaf around in a tobacco sack. It didn't take any particular courage for a man to sit under a tree and let coconuts drop into his lap. Al, of course, was mighty cold and hard and practical at times. He was reserved and never gave generously of himself unless emotionally stirred. Very different certainly from the dreamy, warmly impulsive doctor.

And then one morning a note came to me from Sister Sistine, who had throughout visited him daily. He was dead. The end had come the night before. He had asked her to give me his volume of Robert Louis Stevenson's poems. Before he had become unconscious he underlined in *Requiem*, 'Home is the sailor, home from the sea, And the hunter home from the hill,' and had scrawled his name. He told the Sister that if God had a morning, he would meet me at sunup there. Sister

Sistine thought he was delirious, but I knew what he meant. He had often described the glorious mornings in the Islands. Once he said, 'I hope God will make no lovelier heaven than a morning on our atoll. It would be lost on me if He did. I couldn't bear any more of beauty.'

My throat was tight for days. It seemed such a pity that a man so talented should be so wasted. I came nearer to loving John Fleck after he was dead than I ever had before. If I had time I could easily have dramatized myself in this romantic situation. But we were going out of quarantine and Doctor Seymour had a difficult case waiting for me at the hospital. There was no time to think about my own affairs, as we went back fumigated and once more safe for circulation.

For a long time after this, when I tried to sleep, my mind was a chaos of jumbled pictures, emerging and fading, of patients I had cared for. Faces of injured smelter men with bandages over their blinded eyes, children screaming with fright over painful dressings, paralyzed old Dennis slobbering in his wheelchair, the old squaw with a cough whose half-breed white daughter came to stare at her, a deathbed marriage to make legitimate seven half-grown children. And always, as these changing pictures swam before me, I was aware of John Fleck's burning eyes upon me.

The new patient Doctor Seymour had for me was a sheepherder gone loco from — well, the doctor claimed many a herder had gone crazy trying to figure out which was the width and which the length of those cotton-wadded store comforters they used in camp. At any rate, the poor devil tried to kill himself and only half-succeeded. He shot off his lower jaw and tongue and wandered around for two days before anyone found him. No nurse wanted even to go into the room. No doctor cared to take his case either. But Doctor Seymour did, and I went on twenty-four-hour duty.

'We'll make this sheepherder up with a very rosebud of a mouth before we get through with him,' Doctor Seymour told me.

And that is just what he did, with a series of operations, seventeen in all. All the skin the poor fellow could spare from his shins and an additional amount from others who donated it was used to build up that horribly shattered face. By piecing and pulling, he was at last ready to leave the hospital after sixteen weeks. His mouth was a little puckered pink hole the size of a dime, and in a case was the tube through which he would always have to take the liquid foods to which he was limited. Plastic surgery at that time was not up to the miracles of today.

As we watched him go down the hall, the doctor turned to me with a grim face. 'I hope God Almighty will forgive me for saving his life. It was a professional mistake.'

I was of the same mind.

After the ravages of diphtheria, Isobel Jarvis became the victim of exophthalmic goiter. Her heart pounded, her lovely hazel eyes took on a strained, protruding look, and frequently she was prostrated in bed. From the time she had started on the up grade in the pesthouse, she had been so grateful for my care that all her former resentment vanished, and though I was only a few years older than she, she had taken to calling me 'Ma.' I was fond of her and I still watched over her. She was able to be up and around and doing light tasks when Alan's partner, Jock Gordon, arrived. He and Al were getting their affairs wound up and preparing to leave for the homesteading venture in Alberta. Jock was a fine-looking chap and we liked him very much. He was a Boer War veteran and a bachelor who intended remaining one.

Isobel and I spent hours with the two of them, poring over yard-long lists of supplies to be carried by wagon train and sleds into the wilderness of Grand Prairie. At last the lists were as inclusive as we could figure them and Jock left to order the equipment, planning to be in Edmonton when it arrived and procure means of its transportation around Slave Lake to the Prairie.

After Al too left, Isobel was listless and depressed. Our coming graduation seemed the only interest she had.

The night of the great event came at last. We graduated in the midst of a terrible storm, with high wind, thunder, and lightning attending us. In spite of the storm, Doctor Dundeen, bent forward now and using a cane, came to present the diplomas. He made a little speech to each graduate and at the end jestingly said he hoped, since all the good Scotch doctors were married, that we would remain single. With that he went out, leaning heavily on Mrs. Dundeen's arm and his cane, but still gallantly jovial.

I think the memory of his unselfish last days gave all of us great inspiration for the rest of our lives. But strangely, when at last I held my hard-earned diploma in my hand, there were regrets in my heart as well as exultation. Something precious that I should never have again was gone out of my life.

I am still moved by the wisdom of what Doctor Dundeen told us that night. 'The most thrilling thing in life is Struggle. It is not our master. It is opportunity, teacher, priest, and friend. Without Struggle, life would bore you to death.'

* * *

Julie was a prostitute. A super-prostitute, in fact.

I'd always wondered a lot about her kind, up to the time I was sent down from the Catholic Hospital, some time after my graduation, to take charge of a quarantined house in the red-light district.

My curiosity had first been stirred as a young girl in Los Angeles. The train to the beach used to run down old Alameda Street, through a mysterious section where both sides of the thoroughfare were lined with tiny, green-shuttered brick houses. Names such as Vera and Minna were over the doors. Women with unnaturally pink-and-white complexions, looking very elegant, I thought, in their satin négligées, walked up and down, often with little dogs on leashes.

The first time we passed through this quarter, going to the beach on a picnic, I asked Mama about the houses and pretty women. She looked embarrassed. 'They're fancy women,' she replied, and changed the subject so abruptly that I knew she didn't mean to tell me more. The term meant nothing to me. I thought it charming. When at last, as I grew older, it dawned upon me what their business really was, I was shocked, but consumed with curiosity. What would be in the mind of a girl to make her choose this self-isolated, red-lettered way of making a living — a way so abhorrent to the majority of women?

I had no way of knowing until I cared for sick prostitutes in the hospital from time to time. There was Margaret, the morphine addict. She came to take the 'cure' because she had an aged mother to support, and said she was losing business on account of the habit. Clarabel had the unmentionable infection. In those days even nurses whispered and made signs over venereal disease. Clarabel herself would have been profoundly shocked to stand below such a sign as may now be seen in any city in the land, and see young fellows, clean-looking and well-bred, file into clinics in broad daylight for treatment. This girl was ashamed and humiliated beyond words, not for the way she made her living — she insisted what she did wasn't half as nasty as what nurses had to do! — nor for the manner of getting the infection. It was the fact of her having it that was so disgraceful. And there was Constance. She didn't weigh ninety pounds when she came in for a tonsillectomy. She said she'd be seen in hell before she'd work as we nurses did.

My big chance to get close to the matter came when an epidemic of measles broke out in the red-light district and I was sent down to take charge of one of the quarantined houses. Now at last maybe I'd get the answer.

Doctor Grant, the Health Officer, came to take me, all antiseptically pure in my stiff white uniform, and deliver me to the Minnas and Veras. I'd never been down in the district before. It consisted largely of saloons and boarding and rooming houses, which were said to be always well filled with smelter workers, miners in town for week-ends, laborers and single men. Remembering the Alameda Street little brick houses with green shutters, I was a bit surprised when we drew up in front of what appeared to be an old boarding house, weather-beaten but respectable-looking. It had a long, wide porch flush with the sidewalk. Old apple trees, low-limbed and gnarled, grew in the vacant lots on either side of it. Across the street was a plot evidently intended as a park. Winter-killed trees rose gaunt and dry among the live ones. Dilapidated benches stood on the neglected grass, every one of them near the stage of collapse.

We got out and crossed the porch. The place looked deserted, but I noticed a window curtain twitched. The long hall we entered had closed doors on either side. On the doors, in shining metal holders, were white cards bearing the names of the girls I was to know. Close to the entrance on one side, stairs ran to the second floor. On the other, an archway led into a large parlor. At a glance it looked like any other parlor one might find in a well-to-do home. Two girls in négligées played cards at one of the tables. They didn't even look up. At one end of the corridor a large woman appeared, but stood without speaking.

'Hello, Madame,' the doctor called. 'Here's your nurse.'

There was only an unintelligible grunt in response. Then in a rasping voice she called, 'Sadie! Here!' and vanished into the hinterland.

A thin, scrawny Negress, evidently Sadie, shuffled out and dragged wearily toward us. Her kinky hair was covered by a pink net and her sepia cheeks were highly painted. She looked as though sheer inertia might have driven her out of the prostitute game. Without a word she took my bags and shuffled off.

'Madame's pretty sore about the quarantine.' The doctor chuckled. 'You may not see her for a while, but she'll come around all right. But come on. I'm in a hurry. I'll introduce you to your patients. Luckily they're all in adjoining rooms at the end of the hall.'

We went down the corridor and he opened a door labeled Ragna. Cerise curtains of most violent hue, magazine covers tacked to the walls, several huge advertising calendars, a dresser scarf of electric blue paper — badly stained — these I saw at the first sweeping glance, before the sleeping patient woke and turned over. A round, roly-poly peasant face looked up at me, as free from any mark of infamy as my own, I swear. An ignorant child with a mind too simple to cope with her problems, doubtless. She blinked at me, smiled, and shut her eyes again, too sleepy to be interested.

We moved on to the next. Vivian. The door opened on incredible untidiness. Trashy magazines were piled on every available space and slid on the floor from the tumbled bed. Messy boxes of candy, partially nibbled, were on windowsills, on the table, and under the bed. Vivian was sitting up in bed in a pink satin nightgown which accentuated her frowsy hair and the mass of measles eruption on her face. She was coarse and sullen-looking. I told her I'd be back in a few minutes to put wet compresses on her eyes, and went on with the doctor to the last door.

Julie. The rooms had all been exactly alike originally, with bed, two chairs, small table, dresser, stand, and carpet. Each had a little dressing alcove with running water in it. But how unlike they had become! From the highest to the lowest, from the cultured to the illiterate, let any woman occupy a room for an hour and she will stamp it with her individuality. The air in Julie's room was fresh and there were well-arranged flowers on the table. It had elegance of a sort, with its quiet-toned curtains, books with really beautiful bindings, and two good water-color landscapes. One thing, however, I could see at a glance the girls all had in common: the silk and satin négligées and dressers loaded with silver and cut-glass toilet articles more extravagant than any I had ever seen.

Julie had been crying, but even with her dark eyes red and swollen, she was beautiful. The quality of her was unmistakable. She had not yet broken out and the fine cameo of her face was ivory white. The hair which fell back from her forehead straight and smooth was almost blue-black. Her throat and shoulders were as perfectly molded as the lovely face. I remembered what the doctor had told me on the way down. 'Take good care of that girl Julie. Just to look at her is worth ten dollars.' She acknowledged the introduction with only a faint smile and said nothing.

'Well, these are your patients,' said Doctor Grant. He gave me a few instructions and said he must be off. 'You're monarch of all you survey now.' He grinned at me. 'Good luck.'

I needed it, quarantined as I was in a house of ill fame and as unwelcome as the measles themselves. I knew from the way this girl acted she wanted me to get out. She insisted she wanted nothing but to sleep. The others really needed me more, so I told her I'd see to them first. I returned to Ragna. She was awake this time and seemed delighted to see me. She evidently thought her presence in such a house needed explanation, so began pouring out her story to me the moment I entered.

She had come to America from Sweden in answer to an advertisement in a newspaper. It said that a well-to-do Swedish rancher wanted a wife of his nationality. Ragna said she denied herself in every way to save money earned in the harvest fields, to pay passage to America. Then she ran away from the grandparents who had raised her, confident that she was going to be a wealthy rancher's great lady. She arrived in the United States with very little money and could never find her man. And now she was struggling to save fare back. 'Sweethearts' seemed to be Ragna's undoing. She was too susceptible to flattery and made so many loans that were never repaid that she could save nothing. With her broken English and phrases in her native tongue, it was a richly told tale and would have been amusing if it hadn't been so pathetic.

When I made her as comfortable as possible, I went to help Vivian. She looked more hopelessly repulsive than ever, but she was quite the lady when I went in. I straightened her room and kept changing the moist dressings on her badly inflamed eyes. Suddenly she sat up in bed, hurled the compress on the floor, and yelled at me.

'Hey, you! Hand me that cigarette case!'

I handed her a cigarette from the case and lit a match. She hesitated a moment, whimpering a little.

Then she began puffing and between puffs flung at me, 'I suppose you teach a Sunday-School class and read your

Bible every day. But hell! Can you find a single word in it against smoking a cigarette? You look down your nose at us because of our business, but ——'

She gulped and tears ran down from her swollen eyes. She was a sight as she sat there, hair on end and face a mass of eruptions. I reached out and took one of her hot, pudgy hands in mine. Bewildered, she tried to pull away, but I held it tightly. I couldn't help laughing. Then, as though we were playing the old childish game, she laid her free hand on top of mine and laughed with me.

'What's going on here?' The door snapped open, and there, glaring at us, stood a woman who must be the Madame.

She was big and tightly corseted. Her vast bosom was so pushed up that her triple chins rested upon it. In fact she appeared to be a series of steadily augmented chins clear down to her knees. She looked mad enough to fight. Her yellow hair, coarse and frizzled, bristled around her face above small, light blue eyes. But there was betraying softness in that face. It wouldn't have been hard to imagine her crooning a lullaby to a baby against her breast.

'Shut up, you!' She glowered at Vivian. Then turned on me. 'What's all this racket? I told them to send me a refined nurse.'

'Refined? Maybe you wouldn't know.' I grinned back at her. She gaped in astonishment, then put her puffy hands on her hips, leaned back, and shook all over as she laughed with us.

'Well, you'll make out here!' She turned and waddled off down the hall like some monstrous duck. 'Dinner'll be ready soon,' she called back. There was a lingering attar of gin, perfume, and sauerkraut in her wake.

When I went back to Julie she'd been crying again. I sat down beside her to take her pulse and temperature. 'Don't worry,' I told her. 'You're not very sick, and measles don't leave marks. You'll be as good as new when it's over.'

'What if I am?' There was no lightening of her gloom. 'I'm stuck here until this quarantine is lifted. And not a penny coming in.'

It shocked me that money mattered so much to her. 'Try to relax. A vacation won't hurt you.' I wanted to ask her why she was in such rotten business, but held my tongue. After all, I was not a missionary, but a nurse. I made her as comfortable as possible, all the while wondering about my bags. I hadn't seen where the darky put them. No one had shown me where I was to sleep or bathe or eat. I'd forgotten to mention it to the Madame. I'd find out at dinner.

Sadie, the Negress, came in just then to tell me I could serve my patients' trays if I wished, as the food was ready. She escorted me down to the kitchen, a big, old-fashioned room, poorly lighted and none too clean. She said their cook had run away when the first measles case developed, to keep from being quarantined.

'I ain't much of a hand at cookin' since I's al'us done chambermaidin'. But de girls help out. Miss Chérie, dat French one, she kin sho season vittles tasty. Kin you cook, Mis' Hughes?'

'Order some chickens and I'll make dumplings one of these days. They're my specialty.'

'Umm-m-UMM!' Her eyes rolled delightedly. 'My mouf's waterin' right now.'

The dining room was beyond the parlor and a pleasant enough place. There were bottles of beer and light wine on the table, with glasses at each place. The table was sketchily set, the cloth was spotted, and a tall vase of wilting carnations in scummy water did nothing to enhance the effect, but sloppy old Sadie's food was good. She waited on the table, never speeding up her weary shuffle.

The eight drooping girls around the table were obviously exasperated with the quarantine and made no effort to be gracious to me. There was a fat, sloppy, uncorseted one next to me, round-faced and wide of mouth, whom they called Marie. She oozed laziness from every pore and had an air of utter physical comfortableness. You knew she wouldn't be choosey. Come drunk, come sober, it would be all the same to her.

Directly across from me was Eva, a neat-looking person

who might have been a school-teacher. How in Heaven's name she'd strayed in here I couldn't make out. Then there was one called Babe, so small and elfin she seemed almost a dwarf. She was blond, clear-skinned, and very pretty. And in her eyes was the unmistakable 'Come-hither' look. One Junoesque creature they called Lillian Russell, because she got herself up to look like the famous actress. At the end of the table was Chérie, a French hussy, wicked as brimstone. She was quick and dark and talked in a most theatrical manner, shrugging and gesturing, raising her eyebrows and half-closing her eyes. I was sure she sinned for the love of it. Before long, I thought, unfolding my napkin, I'll know a lot of answers.

The Madame introduced me when the last one had come in. 'Girls, this is Mrs. Hughes, the nurse. You better treat her right. If some of the rest of you come down, she might leave you with a few pox marks.' There was a twinkle in her eye.

'By golly,' I said to myself, 'I don't respect this old gal, but I like her.'

The girls saw no humor in her warning. I could feel the antagonism of their attitude toward me. I was from a Catholic hospital. It smacked of religious intolerance and self-righteousness.

As I cut into my steak, the fat, sloppy girl next to me drawled out, 'Gawd Almighty! You must suffer with all them stays on you. You're stiff as a board.'

'Lady,' I smiled at her genially, 'I never wore a corset in my life. Feel my ribs.'

She did. She pinched up a handful of flesh between her thumb and forefinger so hard that I was black and blue for days. I wouldn't give her the satisfaction of knowing how it hurt. But I hoped she'd come down with the measles. The Madame saw how things were going.

'Marie,' she said, 'a couple of corsets would sure improve your looks. You rake yours out of the closet and put them on the next time we eat.'

It was an absolutely frozen atmosphere. The girls passed

me the food, but no one talked, and it was depressingly stiff and strained. Heavens! I thought. I have to live with these women, possibly for weeks. I'll get indigestion if meals are to be like this. I'll have to break the ice somehow.

Just at this point Madame lifted a glass to me. 'Here's to you. I hope you don't mind if we drink. I'm not offering you any liquor, as I know you'd be insulted.'

'I certainly would if you offered me anything that tame!' I laughed back at her. 'I had my appetite whetted for something stronger.'

She gaped at me in astonishment. Then malicious relish lighted her piggy little eyes. 'Whiskey and soda,' she called to Sadie, who was shuffling through the swinging door. A quick stir of interest ran around the table. I felt the question in the mind of every girl there. Sadie brought the bottles from the sideboard and looked at me inquiringly as she stood ready to pour.

I was never affected by liquor in moderation except on an empty stomach, and now it was empty. What if the stuff should go to my head? I'd have to risk it, for this was necessity.

'Three fingers,' I said casually. 'Neat.'

Stunned silence held the table as I smacked it down. 'Lord!' I exclaimed. 'That's good stuff.'

The change in the girls was immediate. The atmosphere cleared and they talked and laughed and began asking me questions about the hospital and nurses — where we slept and what we ate and what all we had to do. Dinner was really a pleasant meal. The whiskey didn't affect me at all, fortunately. They offered me more, but I told them it was strictly against the rules for me to drink while on a case, so I'd have to deny myself the rest of the time.

When we got up from the table, the Madame told me to come to her room as soon as I was through seeing to my patients. 'I'm the third door from the end, across the hall from Ragna.'

'I don't know yet where my room is,' I ventured hopefully.

'I'll show you when you come down,' she replied.

MONTANA

It was about an hour later that I knocked at Madame's door. I was tired and anxious to be alone and unpack things. My three utterly different patients were a real problem. Ragna had talked such a blue streak I wanted to gag her. Vivian had indulged in an ugly display of temper and refused to have compresses on her eyes. Julie was crying silently, despairingly, too sick and unhappy to try to conceal it from me any longer. I hoped to escape from the Madame in short order.

'Come in!' she yelled in response to my knock.

I walked into a big room, the like of which I know I shall never in a lifetime see again. Rich, deep-piled carpet covered the floor. The draperies were cheap and ornate. Colossal mirrors that must have cost a fortune hung where they seemed to serve no purpose. The Madame told me later they were from a dismantled saloon. There were two ornate brass beds, several heavy chairs upholstered in poisonous greens and blues, and two big dressers.

On the wall above one bed hung a spirited drawing of a bucking bronco and rider by Montana's cowboy artist, Charlie Russell. It was an original. Above the other hung a gaudy chromo of the Christ of the Bleeding Heart, and beneath it was an elaborately carved crucifix. My incredulous gaze moved from one to another of six statuettes of the Virgin, some bronze, some ivory, and one exquisite marble one with the Child.

The Madame smiled at my too apparent astonishment. 'Pretty classy, ain't it? That there picture of Charlie's now — I bought that for twelve dollars when I was a bit tiddley and not myself. Last week I was offered fifty for it. And now, look —!'

She piloted me to a deep closet where masculine suits and clothing had been pushed down the rod, leaving a wide vacant space. My luggage sat on the floor. 'You can hang your things here. George — he's my man — can't come here on account of this damn quarantine, so I thought you might as well sleep in his bed. We can have a nice chummy time of it together.'

I stared at her, for a moment so mad I couldn't speak. I'd slept on army cots, on the floor, and in many crowded and unwholesome places in the line of duty, but to sleep in a Madame's room in her man's bed, enduring a 'nice chummy time' — this topped everything! In another moment I would have undoubtedly exploded, but suddenly it was just funny. And it was the chance of a lifetime to get at some of the things I wanted to know.

'It's mighty nice of you to share your room with me,' I said, and began to unpack.

A few photographs in fancy frames stood on the dressers. One I recognized as George — I'd never known his other name — the wholesale butcher who came to the hospital periodically to contract for our meat supply. I had always supposed him an exemplary citizen and was frankly shocked.

Madame followed my gaze and smiled proudly. 'You know George, of course. You now, with all your notions, you'd never suspect it was me made a man of George. He was just a drunken bum, but about seven years ago I reformed him. Then I loaned him money to begin buyin' beef on the hoof instead of standin' behind a counter and sellin' it by the pound, with the other feller gettin' all the velveteen. And now he's got four markets of his own. He'll marry a nice girl some day.'

'Why don't you marry him yourself if he's your man?'

'Me —? Marry him? Say, he's eleven years younger'n me. Look ——' She reached up and lifted the frowzy hair clear away from her forehead. I stared at the 'transformation' and the head beneath it. Her pate was bald as her knee. 'And I ain't the marryin' kind. I was married once, but I couldn't put up with no man who slept in his sweaty underwear. No, I got a mission in life. I got a work to do. George and me couldn't mix meat and philanthrope.' (She put a heavy accent on the third syllable.)

She gave me a quizzical look and I smiled at her. I was having fun.

'Set there.' She pointed to a big plush chair when I finished hanging up things and had deposited my toilet articles in the top drawer of George's dresser. 'Smoke?' She held out a package of cigarettes to me.

'No, thanks. I haven't taken time yet to learn.'

She loosened her shoestrings and began telling me of her mission in life. She called her way of making a living a profession and said it took lots of experience and good horse sense to run it.

'You pious folks take hospitals and prisons and insane asylums for granted,' she said, 'but you won't admit there's need for houses like mine. Say —! A tough town like this, with the smelter and all —! You'd be havin' women and girls assaulted every day if it wasn't for women like me bein' interested enough in public welfare to save 'em from it. You'll find out, if the church people and W.C.T.U. and reformers ever get the law on this place like they have on some!' She inhaled deeply and blew twin streams of smoke vigorously through those knothole nostrils of hers. 'My, my! What a scandal there'd be if they hit it just right!' She laughed uproariously. 'Some of these she-pillars of society wouldn't talk so smart if they saw their husbands and brothers and sons and a lot of their pet politicians runnin' out of here with their pants off and their shirttails flappin' in the wind behind 'em!'

I agreed it might be embarrassing.

'Well, I'm not worryin' about it.' She pointed to the marble statue of the Virgin and Child which shared table space with a case of poker chips, a decanter and glasses. 'She'll protect me. I haven't missed a Sunday's Mass in ten years until this quarantine. Listen — I give to every charity in this town and I'm supportin' and educatin' three orphans. Which is a lot more than most of these holier-than-thou bitches can say. Come right down to it, a lot of them's kept women — only worse — takin' all they can from their men, but too selfish to give anything in return. If they only knowed it, they're a big help to our business.'

She rambled on, telling me of the different girls in the place. But she was crafty, this old dame. Nothing that would build her up as a public benefactress was left out. I asked her about Eva, the school-teacherish one.

'Say, Eva could have been a schoolma'am all right. She's smart. She reads all the time and can talk politics or the price of farm products or new books and plays with the best of 'em. She's got principles and no one's goin' to shake her. Once before election she threw out one of her best customers because he said he was goin' to vote against her ticket. But she can drink more liquor than any three girls in the house. And the more she drinks, the more of a lady she acts.'

'Chérie interests me. She looks dangerous.'

'Right you are. Don't ever get her down on you. But I like her fine. She's lively and's been around a lot. She'd have went far on the stage as a dancer, but her feet give out on her. Say, you should see her do some fancy numbers when she's in the mood. She was in dance halls for a while, but that was still too hard on her feet, so she had to make her livin' some other way than with them.'

'And what about Julie?'

'Julie now, bless her heart, her old man was a preacher. He thought to dance and play cards was to go to hell in a handbasket. So, see, she runs away. I come across her walkin' the streets — I'm always lookin' for some girl I can help — so I brings her here. And see what I done for her. I makes a Super out of her.'

'What's a Super?'

'Well, she's somethin' special — looks, eddication, and all the rest.' Madame lit a fourth cigarette. 'She don't have to take the rank and file. She makes dates with gents who can pay big in advance to keep a certain night for them, sometimes for months. Then if they don't show up, she has her pay anyway.'

'Do you run the business on a percentage basis?'

'The girls in this house — except Julie — pay me for room and board and a per cent of what they make. There's no big money in it like folks think, except for a Super. Julie pays me a flat tidy sum by the month. Now there's Marie. She never makes more than enough to pay her board. I'd turn her out on the street in a minute, if she wouldn't starve to death. But Babe, now ——'

There was a tapping on the window close to Madame. She raised the blind and revealed the beaming face of George. His arms were full of flowers and what proved to be a three-foot string of sausages. I pretended I hadn't recognized him and left to see if I could do anything for Julie.

The girl was sitting up in bed, forlorn and brooding. 'Hello.' She unbent a little, taken off guard. 'I thought Madame Tiny had you corraled for the evening.'

'Madame Tiny?' I couldn't help laughing. 'Highly descriptive. The woman must weigh at least three hundred.'

'Well, that's not as bad as the name she calls her friend George. His name is Porter, which she twists to "Porkie" — "Wee Porkie," when she's being affectionate.'

'Julie, do all you girls have sweethearts, or whatever you call your own special men friends?'

'Of course. That's natural, isn't it? The difference is, you girls can pick and choose and marry your man. But you're not all so virtuous. I've found that out from husbands. A lot of you just marry for support.' She looked at me defiantly. 'We girls know we can't marry the ideal man who visits us, but every human being wants companionship. And to feel worth while and important in someone's life.'

'No wonder you feel blue sometimes, Julie,' I said by way of a lead. She seemed so burdened by trouble that I thought if I could inspire her confidence she might talk to me. I liked her and sincerely wanted to help.

'Oh, I have no sweetheart. But I'll tell you something you won't believe. It's true, though. I met a man whose wife was in an insane asylum back East. For more than a year he spent every Sunday night up to midnight with me, talking, reading, playing cards — nothing more. And he gave me three five-dollar gold pieces for every date — now don't laugh! — for being a companion to him and seeing to it that he remained faithful to his wife!'

'Faithful —? But Julie, why would a man come to such a place as this in the first place if he wanted nothing more? Hadn't he any friends or club?'

'I sort of trapped him in the first place, though I didn't

mean to. I'd gone for a walk and I was on the bank of the river below town, standing watching the water and feeling pretty lonely. He came walking along slowly with his head down, as though he'd been hard hit with some grief. He glanced up and saw me. I smiled and he hesitated. Then I spoke to him and we talked. We walked a long way on down the river and it was cold and I began to shiver. Then he asked if he might walk home with me. So he did and I invited him in and he came. I'm sure he didn't have any idea where he was going until he got to the very door of this house.'

'Did his wife recover?'

'No, she died that year. And he quit coming. He had insisted he wanted to marry me, but ——' Julie shrugged.

I laid my hand on hers. 'I know, Julie. It's the double standard — old as civilization. A man can do what he will, but ——'

'But no man wants a wife who'd be pointed out as having been on the Row,' she finished. 'Who'd blame him?'

'Were you interested, Julie?'

'I missed him. I ——' She broke off, her eyes bitter. 'But no man can give me what I want. Only the means to it.'

I waited, hoping she'd go on. But she changed the subject. I wondered if I'd ever know the truth concerning this girl. She interested me tremendously. Something deep within was consuming her. I spoke of it to Madame that night when I went back.

'Julie's a mystery to me,' she admitted. 'She's always been standoffish and not very friendly. She won't tell you anything about herself. She was in a bad way when I found her and I told her she ought to go home if she had one, so that's when she told me her pa was a preacher and she couldn't. So I offered her a place with me. She said she wanted to earn a lot of money and I knew she could. But I'll say for her, if anyone's sick or in trouble, Julie's the first one there to help. I know something's eatin' her all right, but I can't figure her out. Maybe she's homesick. I ain't never got over bein' homesick for my folks. They was always good to me when they was sober.'

MONTANA

Far into the night the Madame talked. She was used to sleeping late and didn't realize a nurse's day began very early. As I finally dozed off, she was holding forth at great length on what a wonderful opportunity it was for girls to be in a house such as hers.

'It's high class, this place is. Lots of tone. No riff-raff comin' here, you betcha . . . Real gents . . . Cream of the trade . . . You'd never find nicer girls nowheres, and me just like a mother to 'em . . .'

George's bed was comfortable and the bedding immaculate. I slept well my first night in a house of prostitution.

As I look back on it now, I wonder why the paint and powder of that day looked so wicked. The make-up of a prostitute, put on then to advertise their business — rouge, hoop earrings, elaborate curls, and loud costume jewelry — is so identical with that of today's nice girls. I found out later that as a usual thing, when any of the girls went to the stores or over to Butte to shop, they were modestly dressed and well-mannered. Even the old Madame herself looked like a respectable housewife. I met her once long afterward in front of a market. I spoke to her cordially, but she gave me only a cold stare. When she had a chance, unobserved, she whispered out of the corner of her mouth, 'You shouldn't know me on the street. You gotta reputation as a nurse. You'd better keep it wrapped in a cotton bat.'

It was a strange period I put in down there. Without men as the house was, it seemed little different from a women's boarding house. Seeing the girls as I did, it was hard to believe they were all 'bad women.' Most of them drank and smoked, though not to excess. They read trash and told shockingly risqué stories, but that could be said of many nurses also, Heaven knows. No, they were just girls. Some sweet, some, from their point of view, justified, some ashamed, some pathetic, some brazen.

They spent a great deal of time in their own rooms making themselves beautiful. They knitted and sewed and did fancy work and wrote long letters to families who little suspected the life they were leading. They'd dress in their best and go out and walk up and down on the porch at the time when men were most on the street. 'Lillian Russell,' in a big plumed hat, would go out and sing to attract notice. Her voice was really good. It irked the girls sadly to see the rival houses on either side gathering in trade which they felt was rightly their own. It seemed to me incredible at times that these girls could be making their living as they were, off the butcher, the baker, the candlestick-maker, the doctor, the lawyer, the banker, and if not the minister, the minister's son — judging from the tales they told.

I speculated often on the position of several prominent town women, all of the sanctimonious sort who would gladly have pinned the Scarlet Letter on the bosom of any one of these girls and pilloried her in the market-place. What domestic upheavals there would be in their highly respectable homes if they knew of their men what the whores knew!

No new cases of measles developed and the mild epidemic subsided long before it was time for the quarantine to be lifted. My patients were soon up and around. Ragna had attached herself to me with a puppy-like devotion. When she talked to me longingly of the Old Country, I begged her to quit the life and buy a ticket to home and decency. Her eyes would fill with tears when I spoke of it. But I knew she would never go back.

Vivian had no desire for anything else. She was lazy and not too bright, and to her it was an ideal occupation.

With Julie, except for that first day when I caught her in tears, there was stony calm that I felt was not of the spirit, but from sternly controlled nerves. She made not a single reference to anything in her past. She had put up a wall sky-high between us by something she said about her way of living one day. She was having trouble with her eyes, which were badly inflamed, and I had been reading to her. Suddenly she turned to me.

'Mrs. Hughes, I know you're always wondering why I am in this sort of life. It's that ——' She hesitated. I had a feeling she changed her mind about what she had meant to say. 'I need money. Lots of money. This is the only way I know to make it.' Her dark eyes were defiant.

'Does money compensate for everything you're losing?' I demanded. 'Look here, Julie, your father was a minister, the Madame told me. You've had good bringing-up, so I know this thing is against all your better instincts. Couldn't you —?'

'No, I couldn't! I chose this life deliberately, with my eyes wide open. I know what you're going to say about disgrace and disease and all the rest, so don't say it. This is my affair, not yours.'

'Sorry, Julie,' I said. 'I didn't mean to intrude. After all, "Am I my brother's keeper"?'

Something unfathomable flashed up in her eyes. But she changed the subject.

To keep a restless house of girls interested, we planned parties and games and skits of all sorts. I was surprised at the talent uncovered. Some of the girls sang, some played musical instruments of different sorts. The French hussy was a really beautiful dancer and fascinated us with her half-stripped performances. The sepia-toned Sadie's inertia vanished utterly when she heard music. She did astounding dances that years later were to become a vogue in society ballrooms. It was my first glimpse of a jitterbug.

The old Madame got more and more irate over the situation. She'd tap time to the music with a puffy foot and grumble, 'You'll pay for this slump in business, dearies, and don't forget it!' But her attitude toward me was friendly. I think she had convinced herself that I looked upon her as a public benefactress.

Julie seldom joined in the festivities. Her eyes bothered her, she said, but I knew she spent most of her time reading. There was an attitude of antagonism in her, but I had a feeling it was not directed at me personally.

'Why don't I have wisdom to do something for this girl?' I woke one day full of frustrated exasperation. 'If I don't, maybe nobody ever will. Surely, before this quarantine is lifted, I'll get closer to her.'

But that very night when Doctor Grant came, he put an end to any hope. 'This place will be quarantined for a while yet, Mrs. Hughes, but there's no need of your staying longer. I don't expect any more cases to develop. I need you more on another case and the hospital said I could have you. So pack your things and I'll be back about ten to get you.'

'You mean — I'm to leave tonight?' He'd think me crazy if he knew how little I wanted to leave. I felt utterly defeated as I went to Madame's room to pack. Surely this had been the opportunity of a lifetime, and I hadn't even come within grasping distance of it. I hadn't hoped to reform the place, but I had thought I might be able to put a dent in it somewhere.

The Madame was smoking, corsets off, her flabby bulk filling the armchair to overflowing. 'Leaving, are you?' Her crafty little eyes looked at me wickedly. 'Better stay. I'll give you a job.' She thought it a good joke. So did I. 'It's a damn good thing you're going, Hughsie. You'd wreck my business if you was turned loose on this house.' She grinned at me amiably.

I grinned back. 'If I were, I'd do my damnedest!'

As though by magic the word of my leaving went around the house. Before I had my uniforms off the hangers beside George's clothes, the girls began coming in with gifts. Never have I had such a shower. Silver-backed mirrors, combs and brushes, cut-glass bottles of perfume — all sorts of toilet articles. Several pairs of silk stockings — the first I'd ever owned — underwear too beautiful for words, a négligée of old rose satin, two pairs of satin slippers. From Madame a bottle each of gin and brandy, and a bottle of liquid rouge from Chérie, the sultry-eyed French girl.

'I like you vairee mooch,' she informed me. 'You are — what you say? — ze good sport. But ze chic — non! Zis rouge, it will make you mooch easiaire on ze eye.'

I might say here that it was the only vice I picked up in the Red-Light District. Ragna added to her gifts a very handsome suitcase in which to pack the things.

Only Julie hadn't appeared. Probably she'd been reading

and hadn't heard. I still had a half-hour or so before the doctor would call for me. I left the others and went to knock at her door. Sitting there in the lamplight as I entered, her deceptively pure, chaste beauty caught at me achingly. She had had a very light attack of measles and her skin was again faultlessly clear.

I closed the door and stood leaning against it as she looked at me inquiringly over her book. 'The doctor says you girls don't need me any more, so he's coming for me in about half an hour. I ——'

'You're going away?' She stared at me. I felt a bit sick at sight of the obvious relief which leaped into her eyes. 'Well, I expect you'll be glad to get out of this den of iniquity.'

'No, Julie, I won't.' I walked over and laid my hand on hers. 'All the rest of my life I'm going to be thinking of you. And the thoughts won't be pleasant ones. You see, Julie, I really love you, and ——'

'Oh, God, don't!' The girl's lips went white. In her face was soul-hunger more desolate than I had ever seen. And then she crumpled down over the table, her hand clinging to mine in desperation.

I touched her sleek head caressingly with my free hand. 'Come away with me, Julie. I'll help you get work. Money surely can't mean so much that ——'

'You don't understand, of course.' She sat up, dry-eyed, her face so stricken that tears blinded me to see it. 'You've always taken for granted I wanted money for myself. No one knows except the doctor and the Sisters who took care of me — a lawyer knew too — but I have twin boys, four years old now. The money's for them. I *have* to have it! I can't ——'

'But Julie —! You poor child! This will wreck their lives when they know. Surely your father and mother would help you.'

'My mother died when I was a baby. My father puts the church before everything else. You don't know what a Vermont minister can be. I'm not going to ruin his life by letting him know. I haven't any other relatives. You see, I was never allowed to do anything other girls did — dance, go out with boys. I got to hating school because I was left out of things. I wanted to be a stenographer, but my father wouldn't hear to it. No girl could be virtuous working in an office with men! Finally I ran away and went to New York. I got a job as chambermaid in a hotel.'

My hand ached under Julie's clutching fingers.

'I didn't know anything. I got into trouble. I thought he loved me and was going to marry me. But when he knew, he only laughed. He was already married. I came to Montana to get clear away from anyone who might know me. Finally I got another chambermaid job, but it was in a cheap hotel with poor pay and few tips. I couldn't save enough to take me to a hospital. When my time came, I went in as a charity patient. And had twins!'

Julie laughed hysterically. 'Wouldn't you know that would happen to me? I could imagine my father, grim as he always was, saying, "Whatsoever ye sow, that shall ye also reap." The Sisters told me the babies could be kept in the orphanage until they were adopted. They thought I was crazy when I told them I'd never give them up. I'd leave them there only until I got work and could take care of them myself. If you could only have seen them, Mrs. Hughes! Such fine healthy, beautiful babies. I nursed them for three weeks and loved them so terribly. And now —— Here, I'll show you their pictures.'

She drew a box out of her dresser drawer, opened it and spread on the table snapshots and photographs of two baby boys, from infancy to their present age.

'These are the last ones, on their fourth birthday. I go up to Helena to see them once a month. That's why I was so upset the day you came. I'd expected to be with them. Doctor Morgan, who took care of me there at the hospital, says they're the finest twins he ever delivered. He and the lawyer have done so much for my babies. They're grand men. The doctor begged me to let him adopt the babies. He said he'd give them everything. But they're all I have to love.

I'll be a good mother to them some day, Mrs. Hughes. One year more will do it — just twelve months, and then —!'

'But Julie —! It's appalling for you to go on. Quit now and take your children. They need you.'

There was stark hunger in her eyes. But no yielding. 'I can't, I tell you! Not yet. I'm never coming back to this, once I get them. So I must have enough money to be safe till I get started. I know you are horrified, but I don't want to leave them to work out. I tried that before I came here and I can't earn enough. I've been cheated long enough. I'm going to be with them every minute to make up for lost time. I was absolutely desperate when I met the Madame. She's a shrewd old devil and sized me up at a glance. She was decent enough to urge me to go home to my family, but when she knew how things were — I didn't tell her about the babies, though — she made me a proposition that promised so much I couldn't turn it down under the circumstances. So I left my babies there — and here I am.'

'You're taking a terrible risk. Suppose you contract disease sometime these next twelve months? Julie, how can you look at those precious little boys one minute and give yourself to such degradation the next?'

'It's only my body I give! Don't you understand? *I'm* not touched with this thing. Is a man's heart defiled because he must work in sewers? I hate everything about this life, but it's a means to an end. And the end justifies everything. As long as I was going to be a prostitute, I've made an art of being a Super one. I *had* to get money. Don't you see?'

'But Julie, doesn't the good opinion of people mean anything to you? That doctor who's so helpful with the children, and the lawyer — don't you want fine men like those to respect you?'

A strangely wistful smile touched her lips. 'They are my best clients — those two. They come down often to see me. They know why I'm here and what I'm saving for. They pay me twenty-five dollars for each visit. And they send their rich friends to me. I think maybe they've hinted to them about the boys, because they all pay far more than is expected — and for many visits they never make. That's why I've been able to save as I have.'

I was absolutely deflated. It was a mad world, with honor and decency and mother-love and human kindness all mixed up with things dishonorable and indecent. As I groped for words, a sharp knock came on the door.

'The Doc's here, Mis' Hughes.' It was Sadie's drawl. 'He say, is you ready?'

'Coming. Good-bye, Julie.' I held her close and she clung to me.

'Please forgive me if I've acted ungrateful.' Her voice broke. 'You've been wonderful. Being with you — makes me ashamed. And I can't afford to be. Only one more year —— Mrs. Hughes, I'm going to make this town respect me yet! I'm going to make good. Please believe it!'

I believed it. Even that moment, before the years proved it fact. I kissed her swiftly and fled. I couldn't trust myself just then.

'You've acquired a mountain of luggage, seems to me,' Doctor Grant said, as I joined him. 'Think it will get by the customs officer?'

I laughed, imagining Mother Superior's cold survey of some of those seductive underthings. I looked over all the assembled girls with a lump in my throat. I needed my handkerchief, and realized I'd left my handbag in Julie's room.

'Be back in a minute. I forgot something.'

I hurried down the hall. Julie's door was closed, but not latched. I knocked and pushed it open at the same time. And stopped on the threshold. Beside that bed of infamy, her face buried in the counterpane and her hands clasped tensely before her, Julie knelt in prayer. She had not heard my knock. My bag lay on the table halfway across the room. If I could only get it without her knowing —— Some word of mine then had taken root after all —— A board squeaked under my tiptoeing.

Julie whirled around, still on her knees. I expected tears, but her face was stony calm and in her eyes was tired resignation.

'I'm sorry, Julie. My bag ——'

'I know what you're thinking.' She got up slowly. 'But you're wrong. I'm not asking to be forgiven.'

'Then what in Heaven's name are you praying for?'

All the rest of my life I was to speculate on her reply. Her eyes met mine levelly. 'I'm praying for what I've always prayed for in this house. Business!'

* * *

I nursed at the Catholic Hospital six months or so after my graduation, then decided to go back to Riverton and live at home with my family. They had rented the ranch and moved into a big house Father had built in town. He was making a good thing of his building just then. Between cases I could enjoy them — and enjoy lolling in bed being as lazy as I wished. There were several hospitals there and I knew I'd always have work if I wanted it.

One morning after a fifteen-hour sleep — I'd been on a twenty-four-hour a day case for several weeks — I woke craving a picnic. None of the family was free to go with me, but I packed a lunch and headed out of town for one of the canyons. The late October day was perfect. An Indian summer warmth lay hazily in the great valley. For the moment I hadn't a care in the world. I reveled in the scent of dry prairie underfoot and of pine drifting down from the mountains.

I had walked possibly a mile when I heard an automobile horn honk repeatedly behind me. I turned to see Doctor Ladd's car bearing down upon me. It was one of the first in town and always created a sensation when it ran through the streets.

'Hello there!' the doctor called. 'Where are you going?'

'To a picnic.'

'I'll say you are! Hop in and I'll tell you where.' He opened the door of the car, and I obeyed. 'We'll have to hurry. I'm taking you home to pack your duds to go up to the Pelky place.'

'I don't like your picnic. Who are the Pelkys?'

'They live up in the hills in the Blackfoot country. Used to be pretty prosperous with timber and cattle, but now they're sort of down at heel. Lost four children and now the last one's sick — a boy about twenty-one or -two. Pelky just 'phoned down from the ranger's station, but I can't leave. Don't know a doctor who can. We're swamped with this typhoid epidemic. From the father's description, the kid must have it. You're the only nurse I know with experience enough with it to take full charge.'

'How'll I get up there?' I asked, with small relish for the assignment.

'The logging train leaves in an hour. Pelky'll meet you at the crossroads. Give your patient something to quiet him if hemorrhage is indicated. Check him over carefully and tomorrow drive over to the ranger's station and 'phone me for further orders.' He gave me instructions all the way in.

At my gate he told me to hustle. I scrambled out and started up the walk.

'Take warm clothes,' the doctor called after me. 'And prepare for a siege. I'll call the Sisters at the hospital to see if they'll let us have some equipment. They can send a man over to the station with the stuff. I haven't time to wait to take you to the train, so order a hack right away. And start soon enough to stop at the office for drugs. As a special treat I'll give you a shot of typhoid serum.'

'But I had typhoid in the Islands. I'm as immune as a tombstone.'

'I'll make you as immune as the Washington Monument.'

Mama was picking a chicken as I dashed into the house. 'What —? How're you back so soon, dearie?'

'Chuck the hen, Mama. Another typhoid case. Hurry and help me pack. Up in the Blackfoot country. Pioneering stuff, I judge.'

'More typhoid — Heavens! That means half the winter.'

'Yes, give me heavy clothes. But get me that mosquito netting in the linen closet. You know how flies hang on in the fall.'

As I gathered clothing into a heap, Mama stuffed them into

three grips and then called for a grain sack for the overflow. The hack arrived and I kissed Mama good-bye.

The logging train stood on the tracks next to the lumber yard. It was just ready to pull out as we galloped up. The caboose served as station and carrier for all people connected with the lumber company, as well as for occasional travelers up-country. White duck sacks leaned against one another on the entrance platform of the caboose. They were the contributions of the generous Sisters of Charity to my case. The bulges in the bags indicated enamel hospital utensils and other sickroom paraphernalia.

I introduced myself to the train master, a powerfully built man in brown corduroy uniform, and he told me his name was Scanlon. He helped me aboard.

He grinned, seeing my amount of luggage. 'Sure you got everything?'

'No,' I grinned back. 'I forgot a birdcage full of doughnuts.'

Some dozen lumberjacks standing around laughed boisterously. Scanlon turned on them. 'Who's talking to you?' There was an instant hush. The men looked embarrassed. A few more coarsely clad loggers climbed into the caboose. Then with two short, impatient toots the train of eighty or so cars groaned out of the yard.

The train master came to collect my fare. 'Is the dining car fore or aft?' I asked him.

'Aft,' he replied. 'Aft in my lunch kit.'

'How can that help me?'

'Wait and see. I'll hatch up something when I get things checked up here.'

One end of the caboose was divided into two booths. From the smaller one iron steps led up to the lookout from which the master could keep his eye on the entire train. A bunk ran along the wall of the larger booth. In its corner a miner's stove, with a steaming, sooty ten-pound lard bucket anchored in a griddle hole, gave out warmth and fumes of coal gas. There was a water container and galvanized cup hanging beside it. In the center of the booth was a staunch table, around which four loggers played cards.

At the entrance end of the car there was a little room with a closed door which needed no marker. In this room constantly running water swished through imperfect plumbing. In the opposite corner were piled boxes of canned goods, firkins of fish, kegs of pickles, cases of eggs, and sacks of all sorts of food for the logging camps. Piles of bedrolls, old canvas valises and duffel sacks were everywhere.

By the time I had taken in all these details, Scanlon had finished checking his cargo of men and goods. He placed a lunch box on the table and the card-players immediately scooped cards and poker chips into their caps and left. He motioned me into the booth.

'I always carry extra grub,' he said. 'Never know who's left their doughnuts behind.'

He dipped a handful of coffee out of a sack and threw it into the steaming lard bucket.

'Sure you have plenty for two?' I asked, seating myself quickly before he could weigh the matter. 'I didn't have time to eat lunch after I was ordered on this case.'

'Orders, orders!' he growled. 'I'm always under orders myself. I used to want to be my own boss. But when I got older, I knew the man on call was the lucky one. I've seen millions of dollars' worth of logging business signed right here on this table. I know all the big bosses. And believe me, they are the fellows who can't sleep nights for worry.'

'Well, I'm worse off than either you or your bosses,' I told him. 'I'm under orders from the doctor and I'm the big boss when it comes to the patient and the entire family. I get it going and coming.'

It was while Scanlon was setting out his lunch that I became aware of the lumberjack in the main part of the car, diagonally across from me. He was hunched over, his apelike arms dangling between his knees almost to the floor. His mouth and bloodshot eyes leered at me insinuatingly as he swayed with the motion of the train. He began singing guttural words in some foreign language. I was confident their implication was obscene.

'Shut up!' one of the loggers yelled at him. But the man kept right on with his serenade.

Scanlon turned, and his face darkened into a scowl. 'Cut that out quick!'

The little pig-eyes looked up insolently and the song increased in volume. In two strides the big train master reached him and yanked him out of his seat by the collar. The lumberjack struggled and cursed, but Scanlon dragged him out onto the platform, snatched his duffel bag and bedroll and flung them off the slowly moving train, and then, before the drunken fellow could scramble to his feet, he kicked him down the steps after his belongings. Utterly unruffled, the official turned around and eyed the other men coolly.

'If any more of you fellows want trouble, now's the time to start it. I'd like to eat my lunch in peace.'

We were miles from any habitation. The morning warmth was gone and the day had turned cold and windy.

'I know what you're thinking, young lady.' Scanlon's eyes were amused as he saw my outraged indignation. He showed no concern over the matter. 'You're thinking I'm cruel and inhuman. But from years of experience, I've learned this is the only way to handle these fellows. Now this one' — he paused to pour potent-looking coffee from the black bucket — 'he's so limp drunk he could tumble down the Matterhorn and never crack a bone. He'll unroll his blankets under the lee of a fallen tree or something and sleep the clock 'round. Tomorrow when I pick him up, he'll behave himself. And hold no grudge.'

I choked down my wrath with the scalding coffee and hoped he was right. As we followed along up the Blackfoot River, getting farther back into the hills and timber, I realized more than ever before how bitterly the Blackfeet must have hated to give up this ancient domain to the whites. Few Indians ever came back any more to pitch their tepees and dry their meat on the banks of their river.

No season could be more beautiful than that particular autumn. Crimson maples and yellowing cottonwoods hemmed plots of tall grass which rippled in the wind like mauve lakes. Goldenrod tinged the banks. Thistledown and the spun silk of fireweed sailed white in the deep blue of the sky. Here and there clumps of trees were huddled together and huge weather-tested evergreens on a promontory stood guard over the valley.

I had a quickening sense of adventure as we wound farther and farther back into hills sometimes bare, sometimes timbered. I hadn't realized before just where I was heading, until Scanlon told me the Pelky ranch was just about ten miles from Salmon Lake. I'd camped there with the Bentons two years before. This was Mack's and Jules's country. I'd often wondered if I'd ever see them again, those two strange trappers. Disqualified doctor and unfrocked priest — what rare companions they'd been! I devoutly hoped they hadn't come to grief in some one of their occasional sprees. Scanlon said they hadn't been out for some time, but as far as he knew they were all right.

'Ring the ranger when you get up there. He'd know. They're a great pair, those two, even when they're soused to the gills.'

And then before I knew it, I was at the crossroads. The rough, deeply rutted country road was disconcertingly empty. There was no sign of Mr. Pelky. Scanlon and one of the loggers unloaded me and my belongings on a spot in the big outdoors where the only sign of civilization was the meeting of those two ways.

'I don't like leaving you here alone,' the train master said, 'but it's orders.'

'A nurse takes what comes,' I told him. 'If that stewed lumberjack can make out twenty-four hours on two blankets and a bottle of whiskey, I should be able to survive a half-hour with all this equipment! I'll swathe myself against the icy blasts with that mosquito netting.'

My joke was lost on him. One of the loggers offered to stay with me. 'I'm sorta soused, but I'm never too drunk to be a gentleman,' he assured me. I declined smilingly. The 'go-ahead' signal was given. As Scanlon swung aboard, he called, 'Don't leave this spot, no matter how long you have to wait.'

I'd always thought I wanted to be lost in the wilds some

day, just for the experience. But now, as the little red caboose disappeared in the distance, I didn't relish the idea of sleeping in a hollow log and subsisting on berries. I stretched my cramped legs gratefully, though, and walked up and down beside the track in the crisp, bright sunshine. Two chipmunks chased each other around and over a log. I laughed, fascinated by their antics. After a while I sat down on my bags. The air was sharper and I was getting a little anxious. What if this were the wrong crossroads? What if Mr. Pelky shouldn't come?

Then, afar off, I heard a sound that thrilled me through and through. It was the sound of wild geese in migration. Nearer — nearer — specks no larger than wheat kernels in the sky, growing swiftly into forms of beauty and grace. The geese flew low, and I saw their outstretched necks and folded feet and heard the rhythmic beating of their wings. Thousands upon thousands of them, endless formations honking up over the hills and disappearing quickly in the South. Watching their flight into space I forgot my petty anxiety. The earthy clop of horses' feet startled me. Mr. Pelky was arriving.

He seemed to be all calfskin coat topped by closely cropped whiskers and mild blue eyes. The outfit was a rickety buckboard drawn by dispirited horses.

'I'm awful sorry I kept you waiting.' His voice was kind and gentle. He loaded my possessions in the back of the buckboard with the most painstaking care. I clambered over the front wheel and sat down on the blanket-covered spring seat. Mr. Pelky clicked a couple of times to his horses, called 'Tom — Star —' as though to friends, and we started on the up-hill road. The spokes were loose. They rattled and the wheels squeaked.

'How does the boy seem by this time, Mr. Pelky?' I asked.

'Eddie's bad. But we can't make him go to bed. I guess you can, though. I'm sure you'll have him well in no time.'

'That's the talk.'

As we jogged along, Mr. Pelky told me how they had homesteaded it. He and his wife had prospered on the ranch and built a frame house. 'We've got a real nice parlor,' he said proudly. 'Got a piano too. And a few years ago we had the children's pictures enlarged in crayon to hang on the wall.'

'That was nice.'

'But things ain't so good now. The land's logged off, all that's fit for lumber, and there's no money in stock just now. I don't know, Mrs. Hughes, how I'm going to pay you right away.'

'Don't worry about that. We'll put all our energies into getting Eddie well and strong.'

We had come up out of the sheltered bottom land where the creek ran. A cold wind blew a regular gale. In spite of my fur coat, I was chilled. Mr. Pelky told me we'd stop pretty soon now at the Hills' place, which was halfway, and get a bite of something hot. It was certainly a relief to come in sight of that ranch house. Mrs. Hill welcomed us into her warm kitchen, where we had good bean soup, coffee, and doughnuts hot and crisp from the frying kettle. When we were ready to leave, she gave me a scarf to tie over my head and a couple of extra blankets to wrap around me.

We wound along the stream through timber and underbrush. Mr. Pelky pointed out bits of interest — a beaver dam, beautifully constructed, an eagle's nest on a towering pine, a strip of black stump land where the ranchers had helped the ranger put out a bad fire last summer. About dark we came in sight of the Pelky ranch buildings and corrals. The house stood a little way back from the road. A few bull pines fringed what had been a picket fence around the house and yard. Dried vines covered porches and arched over windows. An old black shepherd dog bounded out to meet us.

'This is Quick,' said Mr. Pelky. Quick wagged a welcoming tail and licked my hand. Some neighbors had gathered at the Pelkys' to help out any way they might, and also to see the trained nurse, a strange bird in those parts. Mr. Pelky introduced them with a wave of the hand. 'These are friends who live eight miles up the creek.' Then he touched his wife's shoulder proudly. 'And this is Mama.'

Mama was small and work-worn. 'I'm awful glad you come.' There were courageous endurance and eager need of me in her face. 'Eddie's up at the top of the steps. He won't come down,' she explained, as she took my wraps.

I went to look up the cold stairway. A lanky, tousled boy in boots and mackinaw sat hunched at the top of the steep, narrow flight. He was shaking with chills, and even in the uncertain light I could see the hot fever flaming in his eyes and cheeks.

'I don't want a nurse!' he cried hysterically, at sight of me. 'I won't go to bed! I don't care if I die. I want to!'

'Who said anything about dying?' I laughed as I walked up the stairs to him. I touched his wrist to count his pulse and get his attention. 'I've nursed lots of people back to health who were sicker than you.'

He jerked away from me, and before I could stop him, he staggered down the steps and ran out to the backhouse. Just then the forest ranger came in to see how things were going. Without introduction, I asked him if he'd go look after Eddie and bring him in, while I prepared a hypodermic. He hurried out and soon returned, half-carrying the boy. There was no persuading the near-delirious youth to be reasonable, I saw, so while the ranger and Papa Pelky were forcibly removing his outer clothing, I managed to give him a shot of morphine. We soon got him to lie down on the living-room couch, where he fell into a restless sleep. I hastily outlined to the parents and the ranger — introduced as Carter James — what had to be done. They were eager to co-operate.

'First, we must make some room into a sort of hospital — a room with heat.'

Mrs. Pelky opened a door. 'Will this do? It's our parlor.' I could see the pride in her face. 'It has a stove in it.'

I glanced over the room. 'Fine.' I was grateful for its several windows and outside door. 'Now take out everything — furniture, pictures, curtains, and carpet. Then we'll wipe up the floor with antiseptics and get a bed in here.'

The ranger pulled off his coat. 'I'll give you a hand. We'll have it fixed up in no time.' He did most of the work and

Papa Pelky helped him. It was he who wiped up the floor and woodwork according to my instructions. Aside he said to me, 'Looks to me as if all the germs in here would get scared and run away the minute they met up with what Eddie's got.' I laughingly explained that the mopping-up was to give Eddie's germs a hot reception, preventing them from spreading to other people.

The two men improvised a table by placing a wide board on two kegs. On this we arranged the hospital equipment in orderly fashion. Eddie's bed was brought down from upstairs and made ready. The couch from the living room was to be brought in for me when we got Eddie off it. We stretched a rope across one corner of the room and threw a blanket over it, and that was my private dressing room.

It was ten o'clock when we finally got our hospital ready. Our patient still slept. The neighbor woman pussyfooted in to tell us supper was waiting. No one had thought of food till that minute. Carter said he'd eaten early in the day, so he'd keep his eye on Eddie while we ate.

The kitchen was fairly well lighted by a bracket lamp on the wall. I was tired and dropped into the first place I came to at the kitchen table. Papa Pelky turned to me apologetically. 'Would you mind settin' over at the end of the table, Nurse? This place next to me belongs to Mama. We never let anyone set between us.'

I tried to relieve the Pelkys' bottled emotions by asking questions about the ranch and themselves. But they couldn't get their minds off Eddie. They wanted to know just what typhoid fever was, how long it lasted, and if it left marks like smallpox. Mr. Pelky ate little and hurriedly, then took the water buckets and went out to the pump to fill them. When we were alone, Mama Pelky said, 'Excuse Papa, Nurse, for askin' you to move out of my place. He didn't mean any harm.'

'Why, I thought it was beautiful of him to want you near him.'

'He's always been like that — all the twenty-three years we've been married. He tracks in mud an' he spills water, but I never have the heart to scold him. He loves me an' the children so much.'

'Tell me about the children, Mrs. Pelky, if you want to.'

She sketched their life on the ranch as we sat at the kitchen table. The grease from the fried potatoes hardened on the plates. A fly struggled in the pitcher of milk.

The children seemed all right when they were born, she told me, but they soon got 'sort of puny. The baby died of pneumonia, but the girls got to school age. Then they both got awful colds and it turned into tuberculosis — that's what the doctor said it was. I fed 'em milk and eggs just like he said, but it didn't help. They both went within the year.'

'And Eddie?'

'Oh, he's always been well, except a winter cough. Maybe we should have made him go to a doctor.' She bit her lips. They trembled. 'There's three of 'em in the graveyard now. Oh, I couldn't bear it if ——' She pressed the back of a closed hand tightly against her mouth. Her shoulders shook with sobs. Papa came in just then. He set the buckets down sloppily and bent over her, putting his cold cheek against her wet one. I slipped out of the kitchen. In all the terrible days that followed, this was the only time I ever saw Mama Pelky cry. It was pathetic — those two growing prematurely old, struggling to make a go of life and losing at every turn.

After supper it took the four of us to get Eddie undressed entirely and into bed. I disposed of my own things as best I could and persuaded the Pelkys to go to bed after the neighbors and the ranger were gone. Then I sat down by Eddie in the still house. He was a lean, strong-looking country boy, with thick yellow hair and eyes like his mother's. In the shaded lamplight he looked younger than I knew him to be. So well worth saving. Sincerely I prayed for strength and skill to pull him through.

Suddenly he roused and reared up on his elbow. He looked about the room in bewilderment, puzzled, no doubt, by its stripped condition. Then his bloodshot eyes fastened on me. They were bright with excitement. He looked as though he were about to divulge some great secret he had brooding in him. But what he said startled me. 'Say, are you as homely as I think you are, or is it the dope you stuck into me that makes you look that way?'

I thought of the sooty stovepipe I'd held up for the ranger to wire, of the dust and grime of my trip, of my wind-rumpled hair. There'd been no time for primping. I probably looked far removed from any spick-and-span hospital nurse he'd ever seen. I started to tell him I wasn't always so messy, but he was off in a stupor again.

With Eddie's temperature at 103° I couldn't have heat enough in the room to keep me comfortable, so I sat awhile in an old Boston rocker, warming my feet at the living-room stove, where I could watch my patient through the open door. As I looked about me, I decided things might have been much worse.

Downstairs, beside the hospital room, living room, and kitchen, there was an unfurnished 'spare room.' The cellar had caved in, Mama Pelky explained to me, so they used the spare room for storing produce. I had noticed briny kegs of fish and pork, piles of pumpkins, squash, and other winter vegetables. There, piled on the floor, was seed corn on the cob. Beans, dried on their vines, hung from the rafters. The sharp fragrance of vinegar and spiced pickles permeated the room. It would be a wonderful place to visit occasionally as an antidote for hospital smells.

The pump, I had discovered earlier when checking on the water supply, was a good two hundred feet up the hill away from the drains. I was certain this clear, cold, isolated well of water was not the source of Eddie's typhoid germs. A simple home-made trough from the well and some storage barrels would have saved these people hours of carrying, but like so many other country dwellers, they hadn't used any ingenuity in making things easier for themselves.

The reflector of the big bracket lamp cast a yellowish light over the room. Fantastic shapes from the leaky roof stained the ceiling. The plaster was off the walls in places and cheesecloth had been pasted over the holes. The windows rattled. I heard a sound like bees humming and found it was made by the wind vibrating the edges tacked over broken panes. Freshly laundered muslin curtains hid the dilapidation of the windows. Clean, hand-embroidered linen covered the center table on which were albums and other books with metal clasps. The what-not held many treasures — on one shelf specimens of wood and stone, on another bric-à-brac, and on a third photographs of children: departed Pelkys. 'Please, God,' I prayed, 'don't let Eddie's fine face be added to this collection.'

Just then the boy cried out. 'Muriel! Muriel! Don't go like that!'

I went over to him, but he was sleeping. On the alert, I listened, but he didn't call again. I dozed in my chair while he slept restlessly until daylight. I was beside him when he awoke.

'Feeling better this morning, aren't you, Eddie?'

'I don't want to feel better. I want to die.'

'Sh-h-h. Your mother would feel terrible if she heard you say that!'

'I know. I guess they'd feel awful if I didn't get well. But Nurse, I don't want to get well, I tell you.' The boy's face was pitiful. 'You don't know half of it.'

I could see I didn't. Eddie grew steadily worse. His temperature mounted. Stupors alternated with delirium, and always when delirious he raved about Muriel. I tried to piece together the snatches, but they didn't make sense. Mama and Papa Pelky evaded the issue when I asked them.

There was much to overcome, flies particularly. But before we had more than put the mosquito netting, tent-like, over Eddie's bed, the weather turned suddenly cold. A Montana winter was upon us. Mama Pelky washed and dried bedlinen patiently, endlessly traveling up and down from the lines in the attic. Papa Pelky carried mountains of wood, his whiskers white with frost, and slipped in and out doing everything he could do to help. He rode to the telephone every day to read my message to the doctor and bring back orders.

The forest ranger came in one morning when Eddie raved the worst about Muriel.

'Is Muriel someone Eddie conjured up?' I inquired, 'or is she a real person?'

'A very real person,' he replied. 'And very pretty. Her family owns the ranch west of this. She and Eddie grew up together and were sweethearts for years. They were going to be married this spring. Eddie worked hard in the logging camp to save money for their house. His father deeded him a piece of land and the lumber was hauled for their house.' The ranger looked down at Eddie with deep pity in his eyes.

'What happened?' I asked.

'A good-looking no-account came through here with a surveying party. Muriel ran away with him and Eddie hasn't heard from her since.'

'Poor Eddie! So that's why he wants to die.'

'Do all typhoid patients rave and carry on like this?' he inquired.

'No, most of them are in a stupor a large part of the time. But he had this on his mind when he took sick and he hasn't the will to live. It's a bad combination.'

Shortly after this Eddie developed a hallucination about a letter from Muriel. Day and night he insisted it should be under his pillow, and all the time he was not sleeping or in stupor begged me to help him find it. His frustrated efforts made him hysterical and exhausted his small strength.

As I quieted him after one of his frenzied searchings, I decided he mustn't be disappointed again. I'd write the letter myself. I spent some time on it and wrote what I believed he'd want the faithless Muriel to say, and slipped it under his pillow when he was asleep. The next time he got to pawing around, he found it. The ecstatic happiness that lit his face was pathetic. His hands shook as he tried to open it and his eager, bloodshot eyes strained to see the words. 'Read it! Read it!' he cried. I took it from him and folded a firm hand over his trembling ones.

The letter was tender and penitent. She was sorry she had gone away. She had been foolish, but she loved him and was thinking of him all the time. She'd be coming home as soon as she earned enough money and they'd be married. And so on.

'Read it again, Nurse,' he begged, as soon as I had finished. So I read it again and again, until he fell into the quietest sleep he'd had in days. A happy smile lay on his lips, and I felt my deception had not been wrong. But I wondered what I'd do if Eddie miraculously regained his senses. Could I convince him that there had never been a letter — that he'd only dreamed it?

But this anxiety was soon submerged in a greater one. A small inflamed lump on my arm, which had appeared after the typhoid shot I'd had before coming up, began swelling and growing more painful. The infection from my arm went down into my hand, and one finger in particular became so badly affected that the giving of baths and treatments was almost impossible, even with Mama Pelky's zealous aid. I was on the verge of telling Doctor Ladd he would have to send a relief nurse to take my place, when Eddie changed my mind for me. Sitting by him one morning, trying to think things out, I was startled by his opening his eyes, smiling up at me, and saying, 'I knew you'd come sometime, Muriel. You thought I was fooled, but I knew it was you several days ago.' He reached out for my hand and clasped it in his shaking ones. 'Your hands are nice and cool. You won't leave me again, will you, darling?'

'No, Eddie, never again,' I whispered, as I choked back the tears. I was grateful for the ranger's arrival at that moment.

'How's the hand, Madam Nurse?'

'Well, the truth is, Mr. James ——.'

'Just plain Carter to you. Leave off the Mister!'

'All right, Just-plain-Carter, I must have relief. The Pelkys can't do more than they are doing. There's no neighbor who can take charge. The only sleep I've had since I came is a cat-nap now and then. And my hand is driving me mad.'

'I'd like to help. I've had first aid in the Forest Service. But this is different. In accidents ——.'

'I know, Carter. There's only one person around here who could help. I think he would be willing to. That's Mack Trevor, over on Salmon Lake. You know him, don't you? He ——'

'The trapper, you mean? What on earth would —?'

'Mack's a doctor — or was, until drink got the best of him.' I told him something of Mack's story. 'I know Mack could take hold here,' I declared. 'I have a feeling he'd be glad to help me.'

'By golly, I'll get him if I have to use a gun! If he gets drunk, we'll put him to bed with Eddie. That should sober him up.'

A bit reluctantly I talked to Mama Pelky about Mack's possible arrival. One more mouth to feed —? But she was enthusiastic. 'My, that's just fine! Eddie knows him and likes him a lot. I've heard him talk about Mack Trevor, though Papa and I never met him.'

But after Carter had left with my message to Mack, I began to feel a bit of uneasiness over the situation. What might these last two years have done to those exiles? If Mack came fogged with drink, incapable of helping, it would be a bad business. I hadn't expected any word of him before the next day, but late that night he arrived.

As he loomed up in the doorway in high laced boots and mackinaw, well-groomed, capable, clear-eyed, I could have wept with relief. He was so big and dependable-looking. More fit than when I had seen him before.

He smiled at me warmly as he advanced to clasp my well hand. 'Here I am, Sister! Sober as John the Baptist, with hip boots on and sleeves rolled up, ready to pitch in. Oh, I brought my girl friend along,' he added, as he took a quart of rye whiskey from his pocket and perched it up on the clock shelf. 'Now you stay there.' He shook a finger at the bottle. 'Not a peep out of you until I'm through here.'

'How's Jules?' I asked.

'He's gone into town for winter supplies. We were just on our way when we met the ranger. Jules sent his best regards and hopes to see you soon. He ——'

'Are you the doctor?' Eddie's voice broke in. 'Did Muriel send for you?'

I nodded to Mack's bewildered look and he said, 'Yep. I'm going to stick around and help the nurse make you better, Eddie.'

'She isn't the nurse!' Eddie's voice was querulous. 'That's Muriel. Don't you remember her?'

'Sure, sure,' declared Mack. 'My mistake.'

Eddie looked pleased to have Mack there, though he didn't seem to recognize him. It was certainly wonderful relief to me. In this sickroom he had a subtly commanding manner that I had never seen in him before. He turned from Eddie to me.

'And now, young lady, let's see your hand.' He scrutinized the finger and the swelling on the arm without comment. Then his eyes looked into mine with that unwavering intentness I so well remembered. 'You line up things here tomorrow so that Mrs. Pelky and I can look after Eddie while you go over to the 'phone and report this condition to Doctor Ladd. You ——'

'I'd been thinking of that, but now that you're here you can ——'

He didn't let me finish. 'You have a nurse sent up so you can get back to town right away and have these abscesses lanced.'

'But Mack, you could —!'

'No, I couldn't!' His face was grim. 'Suppose the scalpel slipped?'

I knew he would not be persuaded. The Hills arrived early the next morning with all sorts of good things to eat, and while Mrs. Hill sat down to talk awhile, her husband loaded me into their carriage and we drove over to the ranger's station to telephone. Fortunately I got Doctor Ladd right away and told him the situation.

'Don't come back,' he told me. 'I'll get a man to run a relief nurse out. She can take care of your infection and tend to the boy under your supervision, while you get some rest. I'll send her up in the morning.'

'I do wish you could see this Pelky boy, doctor. In my judgment there's a bad throat complication.'

'I'll try to get up to bring this nurse back after a few days. But right now we never get our clothes off with the hospitals and the country full of typhoid cases. I've told Pelky to get another doctor if he could find one that could go up there. But he seemed satisfied that we were doing all that could be done.'

I told him about calling in Mack Trevor to help, and he thought it a good idea. 'If it weren't for my hand, I wouldn't feel that things were bad.'

'That's the talk. Say your prayers and keep the powder dry. But' — he almost shouted at me — 'take care of that hand!'

Mack insisted on taking final charge of Eddie that night. There was a camp cot on the porch and Mack pulled it over under the two windows opening from the sickroom. Mama Pelky heaped a feather bed on it and brought out good wool blankets. Cold though the weather was outside, I knew I'd sleep warmly there. I made Eddie comfortable for the night and told him Doctor Mack would stay with him. 'Be a good boy, Eddie. Now let's see who can get to sleep first.'

He looked at me longingly. 'I wish you'd kiss me good night, Muriel.'

I shivered at the thought. 'I wish I could, Eddie, but if I did, I might get the fever too. Then I couldn't stay with you.'

'Stay with me — don't get sick,' he murmured plaintively.

'I won't, Eddie. I must keep well to take care of you.' I patted his head gently and he drifted off to sleep. 'Now, Mack,' turning to him hopefully, 'what about this hand?'

'I'll put a moist dressing on your hand and arm — nothing more.' There was defeat in the eyes that met mine levelly. But his hands were deft. He worked swiftly and skillfully. Standing so close to him, I was startled to discover the abnormality of his heart action. Pretending to put the table in order, I took the stethoscope from its case and, before Mack realized my intention, I was listening to a heart that alarmed me with its labored and leaking struggle to function. I looked up at him in amazement. It seemed incredible that this bronzed, strong, fit-looking man could have such a heart. I thought of the long miles he walked, the sprees he indulged in ——

'How long has this been going on?' I asked.

'Oh, indefinitely — ten years possibly — since before I quit practice. I used to think it would finish me off, but ——' He shrugged.

'Is this something special, or does it always act this way?'

'Well, it's always murmuring and thumping, but frankly, Little Sister, being back in a sickroom this way' — his dark eyes passed over the table of hospital equipment with a glance almost caressing — 'sleeping dogs rear up and growl. Tonight, now ——'

I took a box of digitalis pills from my medicine kit and handed them to him. 'You take these, Mack. You've given them to a lot of people with good results.' Maybe the codeine I'd just had turned me soft, for, as I stood looking up at him, thinking of the losing fight he had put up for years, tears ran down my cheeks. I didn't try to hide them.

'You run along and get some sleep.' He gave my shoulder a pat. 'You can see what goes on in here through the window. And I'll call you if Eddie gets too much for me.'

'Take it as easy as you can, Mack. Good night.'

Mama Pelky and I talked a little at bedtime as we undressed by the living-room stove. 'Tonight,' she insisted, 'I want you to put on this heavy flannel wrapper. Your robe is too thin for out there.' So to please her I put it on and climbed through the window into my Pullman berth. I can still feel that soft bed, the warm brick Mama Pelky had heated for my feet, the blankets smelling of attic sunshine and pitch pine. The morning came too soon and with it pain more violent than ever.

'How'd you make out, Mack?' I asked. He looked surprisingly fresh and was already shaved.

'Bully. Eddie slept pretty well. He ——'

'Muriel,' Eddie's voice broke in, 'could you kiss me this morning — just once?'

'I can't, Eddie. Don't you remember that I must stay well to take care of you?' I lifted his heavy hair and let my fingers play across his forehead in a way he liked. I noticed the throat infection was much worse. His tongue and lips were badly swollen.

The nurse arrived about lunchtime, a young, pretty girl, full of her own importance. Mama Pelky announced fried potatoes and hot biscuits for everyone.

'You run along' — I waved them out — 'while I get things ready to relieve this hand. I'll enjoy a good meal after it's fixed up.'

Soon everything was ready for the nurse to carry on. When the meal was over, the whole family, as well as the driver who had brought the nurse, ganged around the hospital room to see the fun. I sat on a nailkeg with my hand, swathed in alcohol sponges, lying on the table. The nurse put on gloves she had brought from their sterilized covering and laid out her instruments.

'All ready,' she announced cheerily, scalpel in hand.

She made a little jab at the finger, barely scratching the skin. I looked up in bewilderment as I saw her hand falter. Her face was a ghastly white. Before anyone could move, she toppled over on the floor in a faint. Mack threw water in her face and Papa Pelky and the driver lifted her onto the couch. While I, no longer having the spotlight, snatched the scalpel from the floor, germs and all, and made a good lunge into my finger. It was like lifting the lid from a volcano.

'Well, I'll be damned!' Mack stared at me as he turned from the dripping nurse. 'Here, Sister!' His fingers closed over the instrument and lifted it from my hand. There was no uncertainty in his hand as he dipped the lance in iodine and gouged it into the ripe abscess of my forearm. Swift and sure — and the operation was over.

'If you can find a piece of shirt-tail, Sister, we might tie them up.' Mack's eyes were twinkling.

'Here's an old sock, Mack,' indicating the dressing in order on the table. We could scarcely get the bandage on for laughing. The whole thing seemed too ridiculous. There stood Mama Pelky in front of Eddie, screening him from the activities going on in the farther corner of the room. To shut out possible sounds of the operation, she had started singing when we first began, and in spite of interruptions still continued lustily with 'Oh happy day! That fixed my choice —!'

The nurse was revived shortly. Her hair had tumbled down, her uniform was slopped with water, and she sat on the edge of the couch and cried in humiliation. Kindly Papa Pelky patted her arm and said, 'There, there.' The driver stood with his mouth open gaping around at all of us. When I could collect myself, I tried to comfort the nurse.

'You needn't feel so upset. This often happens. The ride was tiring, too, so early in the morning. Perhaps you might as well go back with the car. See! It's beginning to snow. If you got snowed in here, you couldn't get out for weeks.' I watched her hopefully. I knew she'd be worse than useless in such a place as this. I saw eager relief leap into her eyes, but she frowned.

'Who's going to pay me for coming up here?' she demanded.

'You'd better take that up with Doctor Ladd. Of course you've been a great help,' I said sweetly.

It didn't take her long to get off. I saw her and the driver to the car and waved them farewell. Then I went into the kitchen, ate two fried eggs, three big soda biscuits, some fried potatoes, blackberry jam, and two cups of coffee.

The snow continued to fall all that day and the next. Shrubs, rocks, and fenceposts were molded into smooth forms, hushed and sleeping under a glistening white comforter. The men, and even Mama Pelky and I dug paths to the outbuildings and pump. Neighbors were unable to get through the drifts. We missed them and their helpfulness. It took the ranger the best part of a day to break a trail through to us. All hope of Doctor Ladd's coming was abandoned.

We were deep in winter isolation and sank into a deadly monotony of routine. Breakfasting in relays, Mack going to the attic to sleep, Mama Pelky helping me when she could,

Papa stamping snow from his feet as he made frequent trips to the barn and sheds to care for chickens and stock, then tiptoeing around the house with wood and coal; Eddie talking, laughing, raving, then going into a stupor for hours —— All days seemed alike, except that Eddie grew thinner and more hollow-eyed with each successive one. His mouth and lips were terrible to see and swallowing was becoming difficult.

Every night at eleven I checked my patient over and he never failed to murmur, 'I wish you'd kiss me, Muriel.' And I would answer, 'I must keep well to take care of you, Eddie.' And then I'd climb into my berth by the windows.

After Eddie was asleep, Mack would come out and smoke his pipe as he made the rounds of the porch. He would adjust the old blanket over the dog in the box. I could hear the thump of Quick's tail, as though he thanked him for the service. Mack would read the thermometer in the flare of a match and ask about the brick at my feet. He'd stand a few minutes, smoking silently, and look at the white, starlit night. Once he commented, 'Such vast, illimitable space, and we individuals can have and hold such a tiny bit of it.' Then he tapped the ashes out of his pipe, made a last-minute tuck of the blankets at my feet, and with 'No worries now, Little Sister,' went in to Eddie.

Night after night as I lay in my warm bed, supposedly asleep, I could hear him crooning bits of song to the sick boy. This strange, strong man, who lived, as he said, 'by whiskey and skins,' was tender as a mother with Eddie; his very presence soothed him. When I have been world-weary down through the years I've thought back to those peaceful Montana nights when I lay on the snow-covered porch. I can hear the bare honeysuckle vine tapping against the lattice. I calm myself with the memory of that valley falling away mile upon mile, deep in winter white. I smile and something stirs within me as I recall the ever-startling wail of a coyote, which always brought Mack quickly to the window to assure me everything was all right within, in case I'd thought it was Eddie that had cried out.

As time went on, Eddie called incessantly for his sweetheart. 'Muriel! Muriel!' I never failed to go to him. And then one night, as we were beinning the thirteenth week, I knew the end was near. 'He can't go on now more than a few hours,' I said to Mack. He nodded in agreement. 'Poor kid!'

'I'm going to bunk down here on the couch tonight,' I told him. 'We may both be needed.'

I lay down fully dressed and had just fallen into a belated doze when Mack called. I opened my eyes to see him holding the boy as he struggled to get out of bed. Eddie's mouth was stained with blood from a throat hemorrhage. He opened his eyes and saw me bending over him.

'Muriel — you're beautiful. Kiss me!' His voice was a mere whisper. 'Please — just once!'

Touching his raw festering lips even with my fingers had made me recoil. But this was the end. I stooped down, shut my eyes, and kissed him.

'God!' Mack breathed.

I looked at Eddie. A smile had crept over his tired face. Quiet, everlasting peace settled down upon him. We stood a moment, silent and awed at the sudden transformation. In the kitchen a stove lid rattled. Mama Pelky ——

'Here!' Mack pulled me over to the medicine table and handed me a bottle of antiseptic mouth wash. 'Use this, quick.'

Presently I went into the kitchen where Mama Pelky was frying potatoes at the stove. When she looked up, I had no need to tell her.

'He's gone —?'

'Yes, Mama. Do you want to come and see how peaceful and happy he looks?'

Her chin twitched. She shook her head. 'I'll wait till Papa comes in.'

Mack and I dressed Eddie's emaciated body in his best suit and the tie Muriel had given him on his last birthday, and laid him on the couch. We removed every hospital trace from the room and put the furnishings back in the parlor. Then Mama and Papa Pelky came in to see him.

'Oh Papa — see! He's sleeping quiet at last.'

Papa Pelky clenched his hands together and nodded.

Mr. Hill and Papa went to the piled lumber that was to have been used for a home that now would never be, and picked out smooth boards for a coffin. All forenoon they worked in the bunkhouse down by the barn, so Mama couldn't hear the sound of hammer and saw. We lined the crude casket with home-made quilts and tacked a sheet over them. To soften it I laid in the white mosquito netting I had brought with me and covered a small pillow with my white silk petticoat.

Later I went alone into the woods. Despite human suffering, the world outside was a lovely place. Every tree, every twig and limb, shone vivid white in the bright winter sun. Under the snow I found some golden-brown maple leaves, and on the uplands, white snow-berries. From them I formed a wreath to lay on the coffin.

Mack and Carter had gone early in the day to make sure the road was clear to the cemetery, fourteen miles away, and, if possible, to arrange for a minister to come to the ranch the next day to conduct a funeral service. They drove up as I got back to the house and brought in Eddie's casket from the bunkhouse. Mama Pelky was in the kitchen as usual, preparing food. All day she had kept busy.

'The men'll be hungry,' she explained. 'If Eddie was here now, he'd say, "Cook a heap of stuff, Mom."' She bit her lips.

Mack reported that there wasn't a minister to be had. Half the people in the country were down sick. Privately he handed me a letter. It was for Eddie. Muriel's return address was in the corner. I took it upon myself to open it carefully — in case it should be resealed and passed on to the Pelkys unopened. There was no need. Mack leaned over my shoulder and we read it together.

> Dearest Eddie:
>
> Can you ever forgive me for what I have done? I can never forgive myself. If you'll take me back and marry me right away, so my baby can have a father when it is born, I'll spend

the rest of my life trying to make it up to you. He deserted me. I hate him. I know now I do love you, Eddie. Please, please, Eddie ——

I folded the letter and tucked it under the pillow in Eddie's coffin. There were tears in Mack's eyes as well as my own.

The next morning brought dark, cold clouds. We lighted all the lamps on the place and the handful of neighbors who could get through the drifts gathered in the Pelky parlor. I struck a few chords on the old piano and we struggled through 'The morning light is breaking, the darkness disappears' — Eddie's favorite hymn. Everyone joined in the Lord's Prayer. Then Mack began reading, 'Let not your heart be troubled ——' The sweat ran down his face. I thought he would choke, but he carried through to the end.

There seemed to be a simple analogy between the brown, dead leaves on the coffin lid and the lifeless body of Eddie. I spoke of how spring would bring new leaves again, since life always renewed itself and did not really die. Eddie had just gone out of his worldly house. 'There were loving arms to receive him the night he was born,' I said. 'Just so there are loving arms to receive him into a home better perhaps than this earthly one. It must be part of God's plan.' I spoke of the hundreds of boys who die alone every year, out in camps away from home, calling for their mothers. Eddie had been more blest. He'd had every attention that love and skill could give him. We must be thankful instead of sorrowful. Eddie had suffered long and now he was at peace.

A hush fell on those who had been weeping, for at that moment the sun burst through the clouds and flooded the room with amber light.

It was mid-forenoon when the small funeral procession started through the half-cleared drifts for the cemetery. Mack in huge fur coat, with the collar up around his ears, sat with the ranger on the seat of the spring wagon with the canvas-covered coffin behind them. After them came the Hills' carriage. The Pelkys, Hills, and I rode in it. That was all. It was bitterly cold, but to have speeded up the horses going to the graveyard with the dead would, in those days, have been an outrageous thing.

A thin spatter of snowflakes was coming down as we reached the desolate country graveyard. Someone had made a brush windbreak and a pile of pine knots glowed hotly near-by. How grateful we were for that warmth! The grave was lined with fir boughs. Some stranger read a 'dust to dust, ashes to ashes' service, and the men lowered Eddie's coffin into the earth. The stranger said the minister's wife had sent over some sandwiches and hot chocolate. We warmed our feet and ate a little lunch hurriedly.

The homeward trip was swifter. Snow was falling fast and night would close in on us early. The welcome lights of the Pelky house, the smell of hot food prepared by kind neighbors, and the warm room cheered us. Human kindness and comforts — never had they seemed to matter so much.

When for a moment I was alone with Papa Pelky, he put five ten-dollar gold pieces in my palm and closed my fingers over them. 'No!' I remonstrated, but he held my hand tight shut in his two rough, cracked ones.

'It's all I can do for you yet. Hill bought Eddie's cow and calf today.' His voice trembled. 'Eddie'd want you to have it.' I saw how he felt. I thanked him, half-choking with the pity of it all.

Mack heated the brick for the last time and tucked it in the porch bunk. While he and Papa smoked and talked in the kitchen, with what cheer I could offer I got Mama to bed in the warm living room. She tried in her own way to thank me for all I had done for her son as I tucked her in. Once again I wrapped myself in Mama's flannel wrapper and dived into my bunk. Mack came out for his check-up. I saw by his pack and high laced boots that he was going to leave.

'Don't go mushing through the snow this time of night, Mack!' I entreated. 'All this has been a fearful strain on you. Do have some consideration for that heart of yours. Please wait until morning, so you can get a good night's sleep!'

I was frightened. I knew he had put the bottle of whiskey

in his knapsack earlier in the day. In my imagination I saw him drunk against a log, freezing to death.

He shook his head. 'It's clear as a whistle out now. And I have my snowshoes. I need the tramp. I've been shut up here a long time.'

Nothing I could say would change his mind. He lit his pipe. The light from the match was reflected in his eyes and for a moment they were on fire. I wanted him to take half the money Papa Pelky had given me, but he wouldn't hear of it. We talked about the work we had done together, the faked letter that had given Eddie a few hours of happiness, of camping on Salmon Lake again in the summer.

He put a hand on my blanketed shoulder. 'I want to tell you, Sister, before I go, there are some things a man can never forget — that will always inspire him. Like what you did for Eddie when he was dying.'

'I'd never have made it without you, Mack. You've been wonderful and the thought of you will always give me courage when I need it.'

'I don't deserve that.' His voice was husky.

For the last time he covered the dog's box, then tucked the blanket more securely around my feet. For a moment he stood on the top step, sharply outlined under the arch of dead vines. He adjusted his small pack comfortably on his shoulders.

'Mack — your cap! You're bareheaded. Don't go out in the cold that way.'

'No, I've taken off my hat to you in this place and I shall never put it on again. God! What a woman!'

Without a good-bye he plunged down the steps. I watched him plow through the drifts until he was lost in the black shadow of the forest. The shepherd dog, as though he knew something was wrong, crawled out of his box whining, and jumped on my bed. He was filthy dirty and smelled of the cowshed, but I gathered him into my arms. He licked my face and I cried into his fur.

* * *

I first met the Van Fleets, mother and son, when I was on night duty in a Butte hospital where I nursed for a time. The orderly brought them up to my floor about eleven one night when the last patient was asleep and I'd just finished my charts and was about to relax over the evening paper. They were an odd pair, that big old woman and bow-legged runt of a man.

She was seventy-five at least, I judged, but looked strong as an ox. There were more than six feet and two hundred pounds of her. She wore no hat and her shining, yellowish-gray hair was slicked back into a hard turnip of a knot on the highest point of her head. Her pleasant, weather-beaten face and keen blue eyes radiated courage and determination.

'We're the Van Fleets from over Gallatin Valley way,' she announced. She reached around and pulled to the front the embarrassed male who seemed to be trying to hide behind her. 'This is my son, Cal.'

Cal was a man in middle life, so sprung at the knees that his legs bowed out grotesquely. His face was round and florid and a small copy of his mother's, except for his eyes. They were weak and lifeless, and his graying head, with its thick, unruly hair, reached no farther than his mother's armpits.

He acknowledged the introduction with an awkward nod of the head. His mouth was too full of tobacco juice to speak.

'Cal's horse bucked him an' he come down on the saddle-horn and injured himself turrible,' she explained. 'The doctor over home told me to git him to the hospital as quick as I could, as he thought he'd need an operation.'

I rang for the orderly who had left these two. 'Are you in much pain now, Mr. Van Fleet?'

He nodded his head again and looked at the floor in embarrassment.

'Ain't there no privy close abouts?' Mrs. Van Fleet inquired. 'Go find one, Cal, and spit out that quid.'

I pointed out a lavatory and Cal ambled slowly and painfully down to it. His mother watched him lurching along and grinned at me.

'Poor Cal! He got them legs ridin' astride my hip. He was just about two years old when we crossed the plains to Alder Gulch in the early days, his paw and me. Our horses kept a-dyin' and before we got to Montana we had only one left. I had to walk and I carried Cal astride my hip.'

'That must have been pretty tough on you,' I said. 'But this accident — just how is he injured?'

'It's his — you know.' She lifted her brows and gave a few quick nods.

'Oh, yes,' I knew exactly.

The orderly took Cal off to a room when he emerged from the lavatory minus his quid. I asked Mrs. Van Fleet if she had engaged a room at the hotel.

'No, I didn't have money enough for that. We're awful hard put right now. I'll just wait around until I know what the doctor thinks about Cal, and then I'll go down to the depot and set. It's nice and warm there.'

'You mustn't do that,' I told her. 'You sit in that easy-chair in the hall for a little while and I'll get you fixed up for the night.'

The orderly got Cal to bed and reported that his modesty was so much more painful than his injury that I'd better stay away from him. 'I'll make the examination, and you can relay it to the doctor.' The doctor laughed when I told him of the procedure. He outlined the treatment and said he'd be over early in the morning.

Mrs. Van Fleet was sitting in her stocking feet when I got back to her. 'My bunions and calluses are just about killin' me. I ain't used to wearin' my Sunday shoes all day.'

I had her soak her feet in a salts bath, and when she was in bed I pared off a double handful of old horny tissue and got her feet in pretty good shape. Then I gave her a hot drink and she declared she was so comfortable she could almost believe she was in heaven.

Cal was operated upon the next morning. The Sisters had Mrs. Van Fleet stay in the hospital a few days to see how he would get along. Meanwhile, I treated her feet with collodion mixture and removed her remaining calluses. Cal made quick strides toward recovery, so his 'maw' went back to the ranch.

'It's a pretty poor one,' she told me. 'They used to do a lot of placer mining around in that part of the country — took out quite a bit of gold from along our creek, but nobody's seen any pay-dirt there now in years. They washed off the soil and there's nothin' much but gravel patches left.'

I really hated to see the old girl leave. I liked her immensely and she could tell stories of the early days that would lift one's hair. I wrote her a card about Cal every day. Her answers surprised me. She wrote much better than she spoke and could have spelled me down in three minutes.

Cal left the hospital quite recovered and except for a Christmas card the Van Fleets faded from my mind for about two years. Then the bread I had cast upon the waters in the simple matter of bunion and callus treatments began to return to me buttered. I wasn't aware, at first, of the smear of axle grease on the underside.

I was still living in Riverton at this time. Mrs. Van wrote me a letter enclosing money for a ticket and begging me to come visit them right away. She said she had something very important to tell me and couldn't write it. Since a vacation was due me anyway, I went.

The Van Fleets met me at the station with a shabby buckboard and a span of old workhorses. They were so excited they began telling me of their good fortune before I was seated in the wagon. A dredging company had begun working farther up the creek beyond their place and had contracted to pay them a tidy little sum per month for an experimental right to work over the old gravel again. The income looked like riches to the hard-up Van Fleets and they wanted to share some of their good fortune with me.

'And then my calluses was bad again. I thought maybe you wouldn't mind fixin' them up for me.' Mrs. Van looked at me hopefully.

I assured her it would be a pleasure.

The shabby, unpainted little house had a kitchen and sitting room, with an attic bedroom above, nothing more.

There was a brand-new rag rug on the floor of the living room. Mrs. Van pointed it out as her own work. The curtains at the windows were freshly laundered. There were framed pictures of departed Van Fleets, including bewhiskered 'Paw,' and prints of grim gentlemen whom my hostess told me had been prominent Vigilantes in the early days. Above the door was a sampler bearing a red yarn 'Welcome' on a background of forget-me-nots. The bed set up there had a Dutch comfort of down and a beautiful old hand-woven blue-and-white spread. There were curtains on wires to pull across the front of the bed for privacy.

To this day I still remember the excellence of that dinner — fried chicken and vegetables, cottage cheese, cole slaw, hot sour-cream biscuits, mince pie, coffee with cream so thick we had to dig it out of the pitcher with a strong spoon — my mouth still waters thinking of it. After Cal had finished, he read the *County Weekly* while we did the dishes, and then took himself off to bed up in the attic room.

'Now we can talk,' said Mrs. Van. 'You know how Cal is, Mrs. Hughes. He's good, but he's not so smart. I don't want him to know what I'm tellin' you. He might forget himself an' tell someone. Then the jig'd be up. I got a mining man I know — Peters, an old friend of Paw's an' honest as they make 'em — to do a little scoutin' 'round for me. He got a job on the dredger so's to keep an eye on how much gold they're takin' out. We can make an estimate when we see about how it's runnin' an' then I'm goin' to sell this place an' clear out of here for good. I'm plannin' to live near you somewhere. Then I can have my feet fixed up so's I can enjoy myself. I've never saw the ocean or been on a train all night or stayed at a hotel or nothin'. I'll get me a black lace dress, maybe, an' a fur coat. I've worked like a horse all my life — never done any of the nice things I've thought about. Maybe I shouldn't count on it too much, but this has just *got* to happen!'

And it did. It was over in the Puget Sound country that I saw the Van Fleets next. For a long time Doctor and Mrs. Benson had wanted to go to the Coast to live, and their opportunity came while I was out of town on a case. They were gone when I returned, but soon after Doctor Benson wrote that he needed me badly in Seattle. I liked working with him, and ever since I'd glimpsed the Puget Sound country on my way up to Montana, I'd thought of it as the place where I'd some day have a home. I was now a charter member of the Nurses' Association of the Northwest. All things seemed to be working out as I'd hoped. So I left Montana for the Pacific Coast.

My love was immediate and lasting for hill-climbing Seattle, with its endless breath-taking views of water and mountains. After I had been established for some time, Isobel Jarvis came out to join me. All this time she had been struggling along, a victim of thyroid goiter, barely able to support herself with what nursing she could do since our graduation from training school. When I bought a house with several extra bedrooms, Isobel moved in with me. She was always more or less my patient, but she was like one of my own family and continued to call me 'Ma.' Several years later, my parents came to live with us.

It was the summer of the Lewis and Clark Centennial in Portland that the Van Fleets came back into my life. I'd heard from Mrs. Van occasionally, but she'd said little about the dredging and I thought it must be petering out. And then one day she and Cal barged in on us unannounced. They had sold the place with the gold-producing gravel beds for eighty thousand dollars. She said she'd left behind everything that would remind her of the old life except Cal.

The old lady had an assortment of amazingly well-chosen clothes, but Cal was in the dog-house because he refused to wear a collar. They overwhelmed our spinster establishment. Cal was always underfoot as he sat by the kitchen stove. He kept the firebox door open so that he could spit into it the accumulated tobacco juice that bulged his cheek. Fastidious Isobel would look at him in utter disgust. 'If that man doesn't leave this house soon, I'm going to!' she'd threaten.

I'd been expecting my family over to spend part of the summer with us, so had to wire Mother to postpone their starting for a week, at least, while I entertained these self-invited guests. I couldn't fail them. This was the dream of a lifetime come true and they'd turned to me as the only person who could show them what they ought to see.

Day after day on foot, by streetcar and by stage, I took them sight-seeing. They'd never go without me. 'It's lots more fun with you along,' they'd insist. Mrs. Van told me, to start with, that she was going to pay all my expenses as well as their own, so it wasn't hard on me financially. But physically and mentally it was a strain.

In the picture theaters, when Mrs. Van sank her bulk into an undersized chair, the row was successfully blocked for traffic. Her knees took up all the space between seats and she was so heavy she wouldn't try to stand if anyone wished to pass. 'Mebbe you could make it t'other direction,' she'd suggest. 'I've got my shoes off and my bunions hurt too bad to have anybody trompin' on 'em.' She loved pictures, especially Westerns, but sometimes in tense moments she'd so audibly ridicule Hollywood's portrayal of pioneer life that people would turn and glare at her. They were always further outraged by Cal's laborious reading aloud of all captions, and the incessant spatter of tobacco juice between his knees. It was a rare day that someone didn't call an usher and demand he be put out. My embarrassment was acute at times, but their enjoyment was so enthusiastic and so lasting that I felt well repaid for my efforts in their behalf.

Never a word had they said as to how long they expected to stay. It was time for me to be back on duty and I was at my wits' ends thinking of how to get them out of my house and off my hands. The old woman was so generous with her funds and so thrilled and happy over her big adventure that I couldn't ruin things for her by making them feel unwelcome.

But when she suggested one day that we all go to the Fair in Portland — she paying all my expenses — I saw a way out. I told Isobel my plan and she agreed it was a sound one. I'd wire my family to come on and be in the house before we came back from the Fair. Then I'd send the Van Fleets on to Seattle while I stayed in Portland a few days longer to visit cousins.

When they found the house full and not an extra bed to sleep in, they'd have to get some other place and our problem would be solved.

When I was helping Mrs. Van decide which clothes to take with her on this trip, she pulled a chamois-skin bag from a pocket sewed in her corset, opened it and handed me a roll of bills. 'Count 'em,' she said.

Hundred-dollar bills they were. I peeled off one after another. 'Fifteen hundred dollars! Good Heavens, Mrs. Van! You're surely not planning to carry that much cash around with you!'

'I been a-carryin' it! It'd take a dredge to drag it offen me. All my life I never had any money to carry. When I sold that gravel wash and Peters showed me how to write checks an' everything, I says to him, "Peters, I want fifteen hundred dollars in bills to carry around with me."' She chuckled at memory of it. '"Do you want to get robbed?" he says. "You got a checkbook. All you need's a little cash for your purse." We went out of the bank without it, but the minute he went on about his business, I went straight back an' wrote a check for this money. It sort o' scared me an' I felt like folks must be watchin' me. When I handed it to the cashier, he looked as though he thought I was crazy. 'I bristled right up an' I says, "Ain't I made it out right?" An' he says, "Oh, certainly, certainly. I just thought —— You just banked this money —!" I didn't wait for him to finish. I says, "Well, I'm *un*bankin' that much of it. An' I want it in hundred-dollar bills." So he shoved it across to me. An' when I saw how much there was, I sure didn't know what I was goin' to do with it!'

'What did you do with it?' I asked.

'I went over into a corner an' when nobody was lookin' I tied it flat in my handkerchief an' put it in the crown of my hat. When I got home, I made a pocket in my corset — I only had one then. Now I got two new ones an' they both got pockets — I ain't spendin' this. I like the feel of it against me. Makes me know I didn't just dream all this. So if anything happens to me on this trip, keep your eye on my corset!'

'Speaking of anything happening to you, Mrs. Van, do you have your financial affairs in shape so Cal wouldn't have any trouble?'

'Well, no. I haven't made any will yet. I suppose I ought to.'

'You certainly ought. Some shark of a lawyer could bamboozle an innocent, unsuspecting fellow like Cal out of everything.'

'That's what Peters told me. I'll get around to it pretty soon, though I've never been sick a day in my life. Cal's my only living relative, so he'll get everything.'

For a few days I did eight-hour shifts in the hospital. Then the telegram for which I had been waiting came from Mother. 'Following your plan as outlined. Leaving Saturday.' The next day the Van Fleets and I took the train for Portland. We had good seats in the observation car, but neither of them would go into the dining car to eat. Cal got off at every stop and bought quantities of cracker-jack, cookies, candy, apples, and peanuts. They munched incessantly and kept the exasperated porter sweeping up crumbs and shells all afternoon.

We found a good place not far from the Fair grounds, one not so elegant as to overwhelm the Van Fleets. The next morning we started out to do the Exposition. The morning concert was just beginning as we got into the grounds. I piloted the Vans to the hall, and we stood in the rear as the orchestra was just in the middle of a number. It was a magnificent symphony orchestra and they were playing the *William Tell Overture* with verve that would inspire anyone, no matter how indifferent to music. But when it was finished and I wanted to find seats, the Vans were not interested.

'I like music fine,' declared Mrs. Van, 'but Cal and me's goin' to get us a phonograph, so there's no use wastin' time on it here. This boomin' stuff hurts my ears anyhow.'

We wandered around for hours, until Mrs. Van was limping with pain in her bunions. I told her there were benches in the art gallery where she could sit down and rest her feet and look at the finest pictures at the same time. She said that would suit her exactly, as she did like to look at pretty pictures. One of her friends had painted a yard of pansies once, natural as anything, and she'd like to see some more things like that. But we got little rest. We'd hardly got inside the first wing before Cal plucked at his mother's sleeve, his face red with embarrassment.

'Lookit, Maw, I think we'd better get outa here.'

'But I just come. What's the matter with you? My feet need a good rest.'

'Look back there!' He gestured with his thumb toward an almost life-size nude prone on a couch.

'My sakes alive!' The old woman looked at me in bewildered horror. 'Someone ought to be arrested for putting that saloon picture in here!' She took Cal and me by the arms and fairly marched us out of there.

Try as I would, I could get neither of them into any really worth-while exhibits. They liked the amusements on The Trail and walked up and down it listening to the barkers of the side-shows as long as their feet could take it, undaunted by the scorching pavements and sweat that ran down our faces and wilted our freshly starched summer things.

One particularly hot day we ran into a friend of mine from Seattle and we stopped to talk a moment. I introduced Mrs. Van — Cal had moved on to the snake-charmer — but thought nothing of it when she too strolled off. It wasn't until my friend clutched my arm, her eyes twinkling with laughter, that I saw to what good use the old lady was putting this pause. She had seated herself on the edge of the curb, taken off her shoes and was cooling her feet, modestly stockinged, in the water which half-filled the gutter with the passing of a sprinkling wagon. Her smile was as guileless as a child's as she looked up at people who paused to stare at her. 'My feet get awful hot,' she informed them. 'This feels mighty good, I tell you!' There was frank envy in the eyes of more than one smartly shod woman.

Once I got them into the Manufacturers' Building, certain that they would be fascinated if they'd only start looking at things, but Cal paused only a few minutes before a marvel of a modern threshing machine and then looked bored. Mrs.

Van was impressed with a churn that 'turned half ways around an' then back again just for nothin' at all,' and then she, too, was ready for more entertaining exhibits.

We never had any decent food in the grounds. I couldn't sneak off and snatch a bite, as they were so afraid of getting lost that they wouldn't let me out of their sight. Attractive eating places had no charm for them. They haunted the free sample booths and bought edibles at every out-of-door stand on the grounds. Hot dogs, hamburgers, sea-food, popcorn, taffy, greasy doughnuts — we carried paper bags of them all day long, munching as we walked. In this place where we were offered the opportunity of learning about man's progress in science and industry and art, we spent all our time with trick dogs, the monkey that stood on his head, the green-turbaned Turk who swallowed a sword, and such. Strange to say, they both liked the native dive where the Hula girls danced, and we visited it time after time. Cal modestly sat well apart from us and he and his mother never discussed the dances nor admitted to anyone they'd seen them.

The Ferris Wheel and merry-go-round were the only form of entertainment we three enjoyed in common. On them at least it was cool and we could rest our feet. We rode them so much that the operators called Cal by his first name. With the climax of a never-to-be-forgotten day when a man climbed a greased pole and got a thousand dollars off the top of it, our week at the Fair ended. That night I carefully set down what Mrs. Van had spent on me since we left home, added it up, and put the cash in the money I was handling for her.

'Mrs. Van,' I came out boldly, 'I've decided to stay and visit my cousins a few days. I'll put you on the train and start you back to Seattle and you'll be all right without me. Here's the money you spent on me. I'll feel better to pay my own way.'

She didn't like it a little bit — going back without me. But I held out. The next morning, when I walked out of the train shed, I was a free woman again. I heaved a deep sigh of relief and went out to the Fair.

I gave the Van Fleets a few days to get settled elsewhere

and then returned to Seattle, consumed with curiosity — mixed with a bit of anxiety over the old lady. Father and Mother and Isobel were at dinner when I arrived. I soon had the story of our late guests. When they found my family in residence — 'surprising' me when I should return — Mrs. Van went out immediately and scoured the vicinity for housekeeping rooms. 'I'm goin' to keep as clost as I can,' she declared.

'The dear old soul wasn't gone an hour before she was back all smiles over the lovely place she had. Flowers in the yard and everything, in the home of a "widow-woman." ' Mother exchanged a significant look with Isobel.

'Guess what, Ma!' Isobel had the look of one about to impart choice gossip. 'Her landlady — who she said seemed a "nice homebody" — is none other than The Widow!'

'Good Heavens! That hussy!'

The brassy blond of forty or so who lived in the next block across a vacant lot from us had declared herself a widow when she moved into the house some months before. But her home was far from manless. One didn't need to be a detective to figure out how she was making her living. The thought of the guileless Van Fleets in such a place shocked me. But maybe they'd not see anything amiss. And Cal was old enough to take care of himself. Or was he?

I was to wish more and more that the Van Fleets had moved far away from us. For there was no escaping them. My sister Florence and her family had come to the Coast and were living in Tacoma at this time. They could never drive over for a family dinner with us that the Vans didn't appear with a couple of pies or a mountainous cake, or even a turkey — though it would be too late to roast it. Mother and the old lady enjoyed each other and liked to compare pioneering experiences, but we did pine for some privacy.

I could hardly express a wish for anything within reason that Mrs. Van didn't insist on giving me the money for it. I usually refused. Once she said, looking at Cal, 'She might as well take a little now and then, Cal. You'll have more'n you'll ever spend.'

'Well, his wife can spend it for him,' I said teasingly.

He blushed and hung his head like some bashful boy. No one had ever seen him look at a woman. The mere suggestion he might ever marry embarrassed him painfully.

Mrs. Van Fleet had been at The Widow's about two months when she had a stroke. She got better, but wasn't able to leave her bed. Isobel and I and The Widow took turns looking after her. Isobel usually stayed nights. The old woman didn't seem to need much and slept well. Her mind was clear and her appetite, as usual, something with which to reckon. But her poor legs — those strong legs that had carried her across the plains and had done long duty on the old gravel-bed ranch — were useless now.

'You know, Ma,' Isobel said to me one morning after she came home from her night with Mrs. Van, 'I believe old Cal's sweet on The Widow!'

'Poor boob! Maybe he'll stop spitting awhile if he's in love. She'll make quick work of him, I imagine.'

'On the contrary, she's encouraging him, if I'm not mistaken. The old lady's going to leave a lot of money when she dies. Marrying Cal would be an easy way for that scheming hussy to get her hands on it.'

'Well, she's taking awfully good care of the old girl meanwhile, which is all that interests me. Mrs. Van is a hardy soul and may live for years.'

That evening I was called to Tacoma, as my sister had been taken very ill. Before leaving, I went in to see Mrs. Van Fleet, who was feeling much improved. When we were alone for a moment, she looked around cautiously to see if anyone was within earshot, and pulled me down close.

'I've been meanin' to tell you to take the money out of my corset,' she whispered to me, 'but now I'm gettin' so much better I'll be wearin' my clothes again before long. And I like the feel of that money on me. But come a night I don't feel so good, I'll tell Isobel to take it for you. She knows about it already. I told her — just in case — it's yours when I'm gone. But don't you go worryin' about me.'

I had been out of town only a short time when Mrs. Van

had another stroke and had to be taken to the hospital. Isobel remembered the money when she was getting her ready for the ambulance, and, as the old woman was unconscious and couldn't be asked about it, thought she'd better take it in charge. But when she looked in the corset pocket the bills were gone. She hunted around as much as she could, but they had completely vanished. She had her suspicions.

Mrs. Van Fleet died shortly afterward. Cal and The Widow left immediately after the funeral. He'd 'phoned that they were getting married and were going on a trip. He'd see me when he came back. But I never saw him again.

It was two years or so before I knew anything more about him. And then, one day I read in a brief news item that a destitute man, identified as Calvin Van Fleet, had been found dead in his bed in an old beach shack he had occupied alone for about a year. It was evident, when the coast guard found him, that he had been sick and without food for some time.

Poor Cal! I had visions of the furs and gowns and the limousine The Widow was probably enjoying on old Mrs. Van's gravel-bed pay-dirt.

ALBERTA

ALBERTA

When Isobel's brother, Alan Jarvis, was leaving Montana to join his partner, Jock Gordon, in Canada, he had jokingly asked us when we'd be going up to Alberta to visit them.

'When they build a railroad,' we replied.

At that time the railroad seemed an unlikely thing to expect. Northern Alberta seemed as far away as South Africa. But during the years that followed, the long, interesting, though infrequent letters from the homesteaders always ended with some remark about our visiting them. Finally they wrote they were building a cabin for us, connected to their own with porch and storeroom. When at last we heard a railway was really being built, we began to indulge in a lot of wishful thinking.

One day when I came in from a case, Isobel piled in my lap a half-dozen circulars describing the Edmonton, Dunvagen Railroad — later to become the Northern Alberta System — and the vast country it would open up. The first train running through Grand Prairie was scheduled to leave Edmonton in two months. Isobel's excitement was so apparent in her voice and the trembling of her hands as she poured our tea that my heart ached for her. She was young and beautiful, eager for the adventures of life — marriage, home, children, travel. But at that time there was no sure cure for her specific condition, and I knew the chances were against her.

She turned through the folders, pointing out things which interested her particularly. 'I couldn't resist sending for them, Ma. It's fun to imagine going up there, even if I can't.'

'Why can't you?' Desire had seized me and both my feet were itching. 'Isobel, do you really want to go up to that Grand Prairie country?'

'More than anything in the world. Even if it kills me.'

'Do you think you could stand the trip? Once we got up there, I know you could be comfortable enough with the new cabin Al has been writing about and the things we could take up.'

'Ma, do you honestly mean it?'

'Certainly I mean it. If you really want to go. But think it over carefully. We'd be a long way from doctors, and winter is coming on and ——'

'Oh, I know!' she interrupted. 'I've gone over it a million times. What if I should get sick and die! It'd be better than lingering along with dry rot.'

She could not sleep that night for talking of the plan. Why shouldn't we take that first train which ran into Grand Prairie? I let the thing cool a few days to see what her reaction might be. Like most patients with thyroid neurasthenia, she was more or less perverse and often changed her mind and declared she didn't want things I knew she wanted most. But to this she held with growing eagerness. We wrote Alan we were planning to go unless he wrote us not to do so. We knew it would take a long time to get an answer, but meanwhile went on with preparations for the trip.

It had never been to the interest of the Hudson's Bay Company to promote the settlement of Northern Alberta. It would ruin trading with the Indians if bales of rich furs might no longer be exchanged for a string of beads, a little tobacco, or a few yards of bright calico. There had not been even a road into Grand Prairie, but only the Hudson's Bay Company's pack trail, which the homesteaders followed. It ran north from Edmonton to the crossing of the Athabaska River, around the east side of Lesser Slave Lake, and west into the Prairie, through four hundred miles of muskeg terrain. A team with light wagon could get through in the summertime, but there were sink-holes all around Slave Lake where a wheel might drop in or a horse get mired.

Winter was a better time for travel, when the ice was thick over these holes, and homesteaders could take short cuts across frozen lakes and rivers, traveling by compass, instinct, and the grace of God. They freighted on sleds — 'drags' — drawn by oxen or horses, carrying huge loads of farm machinery, household goods, and food to last a year. Women and children rode in crude comfort in a sort of caboose heated by a stove. It took weeks to make the round trip out of Edmonton for supplies and the homesteader must eliminate every ounce of freight not absolutely necessary.

Christmas decorations were not likely to have been included on freight lists. With this in mind, Isobel and I invited all our friends to a party one night and told them we were ready for donations of all sorts to take to Alberta to make a grand Christmas for the neighboring children of whom Alan and Jock had written us. The response in the next few days was overwhelming: clothes, toys, books, tree ornaments, a portable phonograph and dozens of good records. We made joyous plans for a glittering tree and gifts for children who had never dreamed of such things. Many of them had been born in the country and had never seen tinsel or ornaments.

We made reservations for the first train out of Edmonton. The time was drawing near when we should start, but as yet no word had come from Al. But we decided to go, even if we had to turn right around and come back. And so in late August of 1915, just nine years after we'd first talked of this visit, we sailed for Vancouver, B.C. From there we would take the C.P.R. for Edmonton.

It was on the boat that Isobel had her first reaction — entirely mental. The excitement and preparation had probably been too strenuous. I had been unable to persuade her to take suitable dresses and shoes for ordinary house wear. She had pictured herself a cowgirl, riding the range — though she'd never been on a horse — in corduroys and flannels. Now, with her trunks in the hold of the ship, she wept bitterly and blamed me for persuading her to come.

I had gone through many of these spells of hysteria with her, but now, tired myself, I was overwhelmed with fear that the immediate future held little pleasure for me. Isobel really was a sick woman. Suppose this trip might prove fatal to her? I left the stateroom and walked the deck trying to figure out a solution to the problem. Isobel was very dear to me and I wanted her to be happy. But there was no need to sacrifice myself too far if she gained nothing by it.

When we neared the harbor, I told her I had decided it was all a mistake, her going to Grand Prairie, and I was going to refund her money and she could go home on the return boat. I would go on alone, if for nothing else but to save face after all the fanfare the friends in Seattle gave us. I could get work in Calgary or Edmonton in one of the hospitals the folders said were being built. They'd need nurses in this new country. But Isobel wept and said if I did that she'd jump overboard and drown herself. She was sorry she'd been so unreasonable and did want to go on.

It was a glorious morning when we left Vancouver, all sun and soft fall breeze with just enough nip in it to provoke good appetites. The Fraser River country was a little different from anything I'd seen in the States. Clean — that one word described it best — no dust, just trees and tannish-brown grass with an odor of drying aromatic herbs.

At Calgary a young mother with a ten-day-old infant was helped on the train. She refused to have her berth made up and sat bolt upright in her seat, while her baby yelled at the top of its small lungs. I held it part of the time, trying vainly to find the cause of its misery. Finally the conductor, a burly Scot, declared he knew all about babies and would fix it up

I was horrified when he brought a stiff whiskey toddy and insisted I give it to the child. I told him that was outside my province as a nurse and I wouldn't do it.

'Nurse —? Hoot, lassie, I've saved the life o' mony an ane wi' it in my time. The bairn's fair done in. Its blood will be on oor honds for failin' to do our juty, should it gi' up the speerit. Here — watch noo!'

He took the baby over and seemed as much at home with it as I did. I don't know how much Scotch and water he poured down the infant's throat, but it certainly stopped crying. And went right to sleep. The mother left the train at their home station in the night. I've often wondered if the 'bairn' ever woke up.

We got into bustling, wind-swept Edmonton on time and were piloted to our hotel to await the departure of the Edmonton and Dunvagen, which could not make the start exactly as scheduled. It was cold and there was no heat in our room. I persuaded Isobel to go to bed with a hot-water bottle and a good book while I went for a walk. I had to hold on to my hat and try at the same time to keep the gusts from lifting my skirts too high. I noticed everyone I met stared at my legs. It wasn't until I noticed other women's skirt-lengths that I realized the style of short skirts prevailing in the United States had not yet reached Edmonton. Here they still swept the tobacco juice from the walks, while mine were nearly halfway up to my knees. All the way people stared and laughed at me. When at last a boy walking with his mother pointed at me and yelled, 'Oh, Ma! Lookit, lookit!' I went back to the hotel and let down some of the wide hem of my skirt. (And the farther we went on our trip, the longer we had to make our skirts. And even when there was no more to let down, our men in Grand Prairie were a bit ashamed of us.)

We literally blew out of Edmonton as we had blown in. The atmosphere was cleared of dust, however, and the visibility was excellent. Distances were most deceptive in that rarefied air. After we were settled in the combination sleeper-diner-day coach, on the end of the first freight and passenger train that ran into Grand Prairie, we watched hour after hour landmarks on a rise of ground which never seemed to get any nearer. Our compartment was clean, comfortable, and even elegant. On an adjustable table meals as fine as we had ever eaten were served to us. And amazingly, it was a 'Mountie' of huge bulk and height, who, with his badge on his white starched coat, served as porter, cook, and waiter! It seems the cook engaged for the trip didn't appear when the train was ready to leave Edmonton, so this policeman offered to take his place. There were two other Mounted Police, one the tallest man I ever saw. He went into the movies later, I heard. Most of the passengers were Norwegian emigrants from the Old Country.

Some years before this, a band of Norwegians, true to their hardy pioneering instincts, had migrated to a locality out on this 'last frontier.' There were but few women among them, since most of the women and children and parents waited in the homeland for the building of the railroad and suitable houses on the Prairie. The Norwegians in our car were some of these left-behind relatives, en route now to meet their loved ones in this new land. Excitement had been high among them. They looked out the windows, pointed, gesticulated, and all talked at once in rolling gutturals.

At last a dark spot showed on the level prairie. As we drew nearer to it, forms took shape — covered wagons, oxen, people moving about campfires. The emigrants for an hour past had been gathering together their belongings and piling them ready to get off the train: feather beds, belongings tied in blankets by the four corners, strange skin bags bulging tremendously and smelling of cheese. And then the train slowed down and stopped. Emigrants began getting off with their possessions on their backs, and I saw enacted one of the most thrilling and heart-warming scenes of my life. Such screaming and shouting and hugging and kissing and crying, such running from one to the other as long separated families were united. We other passengers just stood staring at them with lumps in our throats. The conductor forgot to pull the cord for the 'Go-ahead' signal.

'Noo, there's what like heaven might be,' he said, wiping his eyes, 'gin there be sic a place.'

We jogged along for seventy-two hours over the new, uneven roadbed, stopping often and long while working crews reconditioned portions of the track. As we neared the end of our journey, Isobel and I were about as excited as the emigrants had been. It was black night and a drizzle of rain was falling when the conductor called, 'End o' Line! And here ye are, young ladies.'

We peered into the dark fearfully. Not a soul was in sight. Not a lighted window nor a building to be seen. As we paused on the platform, a man came around the end of the car swinging a lantern.

'Are Al Jarvis's sister and her nurse here?' he called.

'Right here!' we sang out, much relieved. He held the lantern high and we clambered down the steps, sinking our best shoes ankle-deep in mud.

The conductor peered down at the man. 'Why, 'tis Belmont, noo. I didna ken ye'd come up here. Ladies, this is Laird Belmont.'

We looked at him in astonishment. 'Is that a title or your name?' I ventured.

'Title,' said the gentleman shortly. 'Call me Chester.'

I could see only that he was of medium height, had a round pink face, and small blue eyes that were decidedly shifty. From later conversation with him, we gathered that he was from New Zealand, where he evidently spent his time playing the races. Isobel summed him up neatly the next day. 'Lord Belmont looks to me as though he might have to get away from wherever he is in a great hurry, and hide himself where he'd be hard to find.' Remittance man, obviously.

But at the moment we were interested in other matters. 'Where's Al?' we chorused in unison.

'I say' — our guide waved the lantern around — 'let's get out of the mud before we mire to our knees. Al won't be in until tomorrow. It's a long story. He'll get your other luggage. It can stay on the train here tonight.'

We said good-bye to the conductor and slogged around the

end of the train, and immediately realized that we hadn't seen the town before because it was on the other side of the track — all four lighted windows of it. There were no sidewalks.

'I'll take you to Dunlap's for the night,' said our titled escort. 'It's just about what would be a block away — if there were blocks. Reggie Dunlap's a friend of Al's. Minnie'll fix you up. I live there too.'

We got the story as we waded along through the mud. Jock Gordon had come in to town that day to get the mail — the first time in two months. He found the letters we'd written weeks before and on realizing we were due this very night on the first train, he was completely unnerved. He gulped down four drinks of Minnie's Saskatoon berry wine, asked Reggie to put us up for the night, and set off at a dead gallop for the ranch house twenty-nine miles away, to take the news to Al. He said to tell us he was sorry, but they'd bring in the wagon to get us tomorrow, and would do the honors then.

The Dunlap place, we learned later, was a little better than the ordinary log house of the homesteader. It had a kitchen and bedroom off the main room, and an attic over all. Reggie Dunlap opened the door wide when he heard us coming. He had a boyish face and dreamy gray eyes. We wondered before the evening was over why he ever came to the Prairie. He told us he was a poet and hated ugliness.

Minnie had a round, plump little body which contrasted oddly with her thin, high-cheeked face. She had brown eyes and brown hair and was a pleasant sort of person. She made us feel as though we were long-lost sisters and had our shoes off in no time to clean the mud from them. The bedroom was immaculate. There were fresh straw mattresses on the bunks and clean blankets.

'We'll have some supper ready for you in no time,' Minnie told us. 'Nobody knew just when the train was goin' to get in.'

I never did find out whether Minnie was Mrs. Dunlap or Lady Belmont. No one seemed to know and no one seemed to care. The thin moral line was covered by her good pies and Saskatoon berry wine. From something she said, we judged it was Lord Belmont and his twice yearly check from England that made it possible for the improvident Reggie to spend his time writing poetry.

'Isn't this grand?' Isobel whispered to me as we snuggled down after a midnight supper.

'Happy, are you?'

'Who wouldn't be? Tomorrow we see Al. I wonder if he's changed much.'

When I woke the next morning, I looked out of the window at the country we'd entered under cover of darkness. Half a dozen log and lumber houses, one windowless and tall, one large and squatty, were scattered over a prairie which rolled up into low hills and vanished in the dim blue distance of forest or 'Bush,' as they called it there. Reggie Dunlap identified the larger buildings for us at breakfast. The tall one was for grain storage, and the big flat one was a center where homesteaders gathered for social events and to discuss the problems of the day. There had been a store in part of this hall at one time, but the cost of bringing in goods by ox-team and sleigh hadn't proved very profitable. But now that the railroad had come in, they'd have stores before long.

Isobel had awakened fresh and enthusiastic for our venture. After a hearty breakfast we would have enjoyed walking around the little settlement, but the mud looked bottomless.

Jock appeared about noon with a team and democrat wagon. He had changed a lot. He still retained that upright bearing he had acquired as a soldier in the Boer War and in the service of the Canadian Mounted Police years before, but he was brown and thin and a bit worried-looking. We drove to the railroad and our baggage was loaded on. From the high spring seat Isobel and I waved farewell to Reggie, Minnie, and Lord Belmont, who had come down with us to the train. Jock slapped the reins on the horses' backs, and we were off on the last leg of our journey.

For a time Jock seemed too preoccupied to answer our questions halfway. He told us frankly that Al wasn't very happy when he heard we were arriving on the Prairie.

'I might as well spill the beans,' he said finally. 'The fact is, we're about done in for funds. The garden froze and the wheat crop failed two years running. But we'll make out. You expect these things when you're homesteading.'

'But we're boarders, not visitors,' I explained. 'You needn't worry about us.'

The Prairie was beautiful country and I loved at once its wide stretches of grasslands, low-rolling hills, fringes of timber, and endless small lakes alive with water-fowl. The grass was brown now except along the margin of the lakes, but late-blooming wild roses spread low on the ground and their fragrance filled the air. A couple of coyotes loped up over a hill. We yelled and they ran like mad. The whole country was like a park and seemed high up, close to the sky. Ranches were few and far apart.

Jock told us, as we rode along, that he had to pick up a bedspring and mattress for us. 'Unless you prefer slats and a straw tick. We're borrowing them from the Markels. They freighted in an extra bed when Hallie Markel's father and mother were coming up. Do you remember our writing about Hallie's mother — the one who got lost in the Bush on the way up? They found traces of shelters she'd made, and pieces torn from her clothes tied onto bushes, but winter came and it wasn't till the next summer they found her bones. They were scattered as though wolves had torn the body, but rings were still dangling on a skeleton finger.'

Isobel shivered. 'Yes, we talked about it a lot. It was horrible.'

'Hallie's never been the same since. And now she's acting queer and getting in bad with people. Maybe you two who've never been mixed up with any of it can help her. At first, when neighbors came to sympathize, she acted as though nothing had happened. Got them good meals, talked about crops or kids: never mentioned her mother, nor gave anyone else a chance to mention her. Some of the women up here think you've no respect for the dead unless you have hysterics in darkened rooms and wear heavy black for a year or so, and they were all for getting Hallie into mourning even before hope of finding her mother had been given up. But even when she knew her mother was dead, Hallie wouldn't put on mourning. And now — here's the queer thing — she's got so she won't have anything to do with the neighbors: won't go to their houses or any of their social affairs, and won't let any of them in her house — not even her best friend, Marie de Witt. Yet she'll have her husband take her to the public dances at the Farmers' Hall clear over to End o' Line. She doesn't know many people there and will dance only with Phil, then after a few rounds want to go home. We can't figure her out.'

'What was she like before all this happened?' I asked.

'She was the most popular woman up here. When she first came to the Prairie, none of us thought she'd last a year. Right out of college she was, but green as grass about farm things. Phil's twelve years older than she is and a mighty fine sort. She was crazy about him — still is. Hallie started right in to learn everything a farm woman should know, driving a team, milking, and all the rest. When the folks were getting ready to put up a building for church and school, Hallie drove a team to the Bush to help bring out logs for it. When it was finished, she took charge of the music. Everybody liked her — except a couple of old cats who were jealous. They're the ones having fits about her going to public dances and not wearing mourning.'

'Will she shut the door in our faces?' asked Isobel anxiously.

'No, you're Al's folks. He has a way with people and Hallie hasn't excluded him. She's probably lonely as the devil and might be glad to see someone who's never been associated with any of it.'

It was along in the afternoon when we reached the Markels' place. Isobel and I went to the log house with Jock. The woman who opened the door to our knock was beautiful. Slender, graceful, with a sensitive face pale in spite of suntan. My first impression, as Hallie Markel was introduced to us, was the fear in her eyes. It was as though she were shrinking from an expected blow. But it passed, and there was in them tragic resignation. Her six-year-old daughter, Marigold, strikingly like the father, stood beside her.

Philip Markel was a gray-haired man of middle age. We liked him immensely from the start. He and Hallie didn't seem to belong to the Prairie, but rather to some cultured college town. Their log house was well furnished for a pioneer home and was restful and pleasing. Hallie brought in a steaming pot of tea and a plate of good cake, which were most welcome. Isobel and I tried to be as friendly as possible without being obvious, and before we left had made a date with the Markels to have dinner with us.

It was late afternoon when we came in sight of The Homestead. The buildings looked low and squatty amid such vastness. Two cabins, granaries, log stables and sheds, various pens and corrals, and large haystacks gave the place an important appearance. The cabins were on the bank of a deep ravine where a large waterhole, with springs bubbling up through it, furnished an abundance of clear, cold water. From the trees which fringed the miniature lake, vines, bright with fall color, swung in festoons to the ground.

Al came out of one of the cabins, shouting a welcome to us. He seemed taller and was thinner and flatter-hipped than when I had seen him last. His very blue eyes were keener and had lost their twinkle. They were the eyes of a man who had come to expect hardships. He had not tanned brown as Jock had with sun and wind and cold, but was red from the exposure. His heavy hair was concealed by a stocking cap which hung down to his waist and ended in a tassel. His greeting of us was so casual that for a moment I felt he was utterly indifferent. But I remembered his tendency to conceal his emotions. Old Granite! I was not surprised, when he gripped my hand, to feel he was trembling. We'd heard his sweetheart had turned him down after he left us in Montana. She refused to go to the Prairie to live. We'd wondered about him a lot — whether he'd find anyone up here. Jock told us Al didn't wear that stocking cap to keep his ears warm, but to hide the gray hair he was getting.

The new cabin was for our use, we were told. Its interior was a delightful surprise. Al had been a cabinet-maker and the floor and shelves and such furniture as he'd been able to make in the wintertime were of white birch; the chairs were made entirely without nails and were as comfortable as they were good-looking. We were grateful for the Markels' bedspring and mattress, some skin rugs, and a heating stove. The windows faced east and west and the room was flooded with mellow light from a sun just slipping down over the horizon. I felt at peace with the world and everything in it as I hung up my things.

Al had supper all ready for us, so we went into the other cabin. It was a combination kitchen-living-bedroom and had been built when the need for hurry was upon them. It was very crude compared to our quarters. The usual pioneer furnishings and household commodities were scattered around — water bucket and tin dipper with a tiny rag in the hole that would no longer take solder; cupboards and table, shelves containing boxes of nails and tools and patches for shoes and harness; a sewing basket, and above the washbench a mirror and comb and brush container with a picture of Queen Victoria on the front of it. An almanac dangled from a string nailed to the end of the cupboard, and a map of the United States and Canada decorated part of one wall. In one end of the room were brown-blanketed bunks which served as seats.

I remember to this day the great slices of Al's light bread and the home-canned Saskatoon berries, milder than huckleberries, richer than blueberries. They had been put up in commercial tins with a square of muslin over the top and the grooved lids pressed down. No vacuum cap, no soldering, no sealing wax.

We told the men we had come prepared to stay several months if they would have us, and wished to be a help rather than a hindrance; that we were paying our way and no argument about it; otherwise we'd go home.

Al's grin was a bit grim. 'Well, I'd swallow my pride if it choked me, to have you with us.'

'Just to see you boys and the country and place here — that's worth the effort and expense of the trip,' I told him.

We unpacked the boxes of foodstuffs — things that had

become luxuries to these men on the Prairie. They were as pleased as small boys. We sat up most of the night visiting I asked to have work assigned me and was told I could take care of the chickens and cooking and other household duties with Isobel's help.

After Isobel was in bed, I went outside and stood a moment. Never have I seen stars so large and so near; they seemed to rest in the tops of the poplars. The air was sweet with odor of dry grass, of sod, of new hay. I breathed it in deeply, loving this remote northern country

Privately I told the men the next day how ill Isobel really was, and what a fight she was making to carry on her life, whatever she had left of it, in as normal a way as possible. I warned them that if they made fun of her cowgirl attire, it would spoil her visit and might have bad results on her.

We unpacked our boxes and when the men had gone to work transformed our cabin with books, rugs, cushions, draperies, candlesticks, and numerous other things. The room had so much charm when we finished that we were sure the homesteaders would be blown off their feet by it. Al had told us that with the exception of a huge mouth-organ, the one Emmy Gilmore played for the community dances, there was no music in that part of the Prairie. So it was with great thrills that we set up the phonograph and arranged the records around it.

We set the dinner table with our best cloth and what dishes we had brought with us, put on candles, and had a colorful arrangement of the vivid-hued vines in a low bowl. We had put the table in our cabin, so the boys would get the effect all at once when they came in. When we saw them coming, washed and combed and grinning, Isobel turned on the phonograph and they entered to the rhythm of 'Alexander's Rag-Time Band.' Those music-starved boys flung themselves together in a mad embrace and went through the wildest dance imaginable. Only when they had about exhausted themselves would they stop to look around at all our changes in the room and sit down to the dinner on which we had spent much thought. Even then during the meal one or the other of them would jump up and do a few more steps around to the music. Their enthusiasm over the looks of the place and the meal more than repaid our efforts.

I remember that music as though it were yesterday. Harry Lauder's rolling *r-r-r-r*'s in 'O-o-oh, it's nice to get up in the mor-r-nin', but it's nicer to stay in bed!' The immortal Caruso and the superb Calvé. When John McCormack came on with his lovely 'Somewhere a Voice is Calling,' Al choked over his food and hurried from the table. We ignored it, for we had seen his face. I heard him blowing his nose outside. I wondered if the faithless sweetheart had sung him that song. I was grateful for the strawberry cobbler we had evolved from our supplies. His eyes almost popped out as he dug into it. 'Tastes just like fresh berries, Sis,' he declared. 'Some day we'll grow them up here.' When dinner was finished, I slipped that record into a box under the bed, and to play safe added the one of 'I Hear You Calling Me.'

The days usually began with a burst of sunshine. Al tapped at the window near our bed when he came from the cowshed with the milk, as a sign breakfast would be served by the time I was up and dressed. He always got the breakfast. Great slices of bread would be toasting atop the range, coffee simmering, and the table set for three of us. Isobel always slept late.

Afterwards, the men left for the fields, carrying sandwiches and tea to brew over an open fire. When they were gone, the day was all mine. The air was frosty and clear. Geese honked overhead and often settled down on the margin of a lake near the ranch to feed and rest before taking off again. The trees in the ravine were deep yellow and scarlet now and every vagrant wind brought down bright showers of leaves.

But perhaps the mainspring from which my happiness flowed was the knowledge that I was useful to the lives of these men and Isobel. The men had little time for housekeeping. There were stacks of winter clothing, particularly socks, to be washed and mended for cold weather. To see those hungry laborers coming in to a good hot dinner with no time wasted preparing it for themselves, to notice their keen pleasure over tablecloth and napkins, a candle now and then, and some arrangement of grasses or seed pods or leaves — that was joy.

The days were gloriously sunny. Jock and Al were doing their fall plowing and bringing home each night a load of wild hay. I often walked down to ride home on the load, loving the sweet scent of it. I urged Isobel to join me, but she always refused. She was being decidedly unhappy over her clothes. She was tired of the mannish corduroys and khaki she'd brought, but when I offered to make her some dresses out of goods I'd brought, she wouldn't hear to it. There was little I could do. If I left her, she resented it; if I stayed at home with her or humored her moods, she was uncomfortable. But I knew this obstinacy was covering pain and weakness and the bitterness of one who couldn't bring herself to accept her fate. With all my heart I longed to help her; but she rebelled — and I couldn't blame her. She didn't want to die. Many times she seemed pleased and excited at being up here in this wild country, and would link her arm through mine, squeeze it affectionately and say, 'We made it, Ma, didn't we?' But I had a feeling it would have been much better if I had not brought her up here.

It was Jock who finally suggested we justify Isobel's clothes by giving her a horse to ride. 'The bay is nice and gentle and would be a good mount for her,' he said.

'But you know she's never been on a horse in her life,' I reminded him.

'What's the difference? She's been hating these clothes. It would be good for her mentally and physically to learn to ride. She can take it slow and easy, you know.'

'Jock, I believe you have something there. We'll try it. Get me a nag, too, and I'll ride with her.'

At breakfast the next morning I asked Al if he'd lend me a pair of pants. Surprisingly, Isobel had agreed without argument that riding would be wonderful for her. Her riding clothes were smart and she looked well in them. To have me looking like some circus clown by contrast pepped her up considerably. They all shouted with laughter when I came out. They got a big kick out of my riding costume. The pants came well up under my armpits and the legs were rolled up at the bottom to keep them from dragging, while the extra girth was wrapped around and pinned with safety pins and securely belted to keep me from losing them. I wore a flannel shirt, had a red handkerchief around my neck, and Al's stocking cap snugged down over my hair. What with laughing so much at me and basking in the admiration the men lavished on her, Isobel was in a gayer mood than she had been for weeks.

Her mount was a gentle, swaybacked old bay, while I was to have Jock's perfectly safe saddle-horse. Isobel had the one saddle, since Al had lent his to a neighbor a few days before. She thought she could get on her horse better from the fence, so she climbed up on the rails and the bay was brought alongside. Isobel stuck her foot up over the horse's back timidly and he turned his head to see what such irregular proceeding meant. When she eased herself cautiously into the saddle, the old bay groaned and shifted position.

'Whoa! Whoa!' Isabel jerked at the reins. The horse backed up dutifully and almost flattened her leg against the fence as she kept on pulling. She screamed and he threw his head up and down, bewildered by such strange maneuvers. Al came and led him away from the fence while Jock put me up on the bare back of his horse, Red. Isobel pulled on her reins again and once more the bay began to back.

'Kick him in the sides!' Al yelled at her. She obeyed and the gentle old horse switched his tail and began to trot. I trotted after her. She went up and down a few times and her feet slid out of the stirrups.

'Save me, Ma! For God's sake, save me!' she shrieked. And then she let go the reins and slid off over the old bay's rump. He stopped, turned around and sort of nosed her, as friendly horses do, mumbling her sleeve in his soft old pips. She, seeing him loom above her, apparently intent on eating her, let out such a screech that my horse reared in fright. It was too much for Red. He took the bit in his teeth, laid back his ears, and stretching himself out in good imitation of a jack rabbit in full flight, made a bee line for the de Witt place, half a mile away. He'd often pastured there and he evidently decided it was much pleasanter territory than this noisy spot.

I hadn't been on a horse for years and Jock told me afterward that every time I bounced into the air he could see the sun, Seven Mile Butte, and a big clump of poplars between me and the horse. I believed him. Red didn't stop. I was beginning to be nauseated from the motion and from swallowing blood from my bitten tongue when the runaway leaped up a bank from a ravine and headed straight for the open door of a barn right ahead. I tried to duck, but there wasn't time. He scraped me off neatly and I landed spread-eagled at the feet of two men who had dashed to head him off, but failed to connect in time.

I had never met George de Witt or Jake Downing, his hired man, and they probably thought when they looked at me that they were having something more than an ordinary 'morning after.' I was jarred and a bit scared, but as they tried to lift me I found my greatest suffering was from laughter. I couldn't stop to breathe. When I found voice enough to speak and told them what had happened, they roared with me. We introduced ourselves, the men snorting with mirth every time they took in some new detail of my get-up. My belt had broken and I had to hold up the pants to keep them from falling off. George de Witt insisted I go up to the house to get myself together and regretted that his wife had gone to see a sick neighbor.

He was a good-looking, well-groomed man, who wore his working clothes with a natty air and had quite a way with the ladies, I could see. The house was well furnished for the Prairie, and beautifully clean. I wondered what sort his wife was. He insisted on driving me home, and I accepted gladly, as I was good and sore. Red, meek as a lamb now, we tied to the back of the buggy.

I dreaded to think of the state in which I would find Isobel, but she was a good sport this time. She was still sitting in the hay beside the stack, laughing at herself and me. She thoroughly enjoyed wearing her riding clothes after that, but she resolutely refused to ride ever again.

Jock came riding home one night to announce that the countryside wanted to have a dance at The Homestead, and for us to set the date.

Our cabin was only sixteen by twenty-four feet. The main cabin was the same. How on earth a crowd of people could dance in so small a space I couldn't see, but Al assured me it was more than many had who entertained the whole community. Late in the fall, after the plowing was done and winter wheat planted, the folks from miles around liked to gather at some ranch, bring food and stay and dance and visit all night, then have breakfast before they went home. We set the date eagerly and Jock spent several days going around to invite all the neighbors within a far-reaching circle.

'This is certainly going to be something, Ma!' said Isobel excitedly, when the day arrived. The bed came down and all the furniture in our cabin was carried out with it. A neighbor brought wide boards which we laid on boxes against the walls and covered with blankets for seats. Al and Isobel and I had baked huge supplies of bread, cake, and cookies. The wash-boiler was scrubbed and scalded to be used for coffee.

Early in the evening, in sleighs, democrats, covered wagons, and on horseback they began to come, some from as far as forty miles away. Soon the long table in the main cabin was piled high with their foodstuffs. Pickles and jam, fried chicken and roasts, butter, cottage cheese, and cold pancakes.

Most of the women were in white shirtwaists and black skirts which swept the floor. Their hair was worn in the same style they had worn when they arrived at the Prairie years before. Most of them said, 'Pleased to meet you,' and gripped our hands in friendly sincerity. A few asked me how old I was. I found out later that women of forty or so were considered quite old and they sat it out and let the younger women have the limited dancing space.

In time the fellow who was a master hand at calling off the dances, sang out, 'Take your partners for the Grand March!' I put on a record of one of Sousa's marches. The phonograph was a complete surprise. There was a surprised hush, then they went wild. Old Scots stepped waist-high and reared back until I was afraid they'd topple over. Tears ran down brown and weather-hardened faces. Children, wide-eyed, stood and stared at the phonograph in astonishment, while more timid ones hid their faces in their mothers' skirts and cried from fright. The Reverend McKay, the minister, clapped his hands, tapped his foot, and now and then raised his arms, puffed his cheeks, and went through the pantomime of a bagpipe player. I was never so moved or so happy in my life.

The grand march ended with prolonged clapping. Men wiped their faces, drank cold water, and then went out to the other cabin to have a nip of something stronger. Grapevine schottische, square dances, slow waltzes, then Jock announced we would have the one-step, which up to then had not been introduced into that part of the country. I had taught it to Al, and we went round and round on the too-small floor, giving our demonstration. Suddenly, there seemed to be some disturbance and Madame Cline, a pious old prude, appeared with her good man in tow, he most reluctant, she with head held high, hatted and coated, evidently leaving. We stopped dancing.

The woman pointed in outrage to a picture Isobel and I had brought with us and hung on the wall. It was 'September Morn,' the nude maiden knee-deep in water. 'I ain't goin' to stay in any house that has such nasty pictures hung up to shame folks,' she declared, the hairs in the big mole on her chin fairly quivering with righteous wrath. 'If I'd a seen it when I first come, I'd never of taken off my wraps.'

'But Mrs. Cline, that picture is part of our evening's entertainment.' Resourceful old Jock rose to the occasion. 'You mustn't miss hearing about it or you'd never forgive yourself. Our nurse here from the States, Mrs. Hughes, brought it up and was just going to tell its story when we finished this dance.' While he spoke, he had been taking off our guest's hood and coat, and now he looked at me wickedly, as much as to say, 'Well, damn me! I've done pretty well so far. Now it's your turn.'

I wanted to kill him. I had no idea of what I was going to say when I stood there, with them all looking at me expectantly. My tongue was dry and the back of my neck prickled. But I had to do it. Finally, I made up a long yarn with a religious smack to it about an artist who lost his sight and promised the Lord that if he could have his sight restored, he would always ask for guidance before painting a picture. Shortly afterward, the artist's sight was miraculously restored. In gratitude, the artist then prayed for guidance and immediately he was inspired to paint this picture of a chaste and beautiful maiden to symbolize the fresh loveliness of that September morning when sight was given him to look once more upon the Creator's handiwork in the universe about him.

'But we would not for the world offend anyone who cannot see its spiritual message,' I finished. And I walked over and turned 'September Morn' to the wall. As I passed Jock, I gave him, unobserved, the good swift kick on the shin he so richly deserved.

In relays the guests all filed into the main cabin, where they were served meat and bread and pickles and cake and pie. Afterward, a few of the men bedded down on the hay in the barn, and some of the women laid straw ticks and blankets on the floor for the children and themselves. Others sat up and visited or played the phonograph. In the morning we all had coffee again. Eggs, too, scarce as they were on the Prairie. Then the housewives gathered up their beds, their dishes, their husbands, and their kids and took themselves off, after telling us again and again what a wonderful time they'd had and how they wanted us to come to their homes as soon as we could. Soon the Prairie was dotted north, south, east, and west with our guests going home. Al and I stood on the porch in the morning sun and watched the last group out of sight. Then we went inside and sat down in the confusion of food and dishes.

'That Swede, Olaf — you were nice to him,' Al commented between sips of coffee. 'He appreciated it.'

'I felt sorry for him. He seemed out of place and bashful.'

'I'm glad you paid him a little attention. He's trying hard to improve. He used to be the world's champion cusser. He freights with four pair of oxen to one sleigh, and somehow freighting and cussing go together. One day Olaf was trying to get a heavy load over Wolf Hill. It's a mighty steep grade and his lead team balked on him. Olaf used all the profanity he knew and then began inventing a few new combinations. He was shouting some pretty choice ones when the Reverend McKay came along on his horse. The Reverend was pretty well shocked at the language the Swede was using. McKay told me about it afterward. He told Olaf he should be more patient with the creatures, and that what he needed wasn't profanity but prayer.

'"Prayer?" says Olaf. "You tank dem damn ox pull if Ay pray? Maybe dey tank Ay big damn fool!"

'"Try it," says McKay. "The Lord is powerful to help those who call upon him."

'Olaf looked skeptical, but he was desperate enough to try anything that would move his freight. So he walked around in front of his oxen and got down on his knees. He put his palms together high over his head and looking straight up into heaven he put his very heart into that prayer. "Yentlemen," he says, "for God's sake, PULL!"

'The big beasts looked at him in amazement. This was something new and it made them uneasy. The two balky ones leaned forward into the yoke, dug into the snow, and pulled with all their might, with the others following their lead. They almost ran over Olaf before he could scramble out of their way. By golly, the simple Swede thought it was a miracle. McKay got to working on him and before long we got word that Olaf was converted. Jock and I were so surprised that we went over to the prayer meeting at the school to see if it was so. Sure enough, Olaf was there. There were songs and a fine talk, and when it was asked if anyone wanted to testify, Olaf got up on his feet. He looked around, scared stiff. Twice he opened his mouth, but couldn't make a sound. Then he gulped and got started.

'"Ay yust vant to say, Ay ain't mooch gude on mak' speech. But Ay lofe my Yesus da same as any oder son of bitch in this year rum."

'Sis, do you think anyone laughed? Well, they didn't. They bowed their heads, and I'll be damned if Jock and I didn't get tears in our eyes.'

'Old Granite Jarvis!' I smiled at him. 'But say, wasn't this the same fellow you threw out of your cabin by the seat of his pants because he belched at your table?'

'Sure. Same man. And I'd do it again under the same circumstances. A man can smell of the barn and not know what a razor is, but he needn't eat like a hog and let off wind in your face! But that night was something I'll never forget — seeing old Olaf stand there so scared he could hardly speak and then using his own kind of talk to say what he felt so sincerely. I'll bet the Lord liked that testimony.'

* * *

After the Markels had dinner with us the first time, I made a point of seeing Hallie often. Not asking too much of her in the line of visiting at first, I'd suggest we meet down by the beaver dam and take our mending. We'd sit under the trees on the dry leaves and talk if we felt like it or watch the beavers at work if we didn't. Sometimes we'd build a little fire and make coffee. One night all of us went to the public dance at the Farmers' Hall. Hallie tried hard to be gay, but after a few dances was ready to go home. It was easy to see she was far from normal.

I had an interesting encounter before we left. After the punishment of a schottische with a husky French-Canadian, I sat down on a bench to rest. Philip Markel joined me.

'I suppose you know nearly everyone here, don't you?' I asked. 'Hallie says you've been here ten years. Why did people like you turn pioneer?'

'Asthma got the best of me. I had a good law practice in New York, but clients don't relish a legal adviser wheezing and coughing in their faces. I traveled all over the country trying to find a place where I could get a decent breath. I wasn't able to do manual labor and I was beginning to get desperate when I read about this country opening up. It occurred to me I might drive a team of oxen — wheezing might be as effective as cussing — so I wrote for a job as freighter. And was hired by return mail. The asthma vanished before I'd even reached Edmonton.'

'This is evidently your country, then. Have you had any attacks since?'

'Only when I went back to marry Hallie. I like this country immensely, but it's been a mistake keeping my wife and child here. This life isn't fair to them — so far away from things, so ——'

'I can't agree with you,' I interrupted. 'I spent my childhood under pioneering conditions on the Kansas prairies, and the memory of those days is my most cherished inheritance. The toughness of fiber you get stands you in good stead all the rest of your life.'

'With some, yes. But in Hallie's case ——' He broke off, his eye on a scrawny, sharp-nosed woman bearing down upon us. 'Excuse me. I'm deserting. This old gossip will introduce herself. You're new and she's fairly panting to find out some scandal about you.' Before I could reply, he was gone.

'I'm Mrs. Blossombalm,' the new arrival announced, seating herself so that she could look me over to the best advantage. 'And you're Mrs. Hughes, the nurse that come up from the States with Al Jarvis's sister, ain't you? I see you ain't dancin'?'

'Not for a while, Mrs. Blossombalm.' The name was incredible, especially on such a woman. 'I like to talk and get acquainted with people.'

'Well, young lady, I seen you talking with Markel. You're here with him and his wife, and since you're a newcomer it's my duty to tell you the less you have to do with that Hallie Markel, the better.'

My dislike for this woman increased steadily. 'Why?' I demanded.

'Why? Look at her — dancin' an' carryin' on at a public place. Look at her clo'es — a white waist an' a blue skirt an' a pink pin in her collar. Not a stitch of black. An' her mother's bones not yet in the grave a year out!'

'Isn't her mother about as dead now as she will be at the end of another year?'

For a minute, she was taken aback. Then her ill-fitting teeth rattled as she came at me again. 'Nurses can't be choosey, I suppose. Have to take all sorts of people, crazy or whatever.'

'Is Hallie Markel crazy?'

'Of course she is. Crazy an' indecent an' ——'

'In that case she needs good nursing. And good company.' I stood up and smiled down at her. 'But of course you must be careful of your reputation. Perhaps you shouldn't be seen at dances where she is.'

The venom and spite of this self-righteous old party made me want to choke her. I walked off before the desire should overpower me. Poor Hallie with the tongues of such people against her! I tried in every way I could to help her. It wasn't hard to imagine what the real Hallie might have been, but this woman was not she. Then one day down by the beaver dam, as we met with our darning, I noticed a change in her. Self-assurance was in her eyes for the first time. We talked casually and got at our darning. And then abruptly she laid down her sock and turned to me.

'Lora ——' She hesitated. 'I wish I could make you understand what you've meant to me since you came to the Prairie. For the first time since my mother disappeared, I'm beginning to feel like a sane person. I was afraid my mind ——'

'Shock, Hallie. I know how you tried to go on in a normal way, but these nervous reactions are bigger than we are sometimes.'

'One can't understand — can't even imagine — who hasn't lived through such an experience.' She pushed her mending away. 'After I came up here, it was eight years before I saw my father and mother. I was only twenty-two when I married and I'd always lived at home. Up here I was appalled at first, by the remoteness and vastness of it. I was out of my element and at times so homesick that I felt I just couldn't go on. Mother and I had been so close — I missed her dreadfully. If Marigold had come sooner, it might have been easier. But other women were homesick, too, I knew, and I didn't want Phil to suspect how I felt, so I took hold of myself, determined not to let the hard life beat me.

'Mother missed me as much as I missed her, but it was a long time before they decided to come up here and stay with us. When the date was finally set, I lived in a regular fever. We built another room on the house for them. Alan Jarvis made lovely white birch furniture for it and I braided a big rag rug and made a lot of other things. They were coming with a few other people in light wagons late in the fall.'

Hallie broke off, her lips trembling. But she went on in a moment.

'I felt as though I'd burst with joy when we set off to meet them at Smoky River, two days out from here. And when I saw them and they had their arms around me again —! We talked half the night around the campfire, and then Mother and I bunked together, too happy and excited to sleep. Smoky River has been the rendezvous where new settlers met the land agents to be directed to their locations. Some of this train were waiting for relatives to meet them, so we all camped there the next day and had a good time getting acquainted. That night all the people gathered for a community supper before they were to separate the next day. Mother and I had been together constantly all day, but after supper, while I was helping clear up and get our stuff packed for an early start in the morning, she said she wanted to see if she could find some more Saskatoon berries. She'd found a few late ones along the way, so she started out to find some in the Bush.'

Hallie pressed her tightly clenched hand against her lips. 'She never came back.'

I reached over and clasped her hand, sick at heart for what she was suffering. Her voice choked as she went on, but after a moment it steadied.

ALBERTA

'It was likely more than an hour before we had camp in order and I began to be uneasy about Mother. The men scattered in every direction and shouted and shot off guns. But in the Bush, sound is deadened and echoes are deceiving. She was a good walker and must have gone a long way in the wrong direction before we began our search. All night they hunted. For several days all the people stayed on and everything possible was done to find her. Then the people went on their way and the search was turned over to the Mounted Police and the Indians. For three weeks we stayed there. Night and day I walked back and forth waiting for them to bring her back, until I'd fall exhausted to the ground. I kept water always ready. She loved her hot tea.

'A thousand times I'd imagine I saw her staggering into camp. When I did sleep, I'd wake screaming from terrible dreams of a bear or wolf tearing at her as she lay in the underbrush.'

Hallie laid her head on her drawn-up knees, but she shed no tears. Her calm almost frightened me. I waited.

'The searchers found bits of her clothing tied to bushes, and shelters of sticks and boughs where she'd been. Then nothing. Phil finally insisted we go home. It was getting colder and we could do no good by staying. I felt he was utterly heartless and was so desperate I was beside myself. Then, as I sat humped before the fire that last night, poor little Marigold came and put her cold hand to my cheek. She was shivering, and she asked me why I didn't love her and Papa and Grandpa any more. It shocked me to my senses. I'd almost forgotten them in my own grief. I warmed her in my arms and Father came and sat beside me.

'"Hallie," he said, "if your mother is alive, she'll be found by the Indians or Mounties and brought back. She might be sick in an Indian camp somewhere. But they will hear of the reward I've offered. If she is not alive ——" He talked to me of Mother's faith — made me see how she would want me to go on courageously. I knew he was right and the next day we went home.

'When the neighbors began coming, I cooked good food

for them, asked them about things and kept talking so they wouldn't have a chance to sympathize with me or mention Mother. That would have been too much to endure. I just wouldn't give up hope. I couldn't accept God's letting such a thing happen. After a while I realized people weren't coming so much, but in a way it was relief. At times I'd really believe Mother'd be found, and then utter despair would grip me when I was sure she wouldn't. Every minute I wasn't active I'd feel my reason slipping. I walked miles alone over the Prairie trying to get hold of myself. That's why I've gone to dances.

'One day, after this had been going on for weeks, Mrs. Cline and Mrs. Blossombalm came to the house. You've seen them both and know their kind. They said they'd come to comfort me and knew I needed someone older to advise me. I mustn't take it wrong if they pointed out that I was showing mighty little respect for the memory of a poor dead mother, acting as though nothing had happened, going to dances and all the rest. They had come to pray with me, so I'd see the error of my ways. They got down on their knees and waited for me, but I sat in my chair, so outraged I couldn't speak. They shook their heads, then each of them prayed for me, telling the Lord all about Mother and her sufferings. My God, Lora! It was so terrible I wanted to kill them. Then they got up and brought out a parcel and opened it. They showed me a black crêpe veil and a black dress they'd rigged up and told me I must be decent enough to put on mourning, at least.

'I went to pieces then. I screamed at them to take their horrible things away and get out of my house. "My Mother isn't dead!" I kept telling them. Mrs. Cline looked scared and said they'd better go, but Mrs. Blossombalm shook her finger under my nose and yelled at me, "You're going to listen to what I have to say, young woman!" And then she told me cruel things my friends had said — even my best ones. She said not a person on the Prairie had any respect for me. How could they when it was easy to see I didn't have any for myself — the way I walked around outdoors with my head hanging, as though I were ashamed of myself.

'If Phil had been there, he'd have straightened them out, but he was away, and for the moment I think I was absolutely insane. I told them I wanted them and all Grand Prairie to stay away from my house. I never wanted to see any of them again. When they were gone, I felt as though I were going to die. They understood so little. It was true — what they said about my going around the place with my head down. It was that I couldn't bear to look toward the Bush — and think of what it might be hiding. I was pretty much alone after that. Winter came and deep snow. It was summer before they found — what was left. Oh Lora! What she must have suffered! The nights were so cold — and the wild animals —!' Relief came at last for Hallie's long-pent emotions. She dropped her head in my lap and great sobs shook her. I leaned over and lit the piled sticks under the coffee pot. After a while she grew calm again. And then, as we waited for the water to boil, we talked with complete freedom.

'Let's face things, Hallie,' I said. 'You've had a terrible experience, but the way you've treated your friends since the Cline-Blossombalm visitation has mired you even deeper in misery. Not that I blame you — I'd probably have done worse! — but you took the word of two malicious women as truth concerning friends you should never have doubted. In grief and separation there is something, whether of self or Time or Nature or God — call it what you will — that comes with healing and the promise, "This too shall pass." But unrighted wrongs — they follow us with bitterness to the end of our lives.'

'Mother told me almost the same thing once.' Hallie fed dry sticks into the flames. 'I know I've been wrong. I've had wonderful friends — I must have them again. I want Father to be happy here — he's coming back in the spring — but with all the things I've ruined for Phil and Marigold — how am I going to undo them?'

'There'll be a way. We'll think up something. Only promise me that if any of your neighbors meet you or come to see you, you'll be friendly.'

'I'll be terribly humiliated. But I promise.'

Isobel and I had planned to picnic with Marie de Witt the next day at the lake where the geese fed. When morning came, Isobel decided she'd rather stay at home, but insisted I go on without her.

As Marie and I drove in her buggy through the underbrush and trees nearing the lake, a horseman passed us with a gun across the saddle in front of him. He sang out a 'Good morning, ladies!' to which Marie barely nodded her head. I commented on her lack of warmth.

'I don't like that Simon Jones.' She slapped the reins on the horse's back. 'He's a cheat and a liar. Once, when several families of us were on a fishing trip and I wanted to help with the lunch, I baited my hook and set the line and left it. Pretty soon Simon Jones came up with a big fish on his line. He showed it to everyone and bragged a lot about it. But afterward a neighbor girl told me she saw him take it off my hook and hang it on his own. I'll get even with him some day. See if I don't.'

He had ridden out of sight around a bend of the road. Geese began to rise in the air from the rushes of the lake, their wings whirring rhythmically. I wondered if Simon Jones had come out to kill some of them. I hoped if he were after them, he'd take poor aim. I was saying as much to Marie when we heard several rapid shots in succession. Instantly thousands of wild geese rose in a dense cloud. In their confused fright they flew low at first, barely escaping the treetops. We stopped, and suddenly from the countless numbers over our heads a huge goose careened crazily down toward us, then plummeted straight into the buggy on top of our feet. Its bill was shot off and blood ran from a hole in its breast. For a moment its legs twitched, then it lay still. Quick as a flash, Marie covered it over with the laprobe, picked up the reins, and swung the buggy around.

'We're going home fast. The picnic can wait. Simon will be back looking for this bird. But we're having roast goose for dinner tonight. We'll send for Al and Jock and Isobel.'

She giggled happily. 'A goose for a fish — that's fair enough!'

As we were preparing the goose for the oven, I decided to broach the matter of Hallie Markel to this woman who had once been her best friend. 'Marie, once I asked you something about Hallie Markel — remember? — and you just shook your head and said you didn't discuss her. But you looked as though you wanted to cry. Now ——'

'Well, I certainly feel like crying every time I think of my best friend's saying she didn't want me coming to see her!'

'Who told you she said that?'

'Hallie said that to Mrs. Blossombalm and Mrs. Cline. She said ——'

'Did you believe those old gossips? I should think ——'

'I didn't — at first. I went right over to Hallie's as fast as I could drive. But when I got there all the blinds were down and the doors were locked. I knocked and knocked, but no one answered, though I was sure I could hear someone moving around inside. I saw Phil down by the barn, so I went and asked him about Hallie. Told him to tell her I was there and just must see her. But he looked so upset I was sorry I'd bothered him. He admitted she was home, but said she wouldn't see anybody, and he thought maybe it would be better if we left her alone for a while. So I left.'

'You really believed she didn't want to see you?'

'My French was up. I was good and mad.'

'She was mad, too, Marie. Mad with grief and shock and long uncertainty, and the cruelty of those women coming with their crêpe rags.' I told her of my talk with Hallie. Marie wept remorsefully before I was half through. 'Don't you see how much she needs you? Let's go over there to-morrow.'

'I'm ashamed to go now.'

'And she's ashamed to face you just as much. Maybe two shames will fix things. And there's something else that needs fixing. Listen, Marie. I'm going to give a party ——'

When we went up to the door of the Markels' house the next day, Hallie threw it open before we had time to knock.

'Oh Marie!' Hallie's arms opened to her friend. Marie's eyes were full of tears as they clung to each other.

I went out to the woodpile where Marigold was playing, and stayed there until Hallie called me.

'Don't you smell the coffee, Lora?'

The faces of the two friends shone. Several times, as they passed each other getting food ready, I saw their hands clasp swiftly.

That night I asked Al if he had any objections to our giving a tea-party some afternoon soon.

'Swell idea!' he said. 'Go ahead. Who'll you have?'

'Oh, just some of the closer neighbors. But anyone can come. Particularly the dames who gossiped about Hallie Markel.'

'Jumpin' Jehu! Not those old bobcats! Hallie won't show up if she knows they're coming.'

'Hallie isn't invited. As a matter of fact, the bobcats are the most important guests of the afternoon.'

Isobel laughed at his bewilderment. 'Ma's a snake-charmer, Al. She tames polecats too, and puts bands on buzzards' ankles.'

'So that's what you're up to? Going to have it out about Hallie, eh? More power to you, Sis. I'll be out behind the barn with a shovel ready to bury the dead. But what makes you think the Blossombalm will come, after the way you slapped her down at the dance the other night?'

'Curiosity. You couldn't keep her away.'

Which proved true. Mesdames Blossombalm and Cline arrived together, the first guests at our party. It was well attended and the house was full of neighbors. By prearranged plan, toward the end of the afternoon, when we were having refreshments, Marie turned the conversation to Hallie. Someone immediately declared that woman was going crazy.

'What makes you think that?' I asked.

'Haven't you ever seen the way she looks — her eyes so sort of blind-looking?'

'What do you think about Hallie, Mrs. Hughes?' Marie asked. 'You've been seeing a lot of her lately.'

That statement startled them. They all looked at me curiously.

'A party's not the place to be discussing disorders, but since you ask, I'll say she has as good a mind as I ever knew. If she hadn't, she'd have been in the asylum, after all she's had to endure.'

One remark led to another and the way was opened up better than I'd hoped, so that, without forgetting the social angle, I was able to give them the picture of Hallie's suffering and the unpleasantness heaped upon her. I didn't spare anything, nor did I uphold Hallie in her turning the neighbors away. When everyone was listening, I told how two women had tried to force mourning on her even before it was known whether her mother was dead, and how they abused her with their accusations, and how maliciously they convinced her everyone believed as they did.'

My listeners were deeply moved. 'How cruel!' they exclaimed. 'No wonder she wouldn't see us when we went there!' — 'Poor Hallie! After all she's done for this community — treated like this when she needed friends most!'

When I finished, Mrs. Blossombalm inquired indignantly, 'Who told you that — about the mournin' an' all?'

'You told me most of it yourself at the Grange Hall dance. Don't you remember?' I asked sweetly.

'It was Mrs. Cline told you!' she retorted. ' She ——'

'I never told no such thing!' Mrs. Cline leaned forward and shook her finger at Mrs. Blossombalm. They glowered at each other angrily. 'It was you yourself, Mis' Bloss', who took them black things and insulted her an' ——'

'Don't you dare talk that way to me, you ol' gossip! Wait till I tell them how you lied about all the neighbors an' made that pore girl believe —!'

'Ladies! Ladies!' I remonstrated. 'Surely, Mrs. Blossombalm, Mrs. Cline wouldn't do such a despicable thing. You two had better wait till you're alone to settle your differences.'

'They're settled right now, as far as I'm concerned!' declared Mrs. Cline. 'I'm never going to speak to that Blossombalm woman again as long as ——'

'Stop before you say it!' I broke in. 'You women can't afford hard feelings here on the Prairie. Friends are too valuable.'

Mrs. Cline stalked out, got her wraps, and stalked in again.

'I've got to go,' she said to me. Then she turned to Mrs. Blossombalm grimly. 'Mis' Bloss', I brung you here, but I ain't takin' you home.'

'Oh, come, now, Mrs. Cline! You know you are.' I smiled at her. 'A little misunderstanding between old friends ——'

'I said I ain't takin' her home.' There was a look of dignity I'd never seen before in the woman's face. 'I'm agoin' straight to Hallie an' tell her what I think of myself.' She glared at Mrs. Blossombalm. 'An' of you too!'

'Don't you dare!' The outraged woman dashed for her wraps. She came out struggling into her coat, her hat cocked wildly on the back of her head, just as Mrs. Cline shut the front door. The pursuit was something which took us all to the front windows in unconcealed relish. Mrs. C. lost time in untying her horse from the hitching-rack, and Mrs. B. was upon her as she climbed into the rickety old buggy.

'My land!' exclaimed one of the guests as she watched their excited pantomime. 'If we aren't all a lot of ninnies — letting those women make us believe such things of Hallie Markel! And us knowing her as long as we have — and how fine she was. We'll sure have to make up to her for all this.'

Mrs. Cline gathered up the reins and was about to slap her horse on the rump to take off, when Mrs. Blossombalm's voice reached us in protesting wail.

'But I want to go to Hallie's myself! If anybody's goin' to tell on me, it's goin' to be me does it, not you. You ain't talkin' behind my back. I know you!'

She was between the wheels, grabbing at the dashboard and trying to climb in. Mrs. Cline couldn't start without harming her, so grudgingly moved over in the seat to make room for her. A moment later they drove off. We all looked at each other and laughed.

'Come on,' I said. Let's have more tea. I need it.'

* * *

Winter was upon us one day and the rigors of life increased immediately. I was uneasy about Isobel. She was in no condition to run undue risks, and since we didn't have to live this way, there was no reason she should endure it. But she wouldn't hear of leaving. Christmas was the one big celebration of our visit for which we had planned elaborately in advance, so in any case, we could not think of leaving before that.

We spent hours going over the guest list, checking each family against the gifts we'd brought up with us. We were grateful we'd taken the stork into consideration and brought a few things for the newborn babies, whose frequent advent Al had omitted in his letters describing the population.

'Is that everyone in the neighborhood, Al?' asked Isobel one night, after reading the boys the list for rechecking.

The MacDuffs were there that night for dinner with their four-year-old boy and two-year-old girl. They were good friends of Al and Jock. Ethel MacDuff had come several times to spend an afternoon with Isobel and me, dressed in spotless white shirtwaist and close-fitting long, black skirt, which was still the style on the Prairie, and driving a good team to the democrat. We'd visited at their ranch, too. Just the ordinary log house of the homesteader, but always clean tablecloth and napkins at meals when guests were present, and food the best the country afforded. When Isobel asked whether that was everyone in the neighborhood, I saw a look flash between Al and Jock and the MacDuffs.

'That's all,' said Al.

'They're holding out on us, Isobel,' I said. 'This is a Christmas party all full of brotherly love. Who are you people blackballing?'

'Dirty Potter.' Al shook his head and grinned at me. 'He's never among those present up here.'

'Ma and I were wondering about him the other day,' said Isobel. 'We've heard him mentioned several times, but we've never seen him.'

'Be grateful for that!' laughed Jock. 'Especially if the wind was from his direction. No, Potter walks alone — like the skunk.'

'I wouldn't expose any child of mine to him,' declared Ethel MacDuff, 'so count us out if he's to come!' She laughed as she saw the question in my face. 'Don't think we're heartless, Mrs. Hughes. He's a hermit and wouldn't come if you asked him.'

'If Potter should ever come here for anything, Sis, send him out to the barn or wherever we're at work. Don't invite him in.' I could see Al was really in earnest. 'You girls wouldn't relish him in the house.'

'Well, for goodness' sake!' I snorted. 'One would think I'd been raised in an incubator! What's a little dirt now and then in a pioneering country such as this? I heard you tell someone once he was honest and had proved up on his claim and made his way all right. What more do you want of an old bachelor?'

'All right, Sis. Do as you see fit.' All four of them were laughing. 'But if you must learn the hard way, do it sometime when Jock and I have gone to End o' Line or the Bush!'

I saw Dirty Potter for the first time about a week later. I went to the door one evening in response to a knock, just about suppertime. The man who stood there in rough, mangy-looking fur coat and cap, with matted beard and hair covering everything but his nose and eyes, looked more like an animal than a human. But he spoke clipped Oxfordian English when he addressed me.

'Mrs. Hughes? I am Leighton Potter. I just dropped by with the mail. There was a most extraordinary amount in Jarvis's box and I thought you young ladies might appreciate getting yours. Mail's always an event on an outpost, even with our recently acquired rail service.'

Keen and intelligent were those deep-set blue eyes which peered out from the thicket of hair. I had a feeling of amazing personality behind a grotesque makeup. Here was something too unique to miss. I forgot the warnings.

'Come in, Mr. Potter. We're certainly grateful to you for bringing our mail. Let me give you a cup of coffee right away. I know you must be cold after that long ride. Take off your things and I'll have supper ready presently.'

He laid off his coat, and the man who emerged from the fur was the dirtiest, most unkempt specimen I've ever seen. He accepted the coffee gratefully and walked about with it in his hand, looking at our innovations.

'I say, you've made a jolly improvement here. Feminine touch, what!'

Isobel came in and I introduced them. The sight of him stunned her, but she was absolutely goggle-eyed as she listened to him talk. I was cooking the supper and didn't smell him, until after Isobel, holding her nose, made signs of distress behind his back. It was when he moved up and sat down by the stove that I got the full impact of THE ODOR. It hit me like a blow below the belt. It was incredible that any one man could give off so much of one thing.

Cold as it was, Isobel opened wide the outside door, and behind him made a gesture toward her stomach, as though she were about to be sick. To him she said, 'If you'll excuse me, I'll go over and have a look at my mail.' He was on his feet immediately. 'Quite all right, I assure you.' She threw her jacket around her and went over to our cabin. I had a feeling she wouldn't be back. I shivered from the cold pouring in through the open door, but it was either freeze or be asphyxiated, and the former seemed a happier death. I put some more coffee in the pot and dumped a bit of the fresh grind on the stove to let it smoke. Then I remembered a can of sauerkraut which was potent stuff. I opened it hurriedly and put it over the fire to steam off. It helped a little.

'Jumpin' Jehu! Are you girls trying to warm up all outdoors?' Al's voice called as he came up the path. 'What's —?' He paused on the threshold. 'Oh —! Hello, Potter. How's everything with you?' Then barely waiting for his response Al turned to me and grinned wickedly. 'And how are you, Sis?'

'Fine!' I lied. I wanted to kick him. I wanted to kick Mr. Leighton Potter also for so ceremoniously getting to his feet on the slightest provocation. He kept things stirred up. 'Supper's ready, Al. Is Jock up? Mr. Potter's dining with us.'

'Fine! Fine!' Al was very hearty. 'But the truth is, Potter, Jock and I have to go over to Fallman's on an errand before dark. I'd just run in to tell you, Sis. You all go right ahead and don't wait on us. I know Potter's in a hurry to get back to feed stock before dark.' Al left with a smug see-what-you-got-yourself-into look at me. When everything was ready I ran over to our cabin to get Isobel.

But she refused to return. 'I can't take it, Ma. Remember, I'm a sick woman.'

I seated my guest as far as possible from me at the table and put the dish of steaming sauerkraut under my very nose. I told him Isobel was subject to heart attacks and was lying down to ward off one. That dinner was one of the bravest feats I ever achieved. War nurses have had decorations pinned on their chests for much less valor. I have sat on the dirt floor of a filthy hogan in Arizona and eaten some sort of mess with the Navajos, but their odors were mild compared to this.

Since I had asked him in on impulse, wanting to know more of so mysterious a combination, I plied him with questions as to his early life, schooling, and so on. But while he replied expansively, doing full justice to the meal at the same time — his table manners were impeccable — he revealed nothing more than I'd already guessed. The man should have been a diplomat. If he'd been cleaned up, I could have enjoyed him thoroughly. But never have I said good-bye to a guest with deeper gratitude. It took hours to get the stench of him out of the cabin, though I threw the place wide open before he was out of sight and scrubbed the chairs with disinfectant.

The boys had a good laugh on me, and I agreed vehemently that the Christmas party would be a much pleasanter occasion without Dirty Potter. A few days before Christmas, however, Al suggested we make up a little box of things for Potter and ride over and make a call.

Isobel and I both shuddered. 'A box, yes. Gladly. But why call?'

'Lost your Christmas spirit of brotherly love, have you?' His eyes twinkled. 'Shame on you, Sis. Come on, both of you. We won't stay but a second, but you'll miss the sight of a lifetime if you don't see how he lives.'

And so we packed a box with food, wrapped the package in gay paper, and tied ornaments and greens on top of it with a bow of red ribbon, and went over to Potter's with it. He was astonished to see us when he opened the door and was delighted with our package. He asked us in most hospitably and made no apologies for the unspeakable condition of his cabin.

Al had told us that the man hadn't touched water to dishes or clothes or himself for years, and we could well believe it. How any man of a well-bred background could live in such a hole was beyond understanding. Sacks of flour were stacked along one wall. Chickens roosted on them and had evidently fouled them with their droppings for months. In one corner, half-buried in filthy straw, lay a big shoat. (Al told us later the place used to be full of hogs, but it must have become too smelly for them, for they moved out!) I looked vainly for some evidence of this man's past, for books especially, since he'd quoted philosophers several times at that meal with me. But the only printed matter in sight was a dirty almanac. I eyed several trunks and pieces of good leather luggage speculatively. THE ODOR here was multiplied tenfold.

I had noticed the hoarseness of his voice when he greeted us, but now, when he was suddenly seized with a paroxysm of coughing, I was alarmed. 'How long has that been going on?' I asked. 'Are you doing anything about it?' Isobel and I were already outside the door.

'It's not half as bad as it sounds,' he assured me. 'All I need is some whiskey. Do you suppose you could find me some, Jarvis?'

'I'll try, Potter. Liquor is as scarce on the Prairie as gadflies on a stuffed horse.' He saw the question in my eyes. 'Oh, they start from Edmonton with it, but it's usually drunk up before they get here. And whatever does get here has to be shared with so many there's not much left but a nip for each. It will probably be different now with train service.'

We all gave him advice as to treatment, wished him Merry Christmas, and rushed off, inhaling deeply to rid our lungs of the taint.

It was a couple of days before Al found any whiskey. He rode over to Potter's with it. When he didn't come back right away, Jock got uneasy and finally rode over to see if he might have had an accident along the way. Jock was gone for a long time. When he came back, it was to tell us Potter was dead. It seems the MacDuffs had become worried over their neighbor when they saw no smoke rising from his chimney for two days, and Dan went over to see if he were away. He found him in bed, stricken with pneumonia, and rode at once for the doctor. They'd got in just about the time Al reached there. Since Jock wasn't needed, he came back to tend to the stock and work while Al helped out.

Al and the doctor came along early the next morning. I hadn't seen 'Doc' Stevens before. He was a big, bearded man standing well over six feet, and in his twinkling brown eyes was all the fortitude and understanding it takes to be a good frontier doctor. I liked him immediately. We had tubs on the floor in the boys' cabin, and plenty of bath water heating on the stove. We knew they'd need thorough scrubbing after such a task as they must have had laying out Dirty Potter. I'd put clean clothing on Al's bunk, and we were serving breakfast in our cabin. The men made as quick a job of it as they could, and threw the clothes they'd worn outside in the open air until they could be cleaned. We kept the conversation entirely away from the deceased. We wanted to enjoy the bacon and eggs, toast and coffee.

'Well, I'm glad we took the old boy a Christmas treat anyway,' said Al, after we'd finished. 'He must have got worse fast after we were there.'

'If we'd had Mrs. Hughes on the job over there, we'd have

saved him sure.' Doc's eyes twinkled. 'A trained nurse could have done wonders tidying up that place.'

'With the total loss of one trained nurse,' I replied.

'We didn't do so badly ourselves after we got him cleaned up,' said Al. 'We shoveled out the place and sloshed disinfectant all around. It wasn't half bad as I sat there with my back to the corpse and my feet in the oven, waiting for Doc to get back with the magistrate. They didn't show up till daylight.'

'I'll wager you enlivened your one-man wake with some of that whiskey.' I grinned at him. 'But did you find out who Leighton Potter really was?'

'If the papers and letters we went through sketchily were his own, he's the second son of a member of the British House of Lords. There's one old letter from his father begging him not to leave Oxford, but to think seriously of fitting himself for the station to which he was born. It would take a barrister to untangle a lot of the stuff and make sense out of it, but that's what Doc and I figured.'

'The Honorable Hog!' said Isobel, in disgust. 'Imagine leaving such a life for the one he made here! What on earth would make a man do such a thing?'

'Maybe he got tired dressing for dinner,' suggested Jock.

'I'll bet anything he hadn't had all his clothes off for years,' said Al. 'Doc and I peeled off four suits of rotting underwear, each filthier and more ragged as we got closer to his hide. The smell of him would have shamed any skunk. But when we got him bathed and his hair and beard trimmed, the chap really looked like somebody. Well, at least when he goes to his grave he won't be "Dirty Potter"!'

* * *

A mere scab of dust-polluted snow had covered the Prairie for weeks. But five days before Christmas great feathery flakes began to cover it, piling high on trees and buildings, and burying fences to the top of their posts, until the whole country lay deep in immaculate white down. For two weeks we had been getting ready for the Christmas party, and the deeper the snow became, the lower our spirits sank. For unless a crust formed, strong and thick enough to bear the weight of teams and sleighs, our neighbors wouldn't be able to reach us. But we went on with our plans just the same.

Fearing just such a snow, Al and Jock had brought a beautiful tree from the Bush the week before. When the snow began, they set it up on its standard and brought it in. Isobel and I had been adding to its trimmings daily. The big trunk of toys, decorations, and clothes, so generously donated before we left the States, was dragged out and its contents spread over the tables and beds. Al, Isobel, and I had at last completed the list of neighborhood children, their sizes, ages, and requirements. There were fourteen in all. It had been a big job to allot the gifts, do them up in gay wrappings, and put the names on the cards.

'These mittens are for Maisie,' Isobel would say; 'these dishes for Peggy Munroe; and the skates — would they do for the Nickols boy, Al? He's thirteen years old.'

'He has a short leg, Isobel. Give him some of those books. He's crazy about reading.'

At last the list was filled and a box of things left over — 'Just in case,' Al suggested, 'someone like the Smith woman would spring a kid or two on us she'd been hiding in the root-cellar a few years.'

To add to our happiness, Mother and the homefolks, taking advantage of our twice-a-week mails brought in by the railroad, had sent us not only personal gifts all around, but a huge box containing twenty packages beautifully wrapped in gilt paper and tinsel ribbons. These were intended as a surprise grab-bag for our women guests — the gifts to be exchangeable among themselves if they wished. No one knew better than Mother, who had pioneered a good part of her life, how precious could be a paring knife or a spool of heavy linen thread, buttons and tape, pen-points, stationery and lead pencils.

The day before Christmas our hopes came true and the snow crusted. It was forty-six degrees below zero and there was no danger of a thaw. We finished our decorations, with streamers of tinsel fastened to the walls and caught up in the middle of the ceiling with a cluster of red bells. Lamps borrowed from the neighbors were placed around the room; the bed was moved back in a corner, and boards were laid on boxes and blocks of wood and straw ticks and blankets on the floor, furnishing seats for everyone. Isobel had made many copies of carols, so everyone could sing with the phonograph. We had asked the Reverend McKay to read the story of the Nativity.

On Christmas Eve, our preparations finished, we four sat down to open our own personal packages. Never had gifts seemed so luxurious. Our friends and relatives had outdone themselves — or perhaps it was the remoteness which made all the things seem overwhelming.

'I've just thought of something we should change, Isobel,' said Al suddenly, as he admired his new fur-lined gloves. 'That little Peggy Munroe — give her a doll, the best you've got, instead of those dishes. You see, when I was freighting a couple of years back, I brought a train of homesteaders through from Edmonton, the Munroes among them. Peggy had a doll she treasured more than anything she owned. The Munroes had driven a wagon through from British Columbia. The night we were changing the loads from wagons to sleds, getting ready for an early start out of Edmonton the next morning, Dave Munroe evidently decided he was overloaded for the long haul and threw out a lot of things he thought unessential — Peggy's toys and doll along with them. None of us knew about it until we stopped to eat early the next day and the poor little kid missed her doll. I think Mrs. Munroe cried more than Peggy did, she was so cut up over it. Dave walked over to her and said, "If you're going to turn soft right at the start, you'd better get out and start walking home to your mother!"

'I never want trouble when I'm managing a train on the road, but before I thought twice I hauled off and landed him one on the jaw that pretty nearly put him to sleep. Then I told him to get on his horse and go back and get the doll. I'd hold the train right where we were. He went. But he didn't find the things. Someone else had evidently picked them up.'

'How could a man be such a pig?' cried Isobel indignantly.

'Well, you can't judge a man by one act like that. He's one of the hurry-up sort — never had taken time even to get acquainted with his own child. Then, too, he was under nervous strain, what with bringing everything for a year by wagon, when every inch of space has to count. He'd probably make any sacrifice himself for his family, but he has no imagination.'

It was a small matter to change the cards on dishes and doll. I looked at the doll's pretty smiling face. This gift had taken on new significance.

Christmas Day was clear and very cold. Long before sundown, dark moving specks began to top the distant ridges, and drawing closer materialized into teams and sleighs. Horses blowing and snorting into their breathing bags — the air was too cold to be taken directly into their lungs — lifted their heads and whinnied to other horses. It wasn't long before guests were crowding into the house. Those who had put their covered wagon boxes on runners and filled them with straw had managed to keep warm, but others were chilled to the marrow, in spite of heavy blankets and wraps. The kitchen was soon filled with people drinking hot tea.

By five they had all arrived. Boxes and baskets of food were unloaded on the big table, and tin cups and plates and knives and forks and spoons piled ready for use. The children were served first. They sat on the floor on comforters. Then the elders served themselves. Al presided at the big washboiler, which had been scrubbed and scoured and now held gallons of coffee. The food wasn't at all the conventional Christmas fare. The meat was largely game and the vegetables had been brought ready-cooked to warm up. But each housewife had contributed the best she could from her winter store.

After everyone was fed and the dishes stacked, we all went over to our cabin for the tree. It was a joy to watch the faces of those children, many of whom had never seen a bit of tinsel in their lives. To them the silver canopy and scarlet bells overhead and the gorgeously decorated tree were an overwhelming spectacle. Jock as Santa Claus rather frightened the younger children at first, but they soon recovered when their mothers explained him. I don't believe there was a mother whose eyes were not brimming with tears at sight of those youngsters. I had been looking at the decorations for several days, but now, with lamps all aglow and candles on the bookshelves giving added luster, it seemed truly as though 'the glory of the Lord shone roundabout.'

When everyone settled down, Al explained about the singing and passed out copies Isobel had made of carols. Then Isobel put on a record of 'Silent Night.' As the voices of a choir rang out in the first stanza, there was only a breathless, reverent silence. Then Hallie Markel stepped up beside the phonograph and lifted her hand. 'Come on, now! All sing! Everyone must give something to the Christmas music!' And as her clear, sweet voice rose with the sopranos of the choir, our guests sang. How they sang! There were good voices there, among the men especially. I listened with keen relish as basses and tenors gained confidence and sang with the gusto of the music-hungry.

Sentimental old Reverend McKay had a hard time keeping the huskiness out of his voice as he began the time-hallowed lines, 'And there were shepherds abiding in the fields, Keeping watch over their flocks by night.' Not even a child moved. Strange, unusual things had happened so thick and fast, they sat overwhelmed with mute wonder. Several more carols were sung, and then it was time to distribute the gifts. It took Emmy, rearing back on her heels, head held high, both hands grasping her harmonica as she reeled off 'Jingle Bells,' to bring them back to a world of reality. She stepped around the limited floor space with a zest that was most contagious.

Santa Claus deposited his pack on the floor and distributed the gifts to the children. They fingered their beautiful wonder-boxes carefully. Some of them cried when their mothers insisted they take off the wrappings to see what was inside. The look on the face of little Peggy Munroe when she opened the long box and saw her doll brought lumps to our throats. I saw a dull flush mount her father's face. The grab-bag brought shouts of laughter and cries of real appreciation. Not a man had been forgotten either. There was tobacco or some trifle for each. The Christmas party was magnificent.

Isobel ran the ouija board for an enthralled group after the gifts were all presented. Some were frankly afraid of it. Jock kept the fire going in the toolhouse and some of the men played poker out there. In the kitchen, where coffee was kept hot, there were card games and conversation, with now and then someone catching a nap on one of the bunks or on the floor as it grew later. As usual, the folks who lived near enough to go home to sleep left at a late hour. Those who lived too far away to make it put straw ticks and blankets on the floor, and one by one the tired children were tucked in.

Breakfast was served early. And then our guests gathered up their belongings, heated their hot-water jugs and their rocks, loaded their children in the sleighs and shouted final good-byes. They were full of praise for the Christmas party and thanked us over and over again. As the last ones took off over the snow, we smiled at each other with deep content. We'd had more fun than any of them.

* * *

The time between the parties and dances we attended on Grand Prairie seemed to hold little interest for Isobel. After the excitement of the Christmas party, she slumped mentally more and more. With bitterly cold weather coming on, I was increasingly certain I should get her back to Seattle. A letter which Al received from another sister at Christmas time helped to strengthen this conviction.

This sister, whom they hadn't seen for years, had unexpectedly moved to Seattle soon after Isobel and I left for Alberta. She was outraged that a nurse should have dragged a sick girl off into the wilds as this Hughes woman had done. If Isobel should get bedridden or die up there, it would be a terrible thing. All of which I myself knew.

Isobel hadn't seen Al's letter. Her sister had written more

mildly to her, but urged her to come back to Seattle and live with her and her husband. Isobel went all to pieces when I suggested returning. She said I could do as I pleased, but she was going to stay.

'I'm not your guardian, Isobel, but I do feel responsible for you,' I told her. 'Your sister would never forgive me if anything happened to you up here. And it's not fair to Al to have him worrying about you — which he is. We could be utterly isolated here by storms for days, maybe weeks. And bad weather is coming.'

But all my arguments fell on obstinate ears. Isobel grew more moody and touchy every day, until she became a genuine problem to all of us.

And then one afternoon Lord Belmont rode over with a telegram for me. My father had been kicked in the head by one of his horses and had a concussion of the brain. I was badly needed at home. There were two trains weekly into Edmonton. One was due in twenty-four hours. We would have to make it.

With the boys' help we were all packed and ready to start early the next morning. For once there was no word of dissent from Isobel. It was colder than our thermometer would register, but we made the trip into End o' Line in comfort. The wagon box on sleigh runners had tight canvas over the bows, and with fresh hay loaded in, plenty of blankets and jugs of hot water, we made out nicely. Al and Jock took turns driving and we stopped halfway at the house of friends for hot food. The trip in would have been fine if it hadn't been for my mental distress. I didn't know just how serious my father's condition might be.

It was black dark before we reached town. The train was standing with snow piled high on either side. Al hustled us up on the platform of the sleeper to escape cold so bitter it seemed fairly to strip us of clothing. Jock, hating good-byes, disappeared. The parting was tragically brief. It had to be. The whistle was blowing the final 'All Aboard!' The icebound brakes screeched and Al tumbled off into deep snow. Our long-planned Grand Prairie visit was over.

The train was warm and comfortable and the food was excellent. It was wonderful to have lettuce and fresh vegetables again. They had so long been just a memory. I hoped to see Isobel soon pick herself up out of her depression, but though she ate and slept well, her resentment at being forced to go home took the form of a silence harder to bear than angry words. She ignored me the entire way to Seattle. I might have been a deaf and dumb person she had never seen before.

Her sister met us at the station to take charge of Isobel. She was not slow in condemning my lack of judgment. I agreed with her heartily. And hurried home. My father, I found, had regained consciousness quickly after his accident. He had never been sick a day in his life, and when I saw him first, he seemed so well physically that it was hard to believe the wires were twisted in his thinking. He remembered the events of his entire life previous to his injury, but nothing after it. It was difficult for him to believe the things we tried to make clear to him. Low down on the back of his head a black-and-blue protrusion gave every indication of a blood clot. The doctors said they were willing to operate, but no one could say what the outcome might be.

My father was mortally afraid of doctors. I have seen him stop plowing a field, rip out a jackknife, lay his finger, swollen and painful with a felon, on top of a fencepost, plunge his knife into it to relieve the pus, wrap his handkerchief around it, and go on plowing. But when it came to doctors and operations, he would have none of them. No one wanted to assume the responsibility of the aftermath of surgery in this case, so there seemed no hope of his being cured. At times he seemed perfectly well, then he would have spells of unconsciousness which might seize him any time. Though they lasted only a brief while, they were long enough and serious enough to justify constant attention for him — a circumstance which he, by nature the family dictator, resented bitterly. Mother was soon worn down to a point of exhaustion as she wanted to take all care of him and allow me to go back to nursing under Doctor Benson. But I felt I shouldn't leave her with him.

ALBERTA

I had been back in Seattle just about three weeks when Isobel had a sudden heart attack. The doctor came for me in the middle of the night, as she was calling for 'Ma.' She clung to my hand as I sat beside her and tried to tell me how sorry she was for the way she had acted. I hushed her as gently as I could. 'We had a wonderful trip, Isobel. I couldn't have gone without you. You probably did much better than I should have done in your place.'

She smiled and panted, 'You — don't know — how much it — meant — to go. I've made my — sister — understand.'

'I'm glad we had all that fun, darlin'.' How I wished I might give back life and hope to that frail, lovely body. 'Maybe you could take a little sleep with your Old Timer sitting close by. Will you try?'

'I'll do — anything — you say. If I — don't wake up — remember — how grateful — I am for — everything . . .'

I sat by her as she fell asleep.

But she did not wake ever again.

PUGET SOUND COUNTRY

PUGET SOUND COUNTRY

FATHER TALKED CONSTANTLY of the home he'd built in Riverton. Leslie, who was now associate editor of the town paper, working nights and sleeping days, was living there with a few other men of the night force. I was able to handle Father pretty well, so I told Mother I'd take him back for a visit. He might not want to stay once he got there, so she might as well get some rest until we came back. She could get someone in Isobel's old room to keep her company. I was sure we could fit into that spacious house without disturbing the men. And so it was all arranged.

When the taxi came to take us to the station, Father seemed surprised that Mother was telling him good-bye. 'Why, Molly, aren't you coming, too?' he asked.

'She'll come later, maybe,' I told him.

'I guess that will be much better,' he agreed cheerfully, and turned away without further question. It was a heartbreaking parting for all of us except him. He was as pleased as a child to be going back.

For the most part the train trip delighted him, but occasionally he'd turn to me in bewildered fashion and ask, 'Why are we on this train? Where are we heading for, anyway?'

'We're going to Riverton,' I'd explain again. 'You're going to bud the orchard when spring comes and maybe make garden again.'

'Is Molly there?' He'd look at me keenly, as though to make sure I wasn't putting anything over on him.

Then once again I'd tell the whole story. It was pathetic to see him so childishly happy when we reached Riverton and walked into that house he'd built. I think if I'd dreamed then that the care of him was to stretch over seven long years, my heart would have failed me. We took up our quarters downstairs, well away from the day-sleeping men. We ate with them occasionally, and the brief snatches I saw of them were often a salvation to me.

All winter, no matter what the weather, I took Father for a daily walk. I was afraid for him to go alone, as a spell might seize him. Then, too, he was very headstrong and irresponsible. Once in the early spring, when we were hiking along the river on the railroad track, he decided he wanted to go across the long trestle. The river was a wide, swift one, swollen now with thaws, and a train was about due. I tried to divert his interest to something else, but he kept on toward the trestle. I couldn't possibly hold him back by physical force, so I tagged along, hoping to make him change his mind before he could get on it. But for once I could do nothing with him. Within twenty feet or so of it, I tried to hold him back and reason with him, but he pulled away, thoroughly angry. Then suddenly we heard the train whistle. Father started running ahead, determined to beat it across the trestle. I leaped forward and grabbed his coat, pulling with all my might. By the grace of God, I jerked him off the track and down over the bank just as the train came in sight. I was so shaken I could hardly stand as it roared by.

Father lived altogether in the past and often came out with something which made us both laugh. I racked my brain to think back to incidents which might amuse him.

'Papa,' I asked one day, 'how did you ever get to calling me "Toadie"?' — It was a nickname that, before this accident, he hadn't used in years.

'Oh, that!' He chuckled. 'Well, there was a silly song your mother used to sing about the time you came along. It went like this ——' He sang out of tune, keeping time with his hand:

> Lora, Lora, how we love thee,
> Tho' we see thy form no more,
> Yet we know thou'lt come to meet us
> On that bright and — something — shore.

'I was mad as Sam Hill when your mother gave you that name. You were awfully fat — broad as you were long — and one day when I was looking at you, I said to your mother that her baby hadn't any more shape than a toad. She always hated toads, so she pretended she was mad. After that I called you "Toadie" just to tease her.'

'Shame on you! I never told you, but I used to be so ashamed that you had such a name as Jasper, that I couldn't bear for anyone to know what it was.'

'Sort of smacks of Pearly Gates and Golden Streets, doesn't it? Well, I don't care what you call me just so you never call me "Dad." That sounds disrespectful to me. And "Daddy"! What a milksop of a name to call one's father! If you ever call me "Daddy," I'll horsewhip you!'

When spring came, he puttered around outside with the fruit trees which grew in the back yard, and he planted the garden with his accustomed skill. He seemed perfectly happy, but he missed Mother. She came out and joined us for the summer and gave me time to relax and see a few of the old friends I hadn't had a chance to visit before. When fall came, we took Father back to Seattle. We suspected then it was to be a long siege, and decided we couldn't disrupt our lives altogether on account of him. He went willingly enough. The world was in a ferment that summer and fall of 1914, with Europe plunged into war. We read of Germany's invasions with rising outrage.

We tried to live as normally as possible those seven years that Father was in a mental fog. He wasn't dangerous to anyone except himself. We had to watch him with unremitting vigilance to keep him from wilfully doing things that could end only in disaster. As time went on, he grew physically weak and slept a great deal. I was able to help Doctor Benson in the surgery and on short cases as the occasions arose. There was good income from the ranch and town house in Riverton, so we managed well enough. But in the spring of 1917, when the United States entered the war and doctors and nurses were mustering for Red Cross duty overseas, I chafed at my age and my inability to enlist for service.

While father's sickness hung like a stone around the hearts of all the family, there was some recompense. Before his accident he had no time for the beauty of the world around him — the sunsets, or the waving of the grain in his fields. To him nothing was so important as weather for the crops and bushels to the acre. But there came gradually to him an awakening to other values. Often he'd call Mother or me to see some high-piled cloud bank over the Sound, or to watch the constantly changing tints on Mount Rainier's summit at sundown. As the years crawled by, he became patient and tolerant where before he had been severe and irascible.

And when last I saw him, white and silently peaceful in death, there was the shadow of a smile on his firm lips.

* * *

After Father's death I went back to general nursing again. As I've thought back over those later years, there are odds and ends of cases that for some reason or other stand out in my mind.

Someone asked not long ago, 'Haven't you ever had any nice luxurious cases in the homes of the rich, where everything was made easy for you?'

'Lots of them,' I replied. 'But people are people, whether they are rich or poor, and patients are stripped of most everything but human characteristics when they're shivering with chills or sick at their stomachs. You remember them more than their surroundings.'

It set me to thinking, and I realized that when I first began nursing there was little difference in the care of the rich and the care of the middle class in the West. Many of the luxuries that came later were unheard of then. Doctors were often few and far between. Housewives and mothers, whether rich or poor, engaged the services of a midwife or elderly woman who knew her herbs and poultices. They carried on with no thought of a trained nurse, unless, of course, the patient's condition became critical. Then trained nurses would be called.

Very likely these pioneering experiences developed in me a preference, during my maturer years, for nursing people of moderate means. Later, when conditions altered, my preference still held. While most nurses were delighted when called to the luxurious homes of the very wealthy, with the prospect of a long-drawn-out convalescence to follow, I still felt greater satisfaction in turning a storeroom into a surgery and a workbench into an operating table, with dressings sterilized in the oven of the kitchen stove piled high on a three-legged stool. Never would the nurses of the rich know the thrill of creative triumph that comes from making a first-class bedpan out of a washbasin, a piece of tin, and a few strokes of a soldering iron!

In the homes of the rich, the problem of servants was always a distressing one to me. The kitchen area was sacrosanct, and woe betide any highfalutin' nurse who thought she could violate it to mess up pans making beef tea for her patient or sterilizing hypodermic needles. All stiff and starched in her white uniform and cap, the R.N. must ring for the maid and give her the order. By the time that tired and usually overworked female had climbed the back stairs, taken the order, executed it, and made another round trip to carry up whatever was required, she was hating the nurse whole-heartedly. Why should any maid, getting only twenty or at most thirty dollars a month, wait on a nurse who was paid at least twenty-five a week and often eight dollars a shift?

I've lost my appetite for many an elegant meal as I dined at the family table with the rich, because I knew the maid who made endless trips to carry off only one plate at a time as convention demanded, was suffering hell from the bulging varicose veins that knotted her legs or from corns and bunions tortured by cheap, ill-fitting shoes.

When money was no object, the nurse was usually kept on the case long after she was really needed. She could read aloud to the patient, play games with her, answer the telephone, and arrange flowers. Though I love flowers, I came to loathe the lavish masses of them around the bedsides of the affluent.

Not infrequently, if there were 'money to burn' and the patient was the mistress of the house, she would take advantage of any slight indisposition to play the rôle of invalid. A white-uniformed nurse, the excitement of her favorite doctor's daily visit, perfumed baths and massage, marvelous négligées, anxious friends telephoning and sending books and flowers and baskets of rare fruit — it was all very satisfying for a change when one was worn out with the social whirl. Especially if there were a husband who had become too absorbed in his work and needed to be brought into line with a little overdue attention.

A few days of this, then all glamoured up with velvet robe and feather trimmings, she'd recline elegantly on her divan and languidly admit a few friends to sympathize with her. The next step would be long rides in the country with the coachman in livery and the nurse beside her with two poodles and a Pekinese slobbering over them. About this time I'd be thinking of all those tired, overworked mothers, so ill they should be in bed, pegging away to feed and care for their brood. I would much prefer helping one of them with no fee at all. But, of course, there were outstanding exceptions in these ultra-rich cases.

Nancy Evanston was one of these. She lived in an eighteen-room house in the suburbs of Riverton, the wife of one of the richest mining men in the whole Northwest. With her older children married and her younger ones of university age, she devoted herself to good works, sharing lavishly with the less fortunate. She never forgot that after she and her husband, Newt, had come out from Missouri in a covered wagon, they were mighty poor for years. She'd worn calico and had gone barefooted uncomplainingly while Newt wormed railroad ties out of the forest. When Newt took to prospecting and discovered his fabulous mine, she still didn't forget.

She took riches calmly and lived life her own way, refusing to be daunted by things she didn't know. The six children were a handsome, high-stepping brood, with finishing schools and society weddings for the girls, fine horses and clothes and travel for the sons. They dressed Nancy up and struggled to teach her social usage, but to her these things were not important enough to matter. She impressed even her own children with an individuality so particularly her own that they were secretly rather proud of her as a 'character.' I think she had in her the elements of true greatness. She had poise and dignity and nobility. She talked with Presidents and their ladies with as much ease as she talked with the grocer and his wife. And if she generally looked like a squaw in her clothes, no one cared much.

Except Newt. He had in him a broad streak of snobbishness. He was proud of being a self-made man and didn't mind having been poor in his youth, but he couldn't endure having Nancy debunk all his implications of genteel old family background. She made no bones about their both having come from common folks, poor and uneducated, and laughed whole-heartedly over the way they'd had to live. I nursed one of the daughters for months, and I don't know when I've ever enjoyed anyone so much as I did Nancy.

Newt was big and fine-looking and had another woman in his life. She lived in Butte and everyone seemed to know about her. I never saw her, but heard she was beautiful and sophisticated and knew how to wear evening clothes gorgeously. It was said she listened, gratifyingly impressed, when Newt talked about his aristocratic lineage. He always took her East on trips with him. Montanans in New York City had seen them together, a very handsome couple, in the famous night spots of the period. If Nancy knew, she gave no sign, and never in any way even hinted she suspected her husband of infidelity. She kept right on deflating him when he got to 'putting on the dog,' as she expressed it.

Her sense of humor cost her a fortune. When Newt Evanston died, long before he was an old man, he left each of his children a million dollars, and left another million to the woman 'who has understood me.' To Nancy he left all right and title to the Evanston home and a one-dollar bill.

The most trying people are the stingy rich, who suffer acutely at the thought of paying for services rendered them. Mrs. Bothner was an outstanding example of this type. She was the widow of a millionaire lumberman, had a palatial home and an ugly, feeble-minded son.

When she developed fever after taking serum for typhoid, she thought she was coming down with a violent illness and worked herself up into a terrible state of mind. The doctor put me on the case and warned me what I was up against in the matter of finances.

'She's always slow pay — and if she can get out of it, she won't pay at all. I know this old girl. She's strong as a horse and she's never very sick, but she'll run you ragged waiting on her, to make sure she's getting her money's worth. Then she'll lie there thinking up some other things she might inveigle you into doing to save her paying outside help to do her work. Don't let her impose on you. Don't dive in and do any housework and don't let her fuss at you about the fee. Walk off the case if she does. I'll send her to the hospital.' He laughed. 'That would fix her. She thinks the Sisters are highway robbers and that doctors and nurses are their henchmen.'

Thus prepared, I tackled the case. Mrs. Bothner was quite miserable for a couple of days, and didn't bother me. Then she got better and at once began to worry about things.

'Do you know, Mrs. Hughes, before I took sick, I put a few linen scarves and Battenberg pieces in the hamper in the laundry. The maid never could learn to do linens. I usually get Pamelia to do them — you know the colored woman who goes out by the day?'

'Yes, I reckon everyone in town knows Pamelia. She's a good old soul.'

'Well, it just occurred to me that you might as well do those linen things today. You wouldn't mind, I know, since you have so little to do, and after all I *am* paying you twenty-five dollars a week.'

As a matter of fact, there was very little to do. I was tired hearing her complain, so to satisfy my curiosity as to the 'few' linen pieces I went down to the laundry. This was the day of the doily — doilies here, there, and everywhere. The hamper was piled high with linens, doilies, large tablecloths, and dozens and dozens and dozens of napkins. I shoved them back into the hamper, closed the lid on them, and went back upstairs.

'Mrs. Bothner, did you really expect me to wash all that hamper of linens?'

'Why not?' Her eyes snapped. 'You can take your time ironing it.'

'But I'm not a laundress. I'm a nurse.'

'Look here! I'm paying you twenty-five dollars a week for almost nothing, and I could get Pamelia Johnson to work hard all day — cleaning, washing, and ironing — for just one dollar!'

'That's unfortunate for Pamelia, isn't it? If she'd studied catering as her sister did, who's at the Hook and Fin Club, she wouldn't be working for any such pay. I've spent lots of time and money learning to care for the sick. And nurses' fees are fixed by the State Registration Board. Though, of course, we may take charity cases if we wish.'

'Well, it's nothing short of robbery! What you do for me certainly doesn't take any special skill. How do you expect me to get well if you make me worry this way?'

'I think we might solve that problem by asking Pamelia to come in and take care of you for a dollar a day. I'll go call her right away.'

I whisked out of the room while her mouth was still agape with astonishment. Pamelia was working next door that day. I went over and talked to her as she hung out a washing on the lines. She was a smart old girl and had little use for Mrs. Bothner, who always skimped her on the meals she ate there. I explained the matter to her in detail. She chuckled with vast amusement.

'Since you're all finished up here now, Pamelia, I'll wait till you get your things and you come right back with me. And remember, all you have to do is to listen while I tell you what to do, and then you nod your head as if you understood everything and say, "Yes," no matter what it is. Then I'll go and begin to pack my bag. I guess that will bring her around all right.'

'But Mis' Hughes —— Lor, honey! Sposen she don' haid you off?'

'In that case you just get a stitch in your back and call the doctor. He'll send her to the hospital so fast she won't know what's happened to her.'

Pamelia's ample bosom heaved with laughter. I waited for her and together we went into Mrs. Bothner's room.

Her face was a study. 'Look here! I didn't say for you to go get Pamelia. I was just going to offer you two dollars a day, as there is so little for you to do. If you'll ——'

'Now here is what you do, Pamelia.' I ignored Mrs. Bothner utterly. 'Take the patient's temperature and count the pulse every four hours.'

'Yas'm.'

'Chart it carefully, noting any discrepancy in the diastole and the systole.'

Pamelia gulped. 'Y — yas'm.'

'If the temperature goes above 102 degrees, give a tepid bath under cover. If it is below normal, it may be a symptom of hemorrhage. In that case, keep the patient quiet, and if you think the pulse indicates it, give a hypodermic of about one-eighth of morphine. Be sure your needle and the water you use are sterile. She could easily get an abscess if they aren't. And be sure to put the needle well under the epithelium. If there is any pain in the occipital region ——'

'Lor' God!' Pamelia's eyes were bulging in horrified protest. 'Mis' Hughes, I cain't do none of dem things!'

'You can do all Mrs. Bothner thinks she needs. Don't worry about anything.'

Mrs. Bothner sat up in bed, fairly snorting. 'You get out of here, Pamelia! You know very well you couldn't take care of me. I never heard of such presumption!'

Pamelia made a hurried exit. I knew from the look on her face she was about to explode with laughter.

'And now, Mrs. Hughes' — my patient glared at me in outrage — 'will you please give me a little of the service I'm paying to get? Give me an alcohol rub and then get me some hot tea. My nerves are utterly shaken.'

If ever a nurse was sweetness and light, it was I. I went missionary, having decided the selfish, snobbish Widow Bothner needed salvation as much as the natives of darkest Africa. She really behaved herself pretty well after this incident. She had few friends and was miserably lonely, so having attention when she was ill gave her satisfaction and a sense of importance.

Her resentment of her son's abnormality had made her neglect him shamefully and he seldom came near her. He was a hulking lad of fourteen and I worked with him daily all the time I was there to see if I could arouse a flicker of interest in that blank mind. The results showed me clearly that with proper treatment his case might have been much better. I talked to her about him and suggested ways she might help him and others as well.

At the end of a week, she smiled at me one morning and declared that she didn't know what had come over her, as she didn't feel like the same person. 'You know, I'm really enjoying myself! I woke up this morning and got to thinking of all the lovely things I'll do. Helping poor Herbert now — I'm afraid I've always been too impatient with the child because he got on my nerves so dreadfully. And these old people who can't get out — I'm going to take some of them riding every day. Our carriage horses never get enough exercise for their own good. And with what I'm paying that fat, lazy coachman, he'd better be doing something besides nap all day. And as you say, I can spare a lot of those lilacs without ruining the looks of the bushes. And there'll be other flowers later —— Oh, I know I'm going to make everybody very happy!'

'Fine!' It was obvious her motives were mixed, but after all if she fancied herself in the rôle of Lady Bountiful others would profit.

'You'll help think up things for me to do, won't you?' She was warming to the subject. 'Next week we might ——'

'You won't need me, Mrs. Bothner. This is something you can work out by yourself. I'm leaving tomorrow.'

'Tomorrow —?' She looked at me in indignant astonishment. 'But why ——'

'You're not sick enough to need a nurse any longer. And I'm due on a maternity case. Besides' — I grinned at her — 'as you pointed out to me a week ago, it's a big expense having me here.'

That was a most unfortunate error of judgment — mentioning money. The word *money* was to her what the sound of a tom-tom is to a Zulu. All the gentle little aspirations that had begun to lift their heads were trampled underfoot by lifelong traits leaping strongly into action again. I saw the jungle of selfish stinginess reach out and claim my near-convert.

'You know best, of course.' Her eyes shifted uneasily. 'I'm glad you realize what an awful expense it has been.'

I left the next morning. Mrs. Bothner told me she didn't have any ready cash just then and had mislaid her checkbook, but would send me the amount by the coachman in a few days.

The old coachman drove me home in state in the carriage. When he helped me out, he said, 'Don't be countin' too much on your earnin's, ma'am. You mought get them by Christmas. Then again you moughtn't.'

He was right. I moughtn't. Several 'Please remits' were sent to Mrs. Bothner to remind her of the debt she owed me, but it was never paid. After a couple of months I told everyone I nursed Mrs. Bothner as a charity patient.

I think by the time that got back to her, she believed it herself.

* * *

As I look back in memory over endless instances of high courage, Anna Hillyer always emerges cameo-clear among the brave. Fine and sweet, with fair curling hair and warmly understanding gray eyes full of laughter, she often lamented her quick tears.

'I've always envied people who don't get all red-eyed over nothing. But I cry like a fool when I see a kitten with its little paw bleeding, or when I read a sad story. And music —! It gets me more than anything. Mother's been dead fifteen years and I still choke over the hymns she loved and sang the most.'

'Maybe that's why everybody loves you so much,' I told her.

I met the Hillyers first when their third child was expected. Their little farm snuggled up against the foot of the mountains, and a country doctor, whom I had never seen, had asked Doctor Benson to send out a nurse. One day several weeks before I'd expected to go, I received a call from Doctor Parker, the man in the country. He told me he'd been up to see Mrs. Hillyer the day before and they'd decided I'd better come right away, as her husband was away from the house a lot, working around the place, and there were no near neighbors. I told him I could go up the next day. He promised to meet me at the station of the stub train that served the valley, and drive me out to the Hillyers'.

He was at the station all right — two hundred and eighty pounds or so of him, with a spick-and-span buggy and a good horse. The horse knew his stuff, a fact I was soon to appreciate. The doctor had been drinking, and as we drove slowly up the dusty, swelteringly hot canyon road, he took out his flask every half-mile — to cool him off, he said. I do not doubt that he was a perfect gentleman when sober, but in a drunken state he left much to be desired.

The clothes that were plastered wetly to his huge bulk annoyed him and he began to shed them. First his coat and vest, then his tie and shoes. His socks followed. Finally he pulled his shirt-tails out of the top of his trousers and fanned himself with them. I was mighty glad when he ripped off his collar and flung it into the sage by the side of the road. It was made of celluloid and smelled to high heaven. For some time I'd been afraid it might burst into flames with the heat. My companion up to this time had made conversation of a sort — mostly quite unintelligible — but now, having achieved a degree of comfort, he wrapped the lines around the whipstock and relaxed into sound sleep, his fat chin on his fat chest.

The horse was evidently undisturbed by such proceeding, being used to it, and plugged along at an even gait. It was only eight miles more to the Hillyers', but it was uphill and slow going. It seemed to me we were taking hours to reach there. We came after a time to a very rough stretch. The creek had washed out the road badly, leaving exposed regular boulders and piling drift around them. The horse paused uncertainly. I was impatient. I grabbed the lines from the whipstock and slapped them over his rump. Startled by so vigorous a hand taking over, the animal leaped forward. The buggy careened sideways, hit a boulder, and tipped crazily for a moment. Before it righted itself, Doctor Parker pitched out onto the ground. Fortunately, he landed on a sand spit. He didn't even wake up, but flattened out comfortably and kept right on sleeping. I climbed out and did my best to rouse him, but it was useless, so I got back into the buggy again and drove off and left him.

About half an hour later, I came to a ranch I thought must be the Hillyer place. A man was standing at the gate peering anxiously down the road. He ran out to meet the buggy. He looked stunned when he saw I was alone.

'Mr. Hillyer?' I asked.

'Yes. Are you the nurse? I recognized Doctor Parker's horse and buggy.'

'Yes, I'm the nurse, Mrs. Hughes.'

'Isn't the doctor coming?'

'Not right now. You see, he's dead drunk. He fell out of the buggy back there by the creek and I couldn't get him in again. He's sound asleep by the crossing.'

'My God! What'll we do? My wife's sick right now.'

'Good Heavens! When did she —?'
'About ten this morning. And it's about two now. I——'
'Quick! Show me where she is.'
We lost no time getting to the house. Mrs. Hillyer was in her nightgown, sitting on the edge of her bed, head bowed on the back of a chair in front of her, evidently in great pain. But when she lifted her head as I came in, she smiled at me.
'I'm glad — you got here,' she panted. 'The stork fooled us — this time. He — seems in a — terrible hurry.'
Everything about the place was in as good order as a nurse would have arranged it for a confinement case — even to water boiling in pans on the kitchen stove, for sterilization.
'What do you think I'd better do, Mrs. Hughes?' Mr. Hillyer asked, his big tanned hands clasping and unclasping nervously. 'Should I go after Doc?'
'You might try to wake him by dragging him through the creek. But don't waste any time on him, for I'm afraid he's hopeless right now. I'll need you to help me in a couple of hours, I imagine.'
He set off at a run toward the hitching rack where the doctor's horse and buggy stood.
'Didn't the doctor bring you up?' asked Mrs. Hillyer.
There was nothing I could do under the circumstances but tell her the truth. Instead of being panic-stricken at thought of his failing her in her imminent need, she sat there and laughed until her sides ached. Between pains she kept on laughing. I told her afterward she laughed her baby into the world, for it was born barely fifteen minutes after her husband had gone to rouse the doctor. Fortunately, the two other children had been taken to a neighbor's house the day before, so my coast was clear. I've heard people declare boastfully, with their thumbs in the armholes of their vests, that they didn't believe in prayer. That was because they'd never found themselves alone in a ranch house with a woman having a baby in a terrific rush! Somehow we came through all right. Of the three — mother, child, and nurse — the nurse came out the worst. My knee joints felt as though they were mere jelly all the rest of the day.

The patient was comfortable and the baby bathed and dressed before Mr. Hillyer got back. He came bounding into the house in a frenzy, perspiration running down over his face. When he saw everything was over and all right, he dropped on his knees by his wife's bed and hid his face in her neck, quite overcome. She laid her hand on his head caressingly, her gray eyes misty. But there was still laughter in them.

'Where's the doctor now, Jim?' she asked. 'Did you rouse him at all?'

Mr. Hillyer raised up, flinging his sun-bleached hair back from his forehead. 'I wish you could get up and see. Go take a look out the front door, Mrs. Hughes.'

I did so. The horse and buggy stood close by the gate with the doctor slumped on the front seat, his head sort of hooked over the back of it, legs straight out in front of him, feet on the dashboard, mouth wide open, still dead to the world! Mr. Hillyer described how he yelled at the man, slapped his face, and dashed hatfuls of water on his head before he could wake him enough to try to get in the buggy. He himself had pushed and pried and heaved to get that inert bulk boosted in.

'I think you'd better drive him down to the horse lot, Jim,' Mrs. Hillyer suggested. 'You can turn the horse in there then. And the doctor won't be half so humiliated coming to himself when he's slept off his drunk if there's no one watching him. He can hitch up and go home without being seen.'

Mr. Hillyer looked at me and smiled. 'Anna's the boss, but I'd like to haul that buggy right in here by the bed and have him wake up seeing her nurse that baby! A lot of help he's been.'

I saw the Hillyers off and on over the next two years and spent several delightful vacation days at their ranch. I liked them better all the time. The baby, Denny, was an adorable little fellow, with his mother's blond curly hair and big gray eyes. It was tragic that anything should spoil such happiness as I saw in that home. But Denny suddenly developed a serious kidney infection. They had Doctor Benson go out to see him and he put me on the case.

Never have I so wanted to see a child get well. Mrs. Hillyer was a ghost of herself from lack of sleep and from work and worry when I took over. But she made me promise that if her little son asked for her, night or day, I would call her at once. He loved her to sing to him. Her voice had a lovely quality, and to see her take the sick baby in her arms and rock him and sing to him always brought a lump to my throat. 'She'll never sing again,' I thought, 'if anything happens to that child.'

His favorite song was the old hymn, 'Precious Jewels.' Often, when I'd be leaning over him, he'd put his hot little hand on my cheek and lisp, 'Want Mama sing Jew'ls!' I never failed to call her.

> When He cometh, when He cometh to make up His jewels,
> All the jewels, precious jewels, His loved and His own ——

It came to have a heart-breaking significance for me, for after a short time I knew that, despite all the care and love and skill we could give, the baby's case was hopeless. He lived only three weeks.

Anna Hillyer insisted that I let her bathe and dress little Denny this one last time. Then she called Jim to put him in the tiny casket. The funeral was held at home. The neighbors and friends came bringing flowers from their own gardens. The minister of the country church spoke simple words of consolation. Everyone was weeping except Mrs. Hillyer. White-faced and strained she sat in stony grief too deep for tears. It frightened me to look at her.

And then a young girl from the church choir stood up beside the organ to sing. She'd lived with the Hillyers most of the time since Denny's birth and was devoted to him. The accompanist began the hymn, 'Precious Jewels.' I saw the look of utter anguish that twisted the mother's face.

> When He cometh, when He cometh ——

The fresh young voice faltered at significance too real. I saw the girl's eyes fix on the baby in the white casket, his waxen fingers curled in eternal stillness. The words quavered, stumbled on, then broke off in weeping.

Only for a moment did the startled silence last. Anna Hillyer was on her feet, was beside the girl, slipping an arm around her shoulder. Clear and unshaken her voice took up the words of her baby's beloved song. Night after night she had sung it to him with breaking heart. She could not fail him this last time. Head uplifted, the bitterness gone from her face, her eyes warm again with love and tenderness, she sang the song from beginning to end.

* * *

'I'm sorry, Doctor, but I can't possibly take a case until I've had a couple of days' rest. I haven't had a good night's sleep in months.' Twice within the hour I'd given that reply, and now the telephone was ringing again.

'Hello, Hughsie! This is Ben Herrick.'

'Well, well, Ben! What brings you down to civilization?'

'I need a new river boss up at Jolly Boy Camp. And a nurse. You see ——'

'Don't waste your breath, Herrick. I've just turned down two cases. I'm so dead tired, I ——'

'But this is a vacation. Wait till I tell you. Dad's been up at Jolly Boy for two weeks. I meant to bring him out with me today, as I'm going to the up-river camp tonight, but yesterday he fell down the log-chute into the river, which was pretty much of a shock for a man of his age. Doctor Neeley says there isn't anything broken, but he wants Dad to stay in bed a few days to avoid possible pneumonia.'

'Poor Dad!' I couldn't help laughing. That veteran old lumberman tobogganing down a chute into twenty feet or so of water!

'There isn't a thing to do but keep him quiet and entertained and see that he gets a decent tray from the Mess. You know — play a game of seven-up with him or something. He's always liked you and I'll feel safe leaving him if you're there.'

'All right, Ben.' The thought of forest scents was reviving.
'I'll go. When will you pick me up?'

'I'll be out about two-thirty. I'm taking up supplies, so I drove the truck down, but the seat in the cab is very comfortable. So long till then!'

I had known Ben Herrick and his dad for years. I'd had some tough cases out at the Jolly Boy Camp — men too maimed or too critically ill to be sent into Seattle to the hospital. There was a good cabin there which Herrick used as living quarters and office. In the old days, before Mother Herrick died, when Dad was active head of the company, she always spent her summers up there in the woods. The cabin still bore the touch of her housewifely care in comfort and cheerfulness when I'd last seen it.

Dad was as fine an old rascal as ever lived and was always up to something. I didn't put it past him to be shamming injuries just so he wouldn't have to leave camp. Once he managed to get up in the timber — he was nearly eighty and had attacks which kept him in town — nothing on earth could pry him out but winter weather. He liked the loggers and they liked him. The truth was, his able and very keen son, who was always successful in clearing the river of a jam or closing an important business deal, was most inadequate in the matter of camp maintenance and discipline. That sort of thing got on Ben's nerves, whereas the old man had always liked to putter around making things better for the men, and was a real diplomat in keeping up the camp morale.

Ben was a lovable chap, lean and tanned, with twinkling blue eyes and a shock of yellow hair topping him off like a thatch on a roof. The big company truck rolled up on time, my stuff was put in, and we were off.

'I'm picking up a couple of fellows at a downtown boarding house, Hughsie,' Ben told me. 'You'll laugh when you see them.'

'It doesn't take much to make me laugh, you know. What's so funny about these hombres?'

'You'll have to see for yourself. Remember the river-boss, Erickson, that was up at camp last summer? Well, he and that big Jacques Le Bart had another row and Erickson quit. Now Le Bart thinks he's cock of the roost. He and I've never hit it off very well, and he's going to make trouble sure while I'm up the river at Number Two.'

'That'll be fine for Dad and me. Maybe a murder or so on our hands to liven things up!'

'You're hoping! There's nothing that you and Dad like better than a good scrap.'

'It all depends. I thoroughly enjoy seeing a bully get what's coming to him.'

Herrick laughed. 'Get ready, then. This big bruiser I hired is going to scare tar out of Jacques. Squatty, they call him. Maybe because he's a bit bow-legged — he certainly isn't short. Looks like a bulldog. He has a partner travels with him always, so he's coming along, too. Fellow by the name of Dave. Looks like an umbrella turned wrong-side out. Some team!'

We drew up at the boarding house on Yessler Way. Bedrolls and a couple of duffel sacks leaned against a big wooden box. On the steps sat the most astonishing pair I ever saw outside a circus.

'There they are,' said Herrick. 'Hello, boys.'

Looking at the one I knew was Squatty, I had the awesome impression of some Sandow further enlarged by a magnifying glass, so huge he was and so bulging the muscles of his bare arms. Above his powerful neck was a face so like that of an English bulldog that I almost laughed.

'It's funeral wreaths for Jacques!' I whispered to Herrick.

Dave was a long, lean Jack-in-the-box sort, with a vigorous upward turn to his whole person. His hair went back from his high forehead like quills on a porcupine, and his eyebrows seemed trying to catch up with his pompadour. His nose turned up with such vim that it pulled his upper lip along with it, and the corners of his mouth lifted in a line of perpetual mirth.

Herrick introduced us as they came down to the truck with the duffel sacks. Dave's voice was thin and a bit squeaky. Squatty's sounded like that of a wild lion, but as he smiled up at me, I had the shock of my life. Those pale, squinty eyes which appeared so intimidating at a distance were mild and innocent as I looked down into them, and had in them a kindliness that amazed me. Well, I thought, bulldogs are said to have the sweetest of dispositions, in spite of their ferocious aspects. If Herrick picked this man as a brute, he doesn't know much about human nature.

'I'm glad we're having a lady's company,' boomed Squatty, as he hoisted the big wooden box on his back as easily as though it were a feather pillow.

'What in thunder's that?' asked Herrick, watching the giant slide the box from his shoulders into the rear of the truck.

'Them's his tools,' explained Dave. 'He don't go nowheres without 'em.'

Paul Bunyan implements, forged to scale, no doubt.

'All ready,' said Squatty, as he settled down comfortably on his bedroll, his back against the mysterious packing case.

As we drove along, there were no comments from the loggers. Out of town in the sparsely settled country, where the dense trees seemed to step back to let the highways through, Herrick began talking to the men about trouble he'd been having at Jolly Boy Camp — bad feeling and grouching. The pair listened attentively, but replied only in monosyllables. I wondered why Squatty didn't tell how he'd dealt with such things. River-bosses always boasted of men they'd tamed, of fights they'd had, of arms and heads they'd broken, recounting their own exploits in heroic terms to bolster up their own morale if nothing more. There was something in this setup we couldn't make out.

Just before sundown, we came in sight of the big river. Deep and smooth it ran between rocky cliffs and mountain slopes. We followed the upstream road and it was almost dusk when we saw the camp.

Dave stood up and looked it over. 'Fine smooth water for log booms, Squatty.'

Squatty stretched his big limbs. 'Sure is.' Not another word was spoken.

Outside of a particularly beautiful setting, Jolly Boy Camp

was the usual thing. Half a dozen log and rough lumber buildings were scattered among the trees; there stood the mess-hall, storehouse, bunkhouse, and the rest. Twenty or so roughly clad rivermen, most of them heavily bearded, sat around smoking as they waited for the evening meal. Just as we drew up at the door of Herrick's cabin, the cook appeared in grimy apron at the mess-hall door and whanged away at a piece of iron scraper hanging from a tree. Every man rushed to eat. The whole place had a rundown look which I'd never seen there before. It seemed strange, since I knew the business was flourishing.

I went into the cabin with Ben and found his dad sitting up in bed. No sickly pallor had changed the weather-beaten red of his skin. His thick white hair stood on end as usual. He looked very fit.

'Hughsie!' he yelled. 'For Pete's sake, it's good to see you!' He almost wrung my hand off, then slumped and sighed. 'I need you.' His voice was suddenly weak and I looked at him in alarm. 'Look at this damn mess Frenchie brought me! Nice food for a sick man!'

The plate on his tray was piled high with beef, potatoes, and rutabagas, flanked with slabs of soggy bread and a bowl of canned peaches. I put my tongue in my cheek and grinned at him. Herrick, all solicitous, leaned over his father and surprised me by kissing him.

The old man looked embarrassed. 'You two better get over to the mess-hall,' he growled. 'The food's bad enough without being cold as well.'

Old Frenchie was all smiles when he saw me come in with Herrick. We sat down and he hovered about in his greasy apron, trying to serve us. The food had always been good up here, but now it was carelessly prepared and the whole service seemed slipping. Dave and Squatty sat across the narrow table from us. At the head of the table sat Jacques Le Bart. I took a good look at him. He was tall and too heavy around the middle. His hands were like hams, but they were hung on arms too small for the rest of him. His shoulders were hunched up in a perpetual shrug and his thick neck supported a dark, clean-shaven face. Framed in black curly hair, it was a rather handsome face. He was studying Squatty with sullen antagonism.

'Jacques is taking in Squatty's muscle,' Herrick whispered to me out of the corner of his mouth.

'He'd better. The rest of him wouldn't scare anyone. He's a mystery, your Squatty.'

'I can't make him out. I'd never heard of him until I went into the Employment Agency, but they gave him a powerful boost. Said no bully'd ever cleaned up on him yet. But he's acting mighty tame. I hate to leave until I find out how things are going. If Le Bart should lick him, he'd be more insufferable than ever around camp.'

'Oh, let them fight it out. It will be better. But why do you keep this Jacques on here year after year when he's such a trouble-maker?'

'He's a good worker. He never gets soused. He's always on the job and can clear the river in a jam better than anyone I know. I'd make him boss in a minute, but the men wouldn't stand for it. He's a damned braggart and bully and they don't like him.'

When the men had finished their supper, Herrick crossed over to Squatty and laid a hand on his shoulder. 'Boys,' he said, so all could hear, 'this man — Smith's his name ——'

'I'm just Squatty, fellers,' the big man interrupted.

'Well, then, Squatty,' amended Herrick. 'He's your new boss. I'm going to the upper camp for a few days and I hope things move along all right here. We're behind on the drive right now. If any of you don't see fit to do as Squatty says, you can have your time as soon as I get back.'

The men filed out. Herrick took Squatty over to the river bank to have a look at the logs. By the time I got back to the cabin, Dad had finished his supper. There wasn't a crumb left on the tray. He glanced up sheepishly when he saw me looking at the empty dishes.

'"Tain't good manners to leave food on your plate,' he explained, running his fingers through his hair until it stood on end more than ever.

'"Tain't good manners to lick off all the enamel from the dishes, either,' I came back at him. He grinned at me contentedly.

Herrick came in hurriedly to tell us good-bye. The stable boy had already brought up his horse. 'Mind your nurse, Dad. And Hughsie, take it easy.' Then he tied his sack behind the saddle, mounted, and rode away.

By the time I had hung up my things in my room and tidied up the cabin a bit, Dad talking a blue streak all the time, it was beginning to get dark. A dim light showed in the bunkhouse across the clearing.

'Hughsie,' said Dad, 'as soon as it gets a little darker, you light up the Rochester lamp for me so I can read the paper. Then you sneak over to the bunkhouse — I'll hatch up some errand for you if you want me to — and see what's going on over there.'

'Yes. And then you'll suddenly have a miraculous healing and be up and out yourself!'

'How'd you guess it?' He grinned at me.

'It's written all over you. But you don't get out of that bed, no matter what's brewing. I feel something is. Am I right?'

'Well, yes — in a way. But I don't know what yet. That will keep. Sneak over there and see how things look. You can hide yourself in the thicket by the north window. It's a good peek-hole. The windows are mostly open, so you can hear, too.'

I went across to the bunkhouse half hidden in trees and underbrush, my distaste for snooping overcome by burning curiosity, slipped into the shrubbery by the open window, and took a good look.

The interior was certainly anything but cheerful, but it was much the same as quarters I had seen in other logging camps. Two tiers of shelving, three feet wide, ran around the sides of the room. Each man claimed seven feet of it as his. Old quilts and blankets were messed around, with few attempts made to put a bed in proper shape. The outside night air was fouled by the reek of sweat and dirty bodies, of soiled clothing and stale tobacco smoke. In the corner of the room nearest my window was a pile of broken chairs and tables, probable wreckage of some fight. Nail kegs and apple boxes were now doing duty as seats. Three men played cards on a slab of wood across two powder kegs. A smoke-blackened lamp sat on a shingle at the end of a grindstone. So ineffectual was the light it shed that the card-players from time to time lit matches for a better view of the cards in case of dispute.

Jacques Le Bart sat on a block of wood with a huge palm on either knee. His head was up and he sang an old tune in a wonderfully good voice, but the words, which sounded as though he were making them up as he went along, were decidedly nasty. Lumberjacks milled around the big box which Squatty and Dave had dragged into the middle of the floor.

Squatty looked toward Le Bart and smiled. 'I don't blame you, Jacques, for words like them in such a hole as this bunkhouse is. Come on an' give me a hand openin' this box, will ya?'

'Who the hell do you think I am?' Jacques demanded.

'Oh, that's all right. I had something in the box for you an' I thought maybe you'd like to see it.'

I couldn't see the expression on Jacques's face, but he made no move. 'I'm no damned sissy to be hauled around by the nose!' he growled, and called Squatty a lot of vile names. The loggers crowded around, excitement in their eyes. They were itching to see a good fight and find out which was the better man.

But Squatty seemed deaf to insult. He kept right on opening his box. When he spoke, his tone was casual and, though he didn't lift it, every man in the room turned to listen. 'Fellers, there's only one place around here where we're goin' to use force an' muscle. That's down on the river, battlin' them logs.' He flung out his right arm in front of Le Bart's face. With the muscles knotted up, it was an arm to respect. 'Round the bunkhouse here it's going to be brains an' a bit of a smile. I'm tired fightin'. Ain't no fun seein' a fellow all sprawled out with his face nothin' but a bloody pulp. That's why I quit the game.'

'You're a damn coward!' Jacques was up and advanced menacingly. 'You're afraid to fight!'

'Maybe I am, at that.' Squatty seemed to consider the matter. 'But there's them as wouldn't say it. I don't relish killin' no one. But if you want to settle this fightin' business, I reckon we'd better do it once for all. Right now I ain't got time to fight, but, if you insist on it, take off that new shirt you got on an' hop to it. Ain't nobody stoppin' you. Leastwise not me. But I ain't fightin' back, remember. Just defendin' myself.'

The challenger opened and closed his big fists uneasily. It was obvious he wasn't used to this sort of indifference when a man demanded a proper fight. The man whom he had insulted kept right on working at the box. 'Lay offen him, Jacques!' someone whispered. 'Look at them muscles of his'n.' As the side of the box was pried off, all eyes turned curiously to the contents. An enthusiastic shout went up as Squatty took out a big Rochester reflecting lamp.

'Who'll scuttle for oil?' asked Dave.

Several volunteered. Jacques, looking a bit silly, went back and sat down again. No one was paying the least attention to him in this new interest. In a few minutes Squatty had put up a bracket on a central upright. When the lamp was filled and the reflector adjusted, it transformed the whole place. Once more every eye went back to the box, as Squatty dramatically revealed the rest of the contents. There, packed around with songbooks, stood a small melodeon.

Dave took out an armful of books and began passing them around. A logger stepped up to help him. Squatty pulled out the melodeon and dusted it off carefully. The books distributed to every man, Dave pulled up an apple box and sat down at the instrument. That room was breathlessly still as he played a few chords. Then Squatty began to sing. 'Should auld acquaintance be forgot and never brought tae mind ——?' It was a full, rich voice that came from that big man. And there was a quality in it that clutched at the heart as he sang.

I stood out there in the dark and watched the faces of the men. That song was doing things to them. What memories did it awaken? I tried to imagine as I saw them soften or grow grim or tearful. Themselves as kids with their mothers — children of their own left behind — wives long dead or maybe deserted — lullabies sung in another tongue — or maybe just a little white house and picket fence back in Missouri some place, where the old folks were still waiting for a letter that never came? To this day I choke up when I think of that scene.

There was a dead hush as Squatty sang the first verse through. He raised his hand, beating time as Dave played, and called out, 'Everybody sing!' Sing —? They fairly roared. The building shook with it.

And then I saw Jacques Le Bart pushing through the men to go stand beside the melodeon. He wasn't going to be licked on this count. This was where he shone. Squatty would have to look to his laurels when it came to singing. He bellowed louder than any of them. Squatty smiled appreciatively, stopped singing himself and beat time for Jacques. Then Dave struck up some livelier tunes — 'Little Brown Jug,' 'Clementine,' 'Oh, Susanna.' The men began dancing as they sang, pairing off for amazing performances. I think they'd have kept it up all night if Squatty hadn't signaled Dave to stop.

With the loggers all in this softened mood, Squatty outlined to them the sort of camp life he proposed to have in the future. If it didn't appeal to them, there wasn't a man who need stay. He could fill their places overnight. He told them the place was going to be cleaned up and was to stay clean. Dave was camp tender and would have hot water in the washroom every evening when the men got in from work. He'd shave any man who wanted it on Wednesdays and Sundays. There were going to be games and singing, and a tin can would be nailed on the wall for any extra dimes they could spare as a fund for magazines, extra smokes, and candy.

'Unless we have a log jam on our hands or get some high water, there ain't goin' to be no more workin' on Sundays. Mebbe we kin get up a few ball games. We're all fellers here together, an' if any of you don't like the way things go, speak up an' we'll see if there's a better way. No use grouchin'. An' while we're talkin', what about the chuck here? Does Frenchie put 'em up pretty good?'

'He sure us'ta,' said one man, 'but lately he's been gettin' about as lousy as everything else around the dump.'

I had stayed away from Dad too long. In fact, I had just about forgotten him in the interest and excitement of all this. It was a wonder he hadn't got out of bed and run across to the bunkhouse in his nightshirt when the singing began. But he was sitting in bed still reading when I went in. I told him all I had seen and heard. He didn't seem in the least surprised, but nodded his head in satisfaction.

'Dad Herrick' — I pointed a finger at him accusingly — 'what have you to do with all this business? I'll wager you're behind it, you old fraud!'

'Well, supposing I am? It's my logging business, isn't it? Ben's mother and I started it when he was just a little shaver. She named the camp "Jolly Boy" for him. He's a good boy to his old dad, Hughsie, but he treats me as though I were an old woman. We don't see eye to eye. He starts the men off every year with new tubs and basins and things for the washroom, has all the chairs and tables mended, or gets new ones for the bunkhouse. After that it's just up to the men.'

'I've noticed camp tenders at most of the logging camps I've visited, Dad.'

'Sure you have. We always had a roustabout when Mother was with us. But Ben got the notion it was just needless expense.'

'And you feel it isn't?'

'You bet it isn't. I know. I used to battle with logs and was so dang tired at night that all I wanted was a place to flop down. No logger comes in from the woods or up from the river full of housewifely concern over sweeping out the bunkhouse or airing his bedding or mending chairs.'

'I can well understand that after watching them work!'

'A few of the loggers live around in the country and go home for week-ends. Another bunch goes to town only to cash pay-checks. They put up at hotels, bathe and shave, see the shows and what have you, and come back to camp sober. But the rank and file of the men, while they're hard-working enough, are restless, roving fellows out for excitement and entertainment. They cash their checks, paint the town red, and come back broke, with hang-overs and black eyes, grouchy enough to fight over nothing. That's when the furniture gets smashed up.

'A camp tender'd be cheap compared to what we spend on fight damages up here from season to season. For instance — there was a college kid out from Boston one year, working to put himself through. He was a religious sort, prayed on his knees by his bed every night, and a big Swede who was a rabid atheist was always making fun of him. One night when the Swede had just come back from a big jag in town and climbed into his upper bunk, he saw the kid on his knees across the room and he yanked off his boot and threw it at him as hard as he could. Pie-eyed as he still was, he hit the lamp hanging from the ceiling instead. The kid looked up at sound of the crash and a splinter of flying glass stabbed into his right eye. I spent ten thousand dollars trying to save that eye, but he lost the sight of it. If we'd had a camp tender at the time such a thing wouldn't have happened. Poor kid! He should have stayed in Boston where he belonged.'

'*You* didn't!' I reminded him. 'Weren't you born in Boston, and didn't you acquire a couple of university degrees before coming West? You sure don't sound like a lumberjack when you get up to make a speech. I heard you at the Governor's dinner last year.'

The old man grinned. 'Two degrees —! You forget damn fast up in the woods. You no longer say, "Mr. Jones, will you please pass the potatoes." You beat on your tin plate with your knife to attract attention and then bawl out, "Hey, down there, spuds! And sling along the fat with 'em!"'

'I know, Dad. I can take two biscuits and spit on the floor myself, in camp. Just the same, I wish I had a college education. But tell me how you engineered this Squatty deal.'

'Well, we sign up most of our men from the Eureka Employment Office in Seattle, which is run by an old friend of mine. Jim Boyer and I logged together for years until he got too old for the river. I was telling him about our set-up here one day, how things were running downhill more every year and Ben wasn't handling it right. Jim knows loggers and camps from coast to coast and from the Gulf of California to the Yukon, and right away he wanted me to try out Squatty and Dave. Said they were wizards at bringing up the morale in camp and keeping order. So I had him boost Squatty to Ben for river-boss — he's really tops there, too — and Ben thinks they're his find.' The conspirator chuckled. 'Don't you dare ever hint I was behind this.'

'I won't. Don't worry! Now one thing more. Are you in any degree whatever sick, lame, tight in the chest or anything?'

'Hell, no! Never felt better in my life. But Ben was insisting I must go into town while he was up-river. He's always afraid I'll mess around in things when he's away.'

'Funny he'd think that, isn't it?' I scowled at him. 'Look here, you old scoundrel, was that record run you made down the log-chute deliberate? You might have killed yourself!'

'Deliberate —? Say, do you think a man of my age'd deliberately shoot head-first down half a mile of slide and hit bottom in thirty feet of water? No, that was pure accident, and why I wasn't killed I don't know. But when I got over the shock and Doc said nothing was busted, I decided I might as well make some capital of the thing. If I spread it on a bit, I wouldn't get sent back to town. But gosh! I never thought Ben would bring up a nurse for me!'

'It would have been a darn good joke on you if a prim and proper nurse had come, determined to do her duty! If she'd started looking you over ——'

'Hughsie, you can think up the damnedest things!'

Since reform seemed the order of the day in camp — the bunkhouse was being turned inside out and scrubbed and shined to an unbelievable state of cleanliness — I went to Frenchie after breakfast the next morning and hinted we might slick up the mess-hall a little.

'That man, Dave, you know, Frenchie. He's camp tender

and would help you. You really have about all one man can handle.'

'No! No!' Frenchie gesticulated eloquently. 'Those man, she's look seek. See, Madame Nurse, how I get ze muscle!' He doubled up his fist and lifted his arm that I might see his bulging biceps. 'Me, I will mak' ze sleek house. I will show Madame.'

And he did show us: clean floor and scrubbed oilcloth on the tables. He scoured the black-handled, three-tined forks and short-bladed knives in the sandpile, and afterward held his palm open behind his back for someone to surprise him with a tip. Dad knew his men and saw to it that Frenchie was rewarded. That very day the food began to improve. Before the week was out, it had taken on a quality long unknown in that camp and we knew that Frenchie was once more taking pride in his efforts. He sang lustily with the men every night in a high tenor voice, and taught them some naughty French songs which they all relished. Their rendition of the French words was something wonderful and fearful, Le Bart told me, but they were having fun trying.

It was on the evening of the sixth day that Herrick came galloping into camp and up to the porch where Dad and I sat slapping mosquitoes. He flung the reins over the mustang's head and dropped from the saddle.

'Hello there!' He came up and threw an affectionate arm about his father's shoulder. 'You look like a new man, Dad. Good nursing, Hughsie! Did everything go along all ——'

He broke off in amazement as there burst on the evening air a chorus of men's voices in good harmony, 'Hail, hail, the gang's all here!' Herrick's face was a sight to behold. Bewildered, he looked from one to the other of us.

'Lord God! What's that?'

'It's the heavenly choir, Ben.' The old man grinned at him. 'You see, I've been at Death's door, and I brought back some angels with me.'

Herrick scarcely heard the remark. He leaned back against the porch pillar and just listened. 'Men of Harlech,' they sang, with gusto to stir the blood, then 'Tenting Tonight,' and finally, with amazing tenderness, 'Sweet and Low.' Every little while Herrick would say, 'God!' under his breath.

'And now, boys' — we could hear Squatty's big voice distinctly in the stillness — 'Jacques is goin' to sing "My Wild Irish Rose" for us. When he comes to the chorus, we'll all hum the parts, very soft. Go ahead, Jacques. You've a swell voice for this.'

With the little melodeon leading, he went ahead. I'd heard them nightly and I'd seen the real beauty in their amateurish efforts, but now as I sat listening I had a lump in my throat. There was something wonderful happening here between these two men who might have been the bitterest of enemies.

Before they finished the last chorus, Herrick, without a word, started toward the river in a run. I chuckled to myself. I knew he was wondering if they'd done nothing but sing around here since he'd been gone. I could see him standing on the bank, looking up and down the stream in a stupefied sort of way. Then he was coming back as fast as he'd left. But he paused a moment to look inside the bunkhouse door.

'Dad!' — he was fairly gasping — 'the river's clear! And the bunkhouse is shining!'

Squatty came ambling over from the bunkhouse. 'Hello, Mr. Herrick. Glad to see you're back. Things all right up-river?'

'All in good shape, Squatty. But I'm damned if I can understand what's going on here.' He sank down on the top step weakly. 'How the hell —? The river cleared, the place all cleaned up, you and Jacques not fighting, and this singing —!'

''Tain't nothin' strange, Mr. Herrick.' Squatty's kindly eyes beamed in his massive bulldog face. 'Music done it. There ain't no mud nor bog but that somethin' can't be heard singin' up out of it. And men now — they need to make music. It's like they got a thousand fiddle-strings runnin' through 'em, just waitin' to be played on. They's different kinda tools to use gettin' work done. An' Dave an' me's always got results — even if our tools ain't what you'd expect.'

* * *

Birthdays, I began to notice, came faster and faster on each other's heels — while I personally moved slower and slower. At fifty I assured myself I was still young. At fifty-five I could camp with the best of them, even if I couldn't climb and hike as I once could. But at sixty, when the doctor told me in no uncertain terms that I would have to take a rest if I expected the old pump to continue functioning, I realized the thought of relaxing was wonderful. No night calls, no sleepless vigils.

For some years I had owned a little beach place a short ferry-ride across the Sound from Seattle. I'd go over there and soak up sunshine all summer, then go to California and live on the desert all winter. Mother and I moved to the beach in high spirits. It was good to be free.

The pine tree I'd planted when I got the place had grown as tall as the roof and its drooping lower boughs screened the porch from people going down the road to the little cluster of stores around the ferry landing. We could eat our meals out there in seclusion and enjoy the freshness of beach below and forest above.

I'll never forget that first evening's feeling of utter peacefulness. We sat out on the porch long after we had finished dinner. Dishes could wait. Sunsets couldn't. A red-gold tide rolled in to break on the sands, white sails skimmed its surface, and Rainier glowed brilliantly above the deep green of the timbered islands. We watched the color intensify to awesome glory, then watched its slow fading to the silver gray of twilight. The lights of Seattle threw friendly, shimmering beams across to us. Night birds called up in the woods and a bat darted close to the eaves. We talked the twilight away, mostly of father and things of long ago.

'Well, Mama,' I said finally, 'we're going to have lots of fun from now on. Campfires and suppers on the beach, walks back in the woods, people in for afternoon coffee, trips into town to see the family or go to good shows — it'll be wonderful! I think I'll call you Molly after this, to perpetuate the name. You're far too young-looking to be my mother.'

I couldn't see her face in the fading light, but I heard her catch her breath in a half sob. I stepped to her side and put my arm around her shoulders. She stiffened and sat bolt upright in her chair, pushing my arm away.

'Don't soften me up. There's something I must tell you. I've been putting it off. I don't want to be sniffling over it.' She hesitated a moment. When she went on, her voice was firm. 'Lora, I'm going blind.'

I felt as though I'd been slugged. 'Mama —!' Then I rallied. 'But that's absurd! It's your glasses. I've told you for a long time now that ——'

'I went when you were in the hospital. I never told anyone. I've seen three of the best specialists in town.' She named them, all men whose verdict none would question. 'They all said the same thing. It's cataract.'

Hope surged up in me. 'But Mama — they operate for that. With modern surgical skill ——'

'Yes, I know. They say when one goes entirely blind, an operation is sometimes successful. But at my age they don't think I'll ever reach total blindness. I've passed my eighty-second birthday, remember, and this is the slow type.'

For a moment I could scarcely think, I was so stunned by what this meant. Then I asked, 'How long has this been going on?'

'Oh, for a year I haven't been able to thread my needle so well. About two months ago it got pretty bad, so I went and had my glasses changed. But it didn't help any. That's why I went to the specialist.'

I clasped her hand tightly, stricken that this thing should have to come to her. 'How blind are you now, really?'

'Well, I can see the big print in the paper, and after I get my needle threaded, I can sew fairly well. Depends on the way the light strikes my eyes. Awhile ago when we were watching the sailboats, they were mere smears on the water to me. Oh, Lora, the thought of never being able to do the

things I'd looked forward to doing when I was old — all the
———.' She broke off. 'But you shouldn't be worried with all this. You're the one that we need to think about with that heart of yours so ———'

'My heart'll last longer than it has any business doing. What is it you've wanted most to do when you were old, Mama?'

She smiled wistfully. 'Those silk scraps I've saved all my life — I've made only three quilts of them, and I always meant to make one for each of my children and grandchildren, with all the time I'd have for it when I couldn't do anything else. They'll go to waste now.' Her voice trembled. 'Nobody else cares. There was a piece of Papa's wedding-tie and ———'

'Look here, Molly — for the love of Pete!' I glowered at her accusingly. 'We aren't licked before we start. There's a long time. We'll start those quilts in the morning!'

We consulted all the best specialists in the Northwest, but there was no difference of opinion. Hopeless. And so began the long decline into night.

The change came slowly, as she had been told it would. For the first few years her sight seemed to remain about the same. She could read the headlines in the papers and wrote letters by keeping well within the heavy lines I drew on the paper. We had picnics on the beach and talked long by driftwood fires. We walked up into the cool green of the woods and loved it more each day. We had friends in for afternoon coffee, and many guests for our porch suppers. We stayed at the beach house in the summers and took rooms in town for the winters.

Mother's greatest interest was her handicraft. With feverish eagerness to finish her silk quilts, she plunged us both into an inescapable welter of silk scraps. I helped her every moment I could spare from household duties, cutting, sorting colors, threading needles, secretly pulling out unsightly stitches and putting in others. Rainbow-hued fluff clung to the furniture and rugs. Well did I understand in those years why quilts made of such irregular sewed-and-feather-stitched pieces should be called 'crazy.' It was uncanny the way

Mother's touch took the place of her sight. Fourteen quilts we made, and twelve hooked rugs, before she was satisfied.

'Just to think,' she said one day, when the very special quilt for Bill had just been finished, 'the dream of my life has been realized. Long ago I'd catch myself standing stock-still with my hands in the dishwater, planning the things I'd make some day when I was too old to work. And now they're done. Only I can't half see them. Are they really nice?'

'Of course they are. Everyone says they're lovely.'

She touched my hand caressingly. 'I know you're so good and sick of the whole mess, you never want to see a silk scrap again as long as you live.'

She said it, I knew, just so she could hear me deny it — which I did. But thankful as I was for the absorbing interest this had brought her, she had spoken truly.

The time came at last when all her work, even knitting, had to be abandoned. But she sang her songs, visited with the neighbors, enjoyed the endless letters written her and dictated newsy and witty letters in answer. Life had settled very much into a rut from necessity, but this was my work. I was more and more her eyes — reading to her, writing for her to that steadily increasing circle of second cousins, long unseen and forgotten, whom belatedly she felt she should contact once more.

Even when she could no longer be taken in the car to visit the family or friends, but had to be in bed or in her wheelchair, her active mind reached out in keen interest. She was always a good sport. I can see her sitting on the porch where she loved to be, singing in a voice still clear and sweet,

> Oh, fret not for tomorrow, bid farewell to care and sorrow,
> Let no future evil borrow the joy of today.

I remember how she smiled up at me when I brought out her supper tray. 'You seem pretty gay for an Old Timer, tonight,' I told her.

'Why not? Life will always be good as long as I can have

a whiff of the clam-tide. And the smell of pine. And of potatoes baking for supper.'

The next morning she couldn't get up. She said she'd lost the use of her legs for a time in the night.

'Why didn't you call me?' I asked.

She laughed. 'I thought maybe I was going to trade them off for a pair of wings and I didn't want you heading me off! But I was all right in a little while and went to sleep again.'

It must have been a slight stroke. She never walked again without help. Almost overnight I saw her change into a helpless invalid. We left the beach house for a hotel apartment in town. It was imperative we should be near a doctor, and Mother wanted to be close to Florence and Leslie, who were both in Seattle. For two years, day and night, I scarcely left her bedside.

Then I had a heart attack which flattened me out.

My sister rushed down with the family doctor. Jo, a practical nurse who'd help care for Mother at times, was sent for. There was much palaver — stethoscope, pulse-counting, chest-thumping, blood-pressure. And just where was the pain? Then a conference in subdued tones in the hall. I knew from experience just what they'd be saying. 'Very grave condition — maybe only a few days. At best, complete rest and relaxation in bed, perhaps for months. Hospitalization above all.' Jo hovered around, while I assured Mother I would be as good as new in a few days.

The conspirators came in, looking grave. Mother was up on her elbow, listening. Could I allow them to take me away from her? Absolutely not, except in the dead wagon. I told them so.

There was much persuasion. The doctor told me I'd have to stay in bed for six months at least — maybe a year. What he was trying to make me understand was that only by being entirely inactive could I hope to outlive Mother. But I refused to go to the hospital. I'd nursed many an old girl with a bad heart and pulled her through. Now I'd take a turn at myself. Finally they gave in — for the time. And we began our adjustment to the new order of things.

Jo took charge. She was big and cheerful and we were very fond of her. After a few weeks the pain in my side began to lessen. When it was time for our trays, Jo would put Mother in her wheel-chair and bring her over beside my bed. All through her blindness she had a horror of some fly or spider falling into her food, so I always inspected it as she ate. We had a good radio and a telephone close at hand. After I got better, I read aloud by the hour. Friends came, and the room was always filled with flowers.

From the first I supervised Mother's treatments and slipped out of bed to give her hypos when they were ordered. I sneaked in all the little personal attentions for her I could, and prayed that I would be spared to see her through. My family and friends kept on trying to persuade me to go to the hospital, insisting I was making a martyr of myself. How utterly mistaken they were! That nine months in bed and what I was able to do with it seemed to me the crowning achievement of my life — a benediction, rich and full and satisfying.

Mother and I constantly shocked our friends by speaking of death lightly. To us it was a big adventure on which we were about to embark, and we joked a lot about which one of us would get off first. But I knew Mother was much closer to leaving than I. She was in her eighty-eighth year now.

'Lora,' she said one day, 'if you could have just one of my old keepsakes, which would it be?' — naming a number of relics, such as the little old chest of drawers which had held so many baby clothes, the honey-and-sage pot which always used to stand on the fireplace mantel of the Kansas stone house, and her grandfather's prayerbook.

'No, Mama. You'll be surprised, but it wouldn't be any of those, much as I love them. Nor that invisibly handstitched A.D. 1800 nightcap of our great-great-grandma, museum piece though it is.'

'What, then?'

'It would be that little old worn motto-card you've always had stuck in the corner of your bedroom mirror.'

'Why, Lora!' I could see she was pleased. 'I've wondered

if that would mean anything to anyone else. Every morning I've said those words. They've helped me through many a bad day.' For a moment she was silent. And then in her blinded eyes was the reflection of some glory I could not see. 'When the time comes for me to go, I want to fall asleep peacefully. And when I wake early, I'll say again, "This is a New Day. I will arise and be about my Father's business."'

That afternoon she had a violent attack of angina, but her mind remained clear. She was easier as evening came, and when I sat beside her after the nurse had made her comfortable for the night, she began repeating the Twenty-Third Psalm, as was our usual bedtime custom.

> The Lord is my shepherd; I shall not want.

Line by line we said the words together.

> He restoreth my soul —

I could no longer hear her voice, but her lips moved as I went on:

> Yea, though I walk through the
> valley of the shadow of death,
> I will fear no evil ——

And then her lips were still. She had gone to sleep.

* * *

The morning after the services were held for Mother, I woke with a sense of having new eyes, new ears, a new mind. They were my own again, no longer in the service of another.

Jo came in cautiously, her face sad. She was fond of Mother and had taken care of her a long time. I'm certain she was a bit shocked to see I hadn't 'gone to pieces' now that the long strain was over.

'Didn't you sleep well, Jo?' I asked solicitously.

'Sure.'

'Did you have bad news or something in the night?'

'No.' She looked at me blankly. 'Why?'

'Well, you look like a paid mourner. Mother had had a

good full life, Jo, and her mind was clear and vigorous to the last breath she drew. But she was old and blind and sick, and she was anxious to be off. So to go around looking glum would be a pretty poor way to honor her memory, don't you think? I have a feeling that since Mother had always been gay and courageous, we'll feel closest to her when we're that way.'

Jo gave my shoulder a little pat and went into her room to dress.

'How much coffee have we in the house?' I called to her. 'I'd like a quart or two for breakfast. And suppose you put up a card table. I'd like to get my feet on the floor again. I've been eating out of a trough long enough.'

'You're the big boss,' she laughed back, 'but the doctor's got to OK any coffee.'

I got hot water as usual. Nice start for a day!

I knew the family had long been making plans for my future, in case I survived Mother. Florence had a modern gem of a house, with lovely garden and trees, so her spare room would be an ideal place for me, they said. But I knew how single-mindedly she and her husband were wrapped up in each other. On the long trips his work necessitated, she always went with him. An invalid sister would quite disrupt their lives.

I had definite ideas of my own. But I must develop some strength. A twelve-hundred-pound ox couldn't walk without practice if he'd been tied down in his stall for nine months, even with four legs and a tail for balance. Every time Jo was safely away on some errand, I'd get out of bed to exercise. First, I'd put a pot of coffee on the gas. I hadn't had any for months and I craved it. I made it strong enough to grow hair on the chest and swigged it down with gusto. Then slowly, hanging onto the furniture, breathing deeply, I wobbled up and down the room. When the old heart protested too much, I humored it and flattened out for a while. Then I got up and went at it again.

It was amazing how quickly the sap began to get back in my joints. Soon I could tramp around with my arms extended in front of me, lifting my feet high, like some Scot at his bagpipes.

I'd insisted on staying in the apartment a couple of weeks to get my bearings, and answer 'phone calls and letters. But inevitably my sister set the evening when she and her husband would drive down for dinner and cart me off with them. The morning of that day I called Jo to me.

'Madam, I want my clothes. From the skin out. I'm getting up.'

'But Hughsie, not until we ask the doctor!' she protested. 'You might have one of those spells again.'

'All right, what if I do? I'll die like a man — with my brassière on! Get this now, once for all, Jo. I'm not going to lie in this bunk just to live — so I can lie in it some more!'

She looked at me a bit wild-eyed. I'd always been docile, but this was mutiny. 'Git!' I made a pass at her. She laughed, rather mirthlessly, and began collecting my stuff.

As I dressed in the bathroom, my eye fell upon the remaining medicine of that bottled and boxed supply Mother and I had had measured out to us the past year. An overwhelming urge seized me. I grinned to myself and picked up the wastebasket. When I was dressed, I carried it out with me, well filled.

'Hi, Jo!' I called. 'Come on, we're going to have fun. Here's digitalis to make the heart stronger and here's triple bromide to quiet it down. Here are bile pills and liver pills and physic of various sorts. Here are tablets to make one sleep and capsules to perk one up. Here are mixtures to take before and after. Come over to the window. I want to show you something.'

Jo came uneasily. I think she was beginning to wonder if I weren't a bit unbalanced. Under this rear window, three stories below us, was a rubble pile in a vacant lot.

'See that broken demijohn on top of the pile down there, Jo? I'll give you fifty cents for every time you hit it with one of these bottles.'

'You mean —— You're throwing away all this expensive medicine?'

'Why not? Look at all ninety-two pounds, dressed, of me. I'm no recommendation for the stuff, am I?'

'Well, you're alive, aren't you? This little bottle of pills cost four dollars, and it's half full! You might sit down in the lobby and sell all this at bargain prices to get some of your money back.'

'That's an idea. You can sit beside me, with all your magnificent one hundred and sixty-seven pounds, and five feet, eleven inches. We'll hang a sign on me, 'Before,' and one on you, 'After taking.' You'll have to wear tights, of course.'

She snorted, spat on her hands and started to fire away at the target. She scored six hits.

'Ha! Three dollars! Hughsie, I wish we had five hundred of these bottles.'

'Just how would you spend two hundred and fifty dollars if you had it?'

'For a railroad ticket to California. I haven't seen my sister in Alhambra for years. You know how it's been — one thing after another. I've been tempted to go visit her as soon as we get you settled.'

'Jo, can you keep a secret? I'm not going to Florence's. Sit tight. Keep your feet in the stirrups and hang on to the saddle-horn. In ten days our rent is up here. In nine days you and I will be heading for Los Angeles and way points — Alhambra, for instance. Imagine! The rest of winter in California sunshine.'

'Do you really mean it?'

'I was never more serious in my life!'

'But Hughsie, is it safe to start out? You might ——' She hesitated.

'I might die on the way? What of it? There's always a baggage car ahead. And plenty of high banks where a body could be dumped into the river. I've always wanted to be a water-ouzel.'

'But what will the doctor say?'

'I told him four days ago. He thought it might be a good idea — change of climate and all.'

Jo was almost beside herself with happy excitement. I

gave her the list I'd been making of things we needed done to get ready for the trip. And I told her of my efforts to get back strength.

'I knew about the coffee.' She grinned at me.

'We can get together on our financial arrangements and then you can hop over to the station this afternoon to get the tickets and make reservations. I want those tickets to flash on my family tonight.'

'Don't you want to get in the wheel-chair and let me take you along? I often took your mother around that way. It isn't far. I'll wrap you up well.'

'Whoopee! I'll do just that.'

It was wonderful to be lined up before a ticket-window again. A station, since the time long ago when Mother bedded us children down on the floor of the one in Kansas City, had always seemed one of the most interesting places in the world to me. Now, after being shut up so long, I felt as though I couldn't bear to leave it. The people, the hustle and bustle, the puffing of the engines and clang of bells, and at last that same old 'A-a-all abo-o-oard!' echoing through the vast building — it was wonderful! Jo, calm as she always seemed, was under the spell too, and her face shone. Our business attended to and a telegram sent to Jo's sister to rent us an apartment in Alhambra, we celebrated at the lunch counter with coffee and ice cream.

My brother Leslie was with Florence and her husband when they came that evening. They were much pleased to see me up and dressed and looking so sprightly. I didn't mention my plans. Jo had a good dinner and we tried to forget that Mother would never eat with us again.

Leslie, who had an apartment not far from the others, said, as he was carving, 'Well, Sis, I'll be seeing you oftener when you're living near me.'

I feigned surprise. 'What do you mean? I'm not going to live any nearer you.'

Florence looked at me as though she, too, thought I were a bit off. 'Why do you say that, when you're practically on your way to us this minute?'

'Oh, that! I may go over for a couple of days to visit. But not to stay.' I drew the envelope from under my plate and produced the tickets. 'Look!'

Jo and I laughed to see their faces. Florence gave me a fishy eye.

'I ought to have known you'd pull something like this. For a person who's been sick as long as you have, you're pretty high-handed!' She grinned at me affectionately.

When we told them our plans, no one blamed us for wanting a change. And I'm confident my adored sister and kindly brother-in-law looked at each other in the privacy of their room that night with a sigh of relief.

The trip to California was ideal. I stayed in my berth all the way and landed in Los Angeles rested and happy. There was a host of friends and relatives to meet us. One would have thought I had just returned from Mars, or been made the richest woman in the world — as in truth I felt I was, if friends are riches.

Our apartment was comfortable and I settled down to a lazy life. I spent days out-of-doors in my wheel-chair, or in the back seat of some friends' car as they went on all-day business or pleasure trips. It wasn't long before I graduated from the wheel-chair and sold it. To celebrate, I financed a trip for us to Knott's Berry Farm and to a performance of *The Drunkard*, which kept us chuckling for weeks. I slept and ate and had a grand time and grew stronger steadily.

By early spring I was feeling quite human again. I'd reached the stage when I was wondering if I hadn't better go home, when new adventure loomed. Among the friends of all sorts and ages I'd collected over the years was a breezy outdoor person, Zeeta. She was decades younger than I, but we forgot that disparity in mutual enthusiasm for talking nights away over coffee-pots and campfires, whether on beach or mountain-top. We'd made lots of trips into the desert together. Before Boulder Dam was built, we had once camped ten days on the edge of Black Canyon, waiting for the snow to melt enough so we could get to the Grand

Canyon. But it hadn't obliged us. For years our great ambition had been to make a leisurely tour to the Grand Canyon and other points.

Zeeta had been in Alaska for several years — writing me most thrilling accounts of life on an isolated island fox-farm — and now one day came a telegram from her: 'Hold everything. Coming outside. Shipping car. Grand Gully for us at last.'

Howls of protest went up from my protective friends and relatives when I told them of the telegram, and assured them I was going on that trip. It was utter folly — a woman in my condition — at my age — I'd undo everything I'd gained since I came down. I laughed at them. There was mounting zest in every new day that brought it closer.

We had a hilarious reunion when Zeeta arrived, and immediately began investing in necessary camp equipment. Tent, primus stove, air mattresses, down covers, and sleeping-bags — the latter in case we wanted to avoid auto camps and take roads marked, 'Dangerous, but Passable,' to sleep in the open. In a short time we struck off.

For sixty-eight days we meandered blissfully around in the waste spaces. I took my daily siestas in the shade of the car, or in the car itself if the air were cool, while Zeeta hunted rocks and relics. We ate dust and dripped sweat in Death Valley, hunted for the old camping place at Boulder Dam, for days hung our feet over the rim of the Grand Canyon, reluctant to break its spell. We picked up half a ton of petrified wood in the Painted Desert, stood in awe on the brink of Bryce Canyon, and went down on our knees before the majesty of the Great White Throne in Zion Park. We wept with the beauty of an organ concert in the Tabernacle at Salt Lake City, gambled at Jackson Hole, worshiped at the little Roadside Chapel beneath the shadow of the Tetons, and warmed our feet beside the hot springs of Firehole River, while waiting for Yellowstone geysers to play.

As though this were not enough, we backtracked and crossed over to the Craters of the Moon, whose black lava-fields were abloom with wild buckwheat. I'm still haunted by memory of those nightmarish, forbidding cones into which we peered. At last, heading back to Washington, we swung over to familiar ground and sat again listening to the thunder of mighty Coulee Dam, and felt sympathy for the Indians mourning above the river for their disrupted fishing and for tribal haunts now submerged fathoms deep. We had been just behind Spring all the way, and flowers bloomed everywhere.

When at last I was back home again in my little beach house, I laughed to myself. The old heart wasn't what it should be, but it had held up. I had urgent invitations for visits that would take more time than I had to give. My brother Bill's Montana ranch in the fall, with a trip through the Black Hills promised. Winters in California. The sea, the desert, the mountains —— Life was good as its last lap began.

Of course, my hope of going around the world by airplane had to be abandoned. With war upheavals in Europe again, I'd probably never be able to reach it even by water in my day. A second World War, of unthinkable magnitude, was approaching. I looked out over my peaceful land and water and refused even to think of it. And there was my ambition to come down by parachute from great height — that, too, must be abandoned. I knew it was for the young and venturesome. I was only venturesome.

But one dream still remained: the house I wanted. I'd dreamed of it for a long time. My little place was badly in need of repair and I didn't intend putting any money in it. I knew the location I wanted and the sort of house that should be built on it, against that day when I could no longer travel around. Just beyond the reach of the winter's high tides my house should stand, on a curve of beach which holds so much of beauty one could ask for nothing more. Mountain ranges, snow-capped and rugged, lift themselves above the foothills on the far horizons; the Olympics on the west, the Cascades on the east, with Rainier looming unbelievably large across the islands of the Sound. There would be a spacious living room in my house with a generous fireplace and high, beamed ceiling. And windows everywhere.

I knew an architect who was as enthusiastic as I over the site, and together we juggled all the features I wanted into a workable scheme. For days we drew designs together, studied the lay of the land from every angle and went back to change a line or add another window, until finally in penciled drawing lay tangible evidence of many a day's dreaming.

My friends were most dubious about the whole thing. 'It seems terribly foolish,' they protested, 'to build a house at your age!'

'If I had only a year to live, I'd still build it!' I declared stoutly.

It was begun under such fire of criticism that I called my dream-house 'Folly-on-the-Shore.'

But each stage of its building filled me with new pride of ownership. I was thrilled by the neat precision with which rafters were placed on uprights, with the fitting of brick on brick as the chimneys climbed roofward. I loved the rip of saw through rough fir boards, the good hard ring of hammers, the all-pervading smell of pitch. These things took me back to my childhood days when Father was putting up the walls of Grandma's house, climbing over the roof of Uncle Sam's as he nailed on the hand-made shingles, or helping with the new church whose steeple towered so impressively above the spireless log building the Kansas congregation had outgrown.

As 'Folly-on-the-Shore' took form, it emerged a quite sane and sensible house. And then, when at last it was finished and furnished, I moved in. Familiar rugs and chairs, books and pictures, acquired new interest in this setting. I fairly gloated with housewifely pride over conveniences I'd never had in the other place.

'But won't you be terribly lonely?' the skeptical repeatedly asked.

'No, indeed,' I always replied. 'I'll have lots of old friends visiting me.'

I'd thought long of those guests. I was anxious to review old times with them again in ample leisure. I'd bring them together before my fireplace and put them in a book. There was Julie, who eventually married Doctor Grant, the Health Officer, and had a very happy life with him and her boys. And there was Mack, whom I never saw again after that last night at the Pelkys'. He died of a heart attack in the woods some months later. There were many others. I'd often told their stories. Surely it would be easy to write them.

I'm a wiser and sadder woman now. Such is the duplicity of the pen that these bits of human interest I'd thought to put together in straightforward simplicity at times outdid Mother's silk scraps in shaping crazy patterns. But at last the book is done.

And now, as I sit here at my front windows, my heart is full. It is a rare day of brilliant sun on blue-green water, with a few white clouds scudding south. Smoothly as swans the ferries move against the timbered islands and disappear. Mountains and landgirt water — so long it has been secure and peaceful. But now I know the channel over there is mined. Two vessels stand guard and ferries must signal to be allowed to enter. From here the lighthouse point looks much the same, but I know its beauty is despoiled. The red-boled madronas which once overhung our beach fires are cut to make way for great pipelines and hidden oil tanks of concrete and steel. A power-house and barracks stand where stately firs and cedars once shut in the rocky cove that was so particularly our own. Away in the distance barrage balloons hang twenty-four hours a day over unseen shipyards, where endlessly changing shifts take over work that must not stop.

I had wanted to relax when I finished the book — or had I? — but some months back, while I was still knee-deep in manuscript, my house was changed overnight into a Red Cross Unit. One end of the living room was piled high with sheets and blankets. Stretchers leaned against the walls. There were innumerable boxes and cartons of drugs and splints and bandages. It took a long time to pack them all away in closets and drawers, so that I'd have room to move around. The war was suddenly real to me as I checked those familiar supplies with Doctor Knox when they were all in place. He is an old retired Army doctor, plunged again into active service since the attack on Pearl Harbor.

He turned to me after he finished the survey. 'I'm naming you Supervisor of this Unit, Mrs. Hughes.'

'What can I do, Doctor?' I thought enviously of those strong, lovely young nurses pictured daily in the papers as they left for foreign service. They knew ten times more than I did when I went to Honolulu to nurse soldiers. 'I'm seventy years old. My hands are too slow and my heart is too fast. And I can't lift or carry any more.' I wondered if he knew how proud I was of that assignment.

'No, but you can keep your head and be calm in an emergency.'

'Calm?' I laughed at him. 'I'd undoubtedly hold my ground all right. Man, if we were bombed, I'd be so scared I couldn't move!'

But he had no taste for jest. He was probably thinking of Corregidor and that missing grandson of his, who might be a prisoner of the Japs or might be dead. His thin old hands reached out and grasped my shoulders. His eyes were suspiciously bright as he spoke.

'Carry on, Nurse Hughes.'

I brought up my hand in smart salute.

'Ready, Doctor!'

THE END